'I FOUGHT THEM ALL'

'I FOUGHT THEM ALL'

*The Life and Ring Battles of
Prize-fighting Legend Tom Sharkey*

Greg Lewis
Moira Sharkey

"Hugely entertaining… a great contribution to ring history"
PETE EHRMANN, BOXING JOURNALIST

First published in 2010 by
Magic Rat, 12a Lansdowne Avenue West,
Canton, Cardiff, Wales, CF11 8FS
magic.rat.books@googlemail.com

Copyright: Greg Lewis and Moira Sharkey 2010.

The right of Greg Lewis and Moira Sharkey to be identified as
the authors of this work has been asserted in accordance with sections
77 and 78 of the Copyright, Designs and Patents Act 1988.

The writers will be joint owners of any and
all copyright interests in the text of the work.

A catalogue record for this book
is available from the British Library.

ISBN: 978-0-9562722-1-8

All rights reserved. No part of this publication may be
reproduced, stored in a retrieval system, or transmitted in any form
or by any means, electronic, mechanical, photocopying, recording, or
otherwise, without the prior permission of the publishers.

Typeset in Adobe Caslon Pro by
Steven Levers Publication Design, Sheffield

CONTENTS

Chapter One – *"Sailor" Tom* 7
Chapter Two – *Master At Arms* 23
Chapter Three – *"Sharkey: You're pure gold"* 45
Chapter Four – *The Fight He Won Flat On His Back* 75
Chapter Five – *A Celebrity Homecoming* 109
Chapter Six – *Hard As Nails* 141
Chapter Seven – *Fair And Square* 171
Chapter Eight – *Ninety-Nine Minutes of Hell* 191
Chapter Nine – *Blood, Sweat And Tears* 219
Chapter Ten – *"I'll marry you, but give up the gloves."* 247
Chapter Eleven – *Down But Not Out* 277
Chapter Twelve – *No Crown, Only Glory* 291

The Creed of a Man of the World 299

Notes 301

Bibliography 321

Authors' Note 325

Index 327

CHAPTER ONE
"Sailor" Tom

It was a long shot but the sports writer on the *San Mateo Times* was not going to miss this story.

A veteran sports star, whose international fame had once seen him a favourite of a President and earned him a film-star's fortune, was rumoured to be serving gamblers at a local race track.

The reporter headed to Tanforan to track down a hero who had fallen on hard times.

It was 1932 and Tanforan too was making its own comeback. Since it reopened two years earlier, it had been attracting crowds of up to 25,000 but betting on horses was actually illegal across the state of California.

The track's owners got round the law by selling "options", shares in a horse which could be sold for profit if the animal won a race.[1]

It was in this way, the hack heard, that the former sports star was making a living. Could it be that race-goers were placing bets with a legend; one of the greatest boxers the world has ever seen?

The reporter sifted through the crowds to the stalls where the options were sold. There, he immediately knew he had got himself a scoop.

Tom Sharkey may now have been only a little short of his sixtieth birthday but there was no mistaking the huge powerful chest, the massive shoulders, the misshapen cauliflower ear, the giant hands and the smiling blue Irish eyes.

Here was the man who had fought the hardest and the meanest at a time when heavyweight boxing was only just getting used to gloves, and when perhaps the greatest set of contenders to ever fight the world title were circling each other in and out of the ring.

Yes, here he was. Down, but not quite out. Still fighting.

The eyes were a particular give away, when matched with the patter: the look back to the glory days, the dismissal of the fighters of today. The eyes, when Sharkey spoke, were windows back onto the glory days of boxing.

Now, with the press back on his trail the showman returned to the spotlight.

But would the people remember? It had, after all, been almost thirty years since Sharkey's last official professional fight.

The San Mateo Times felt people should remember, describing Sharkey as "the Irishman who, as a little boy of nine, ran away from his home in Dundalk, Ireland, working his way on sailing vessels out to China, India and down to Australia, where he fed the native pearl divers coconut milk as they came up for air from their work, who came to Brooklyn to join the United States Navy."

And who "rich in money and crowned with success, went home…as the prodigal son to buy back for the family the old farm from which they were evicted when he was a baby."

Tom sat down with the reporter, making space in his option-selling stall and asked if it was alright if he smoked while they talked.

The writer sat opposite him and his hand must have trembled. He knew something of Sharkey, but not all. His article, like much else written about Sharkey, is filled with inaccuracies and claims which no-one can substantiate. And, as usual, far from making an effort to correct the untruths, Tom chose to seize on them. Both the writer and the interviewee clung to the legend, perhaps, and not the man.

"Tom Sharkey is Rudyard Kipling's man," says the writer. "Kipling would like to know and write about this man of the world since nine – he's been up and he's been down.

"He has seen the black holes of Calcutta, the dives of Hong Kong, sailing vessels to Buenos Aires and Algiers."

He led "a sailor's life in the navy where he learned to fight".

So, how much of the legend was the truth?

His was a life which spanned eight decades, forged in a childhood of poverty and political upheaval, and honed in fistic battles in dark shipyards. He recreated himself in America and fought some of the greatest battles in early modern boxing, and along the way he became a celebrity and very, very rich.

The real man in many ways was greater than the legend. But one cannot be separated from the other.

Tales, both tall and true, of physical strength, great warriors, storytellers and poets are integral to the long proud history of Dundalk.

So, it seems entirely appropriate that it was here, in this town nestled into a sheltered bay on the eastern coast of Ireland, that bard, gambler, adventurer and the most courageous man to ever fight for the heavyweight championship, Tom Sharkey, entered the world.

Sharkey, in his own words, "fought 'em all" during that fascinating period when fighters first put on gloves, during the sport's metamorphosis from prize-fighting to boxing, but when blood spill spattered referees and no decision was quite clean except a full, total knock-out.

He was a pioneer. A pioneer who left Ireland for the United States, working his passage at sea, who learned to mix it with his fists in the dockyards and never stopped being that untutored, firebrand of a scrapper – even when the world title was the prize.

But it began in Dundalk, not far from where all Irish life began, just to the north at a place called Ballymascanlon. It was here that the first settlers made their homes about 4,000-3,500 BC, leaving behind the Proleek dolmen, a huge stone doorway made of two massive standing stones - each more than twice the height of a man - and a cap or roof stone, estimated to weigh anything up to fifty tons, laid across the top. It may have been used as a portal to a burial chamber but it symbolizes the birth of a nation.

How the ancients put the dolmen together is anyone's guess but it remains a source of great legend. Some believe the early Irish were a magical people who lived underground and buried the important members of their society beneath these great stone monuments.

Another local legend features Cúchulainn, a great warrior whose father is supposed to have lived inside a great earth mound overlooking Dundalk. The name of Dundalk itself would be created from the Gaelic, Dún Dealgan, or the Fort of Dealga, a local pre-Celtic chieftain.

The poets in Celtic society were known as the "fili" and it is from their work that many of the myths and legends about the modern county of Louth survive. People like Sharkey took the myths with them when they left for the Promised Land, where they then created their own tales of strength and courage, real and mythologized.

The creation of the town has its roots with the Normans who arrived in Ireland in 1169 and took over large areas of the country. By 1185 a Norman nobleman named Bertrum De Verdon had built a manor house at Castletown Mount. The town grew up around an easy crossing point over Castletown River which rises in County Armagh and flows into Dundalk Bay just north of the town. Its location, midway between Belfast in the north and Dublin to the south, would also contribute to its development.

Even today the layout of the original town, from the bridging point on the river, and along streets which originally followed a gravel ridge - present day Bridge Street, Church Street, Clanbrassil Street, Earl Street and onto Dublin Street - in the direction of the Irish capital is easily discernible. On the outskirts, where Dublin Street becomes Hill Street, is where Tom Sharkey was born.

Visitors leaving the town on the busy Dublin road would – and still do today – have crossed a railway bridge and headed down Hill Street. The houses are different now though, but in the 1870s the left-hand side of the street was taken up by a row of white cottages. Each had a thickly thatched roof which hung down low over its frontage like the peak of an old corduroy cap. This was Tom's birthplace.[2]

Tom's parents, James Sharkey and Margaret Kelly, were both natives of Louth. It is understood that James had been born in August 1823 at Annagasson, eight miles outside Dundalk, to a William Sharkey and Jane Clusky, and that Margaret was born in June 1838 at Barrack Street, Dundalk. They had been married about ten years when Thomas Joseph (or Tom as he became known) was born and they already had a growing family.[3] Thomas is a family name held by both James' brother and Margaret's father. Their first child, Richard, had been born in February 1864. A daughter Mary followed the next year, then another son, James, in 1868 and a second daughter, Elizabeth, in January 1870. Tom was the fifth born child, entering the world on November 26, 1873.[4] When Tom was barely two, the couple had another child, Rose, and then in quick succession the family suffered two terrible but not unusual tragedies for the time. A son, Owen, was born in the June 1877 but he died the following summer. Within nine months of his death, Margaret had given birth again to another boy, Patrick, but he perished too after only a few months. Their tenth child was born in October 1880 and was named John.

James and Margaret had seen their home town move through times of tragedy and expansion.

In the 1820s Sir Walter Scott had described Dundalk as a "poor little town by the shore" and during 1832 and 1837 – as Tom's father James was struggling through his childhood and early teens - there were cholera epidemics, the second taking the life of a prominent local physician, Dr Fitzpatrick, who died while fighting to save his patients. Another doctor, Dr Laurence Martin, died of fever while helping the sick during the famine in 1846.

All the same, in 1843, William Makepeace Thackeray described Dundalk as a "bustling little town" where a great number were employed in the "foundries and workshops" of a Mr Shekelton. The conditions for workers, of course, would be hard. Dundalk's workhouse, built to house 800 people, had to be supplemented by rented accommodation for another 400 penniless townsfolk.

Out of poverty and injustice came politics. In 1842, politician Daniel O'Connell spoke to 60,000 people in one of his mass rallies to gain support for his campaign to repeal the Act of Union between Britain and Ireland. The following year he returned and was heard by a crowd estimated at 300,000.

By 1873, a generation of Irish people had been living with the effects of the Irish Potato Famine. They were impoverished and many were still leaving in their droves for other promised lands. The people struggled against English rule and on a day-to-day basis English landlords.

The Dundalk Democrat in the week Tom was born was packed with advertisements for lotions and potions to give good health, Cholera prescriptions, Notices of Home Rule meetings and comment pieces written about the occupation of Ireland by the English.

For a number of years anger had been growing about the conditions in which tenants were forced to live. In the late 1870s a Land League had been formed to campaign for reform and improvement of the living conditions. When the dispute became more intense and violent, an attempt was made to put it down with the passing of a Coercion Act, which gave the authorities power to arrest and keep in prison, without trial, all persons "reasonably suspected" of breaking the law. The hugely popular Irish politician, Charles Stewart Parnell, led opposition to the act and there were some reforms by William Gladstone. However, the Coercion Act had caused the arrest of a great number of "suspects", including in 1881, Parnell himself. While locked up, Parnell and the others issued the "No rent manifesto" - advising tenants all through Ireland to pay no more rent. Although the call was largely ignored, the state of the country continued to get worse. Eventually, the authorities repealed the Coercion Act and released Parnell and the others.[5] There were massive celebrations across Ireland. In Dundalk the crowds congregated to "proclaim aloud their allegiance to the Irish National Land League". The celebrations would have had an effect on every Catholic resident of the town – even an eight-year-old boy – particularly as the torch-lit event was played out against a town covered by snow. There was a "scene of unparalled excitement", said the Dundalk Democrat. The march led right through the town with more than twenty torch bearers at its head. The intense lights from the torches "lighted up the streets as they passed along". As cheers went up from the crowd, all the homes of the town were lit up and a bonfire blazed in Roden Place. And all the while the local musicians of the Emmet Band blasted out a "series of national airs", just as they would some years later to celebrate the return of Tom Sharkey to the town.

By the time of Sharkey's childhood, the long central street of the town and the lanes which crossed it had become home to a series of markets. There was a crowded butter market on Bridge Street, a linen market in front of Market House, where weavers and dyers would come to sell their linen and cloth, a meat market, and the centre of the market in Church Square, with two or three rows of stalls where farmers sold wool, women laid out threads and worsted wool for knitting out on sheets for passers-by to peruse, and potters sold their dishes, plates and jugs.

All along busy Clanbrassil Street there would have run carts pulled by horses, the wide road lined by shops with their decorated awnings and the lines of barrels which stood outside premises like those of T Connolly & Son, wine merchants.

One of the main buildings in the town, then as now, would have been St Patrick's Cathedral, an impressive sandstone building described shortly before Sharkey's birth as "unquestionably, one of the most perfect and beautiful modern churches of its style in Ireland".

However, the two aspects of Dundalk life which would have the most influence on Tom's life had their roots in the 17th Century expansion of the town by Lord Limerick (James Hamilton), Earl of Clanbrassil, who built streets, parks, a harbour, factories and a sea wall. It was he who laid the foundations for the industrial town which blossomed during the 19th century, with the trains from the newly-built railway and the boats which would use the expanding docks or quay.

It was the railways which gave James Sharkey his income and ensured the family's fortunes actually improved as young Tom grew up. And it was the town's quay which would fascinate the little boy and would eventually draw him away before he was even an adult.

In the 1840s the opening of the railway lines from the town to Enniskillen and to Drogheda played a huge role in Dundalk's continuing development. At one time most of the men of the town were employed on the railway. James Sharkey started work for the Great Northern Railway Company in about 1855 and he was a popular man, "universally liked". The railways grew with the amalgamations of the 1870s when first the Dublin-Drogheda and the Dublin-Belfast companies were brought together, and then Dundalk-Derry was added. Later the Belfast-Omagh-Clones line became part of the system. Large sheds for the repairs of locomotives, carriages and wagons were opened at Dundalk in 1880.

As the railways expanded, James' loyalty and dedication were rewarded. He had been a labourer for many years but he learnt how to read and write and worked his way up to signalman. He worked just a short distance from the small cottage in Hill Street that he and Margaret called home.[6]

The small cottages were for the poor, however. While Hill Street was improving, it was still a "dilapidated, troublesome neighbourhood".[7]

According to Dundalk historian Jack McQuillan: "Stories are told of the young Sharkey gathering the surfeit of corn in competition with the other youth in the distillery to bring home for feeding the pigs, which his parents kept at home, a common feature in those days. More often, however, he was to be seen in the quays, where he was as well known as in his own Hill Street, due to his interest in boats and the sea."

The whole town had an interest in boats and the sea, and the effect on Tom was life-changing.

In the final years of the 19 Century, the largest space in every paper was devoted to promotions for Steam Packet Company's voyages to Liverpool, Glasgow and on to America. The cost of a cabin from Newry to Glasgow was 8 shillings while steerage and deck return was 12 shillings. Passages to America cost between £6 and £20. There were other advertisements for the Anchor Line with its destinations: "Transatlantic, peninsular, Mediterranean and oriental". There were fortnightly sailings to New York from both Dublin and Derry.

As a young man, Tom became used to hanging around the quay. He saw people leave and was probably aware that most would never return. At some point in his childhood, his uncle Tom – a brother to James Sharkey - left and would later become a New York fire-fighter.

One writer who visited the quay in 1881 said there was "scarcely a more touching scene to be imagined than that which may be witnessed on the deck of an emigrant ship two or three hours before she weighs anchor for her destination".[8] Heading towards the quay from the town, the first sight which would greet a walker would be the high masts, fluttering with the flags of many different nations. On board the decks of the boats was a "bustle of excitement" as huge piles of baggage were wound up the ship's sides and delivered into the hold. The people themselves acted in different ways as they prepared for their new life, mulling over what that new life would bring them.

There were woman sitting on benches with cooking tins at their feet, embarking on the life of a domestic servant. There were whole families, driven by a dream that they could pack up a life of troubles and find fortune on the other side of the Atlantic. There were farm labourers venturing off for the wilds of Canada, where a free plot of land awaited them. If they could clear it and make it earn them a living, they would have a new future.

Their old lives stood around them in the heart-wrenching form of relatives and friends to be left behind. There were cheers now as the adventurers faced their last moments in Old Ireland but there was always a sadness between the celebration and good wishes, the glint of a tear above the softly turned up mouth of a smile.

There were kisses and hugs on deck before a bell rang: it was time for the visitors to leave the ship as it made its final preparations for departure. Then came "a scene which is never likely to be forgotten by those who have looked upon it. There is sobbing and weeping. The visitors slowly and reluctantly enter a boat which is to take them ashore. The anchor is weighed, the ship drops slowly down the river, the emigrants acknowledge the waving, farewell adieus of those upon the land".

There were claims by the adult Tom Sharkey of a terrible sadness at home. Tom would say that one of his brothers – he claimed he was a twin – was "killed by a runaway horse when he was about eight years old", but there is nothing in the documents or newspapers of Dundalk to show this to be true. He may have been confused or misunderstood or possibly Tom who liked a good sob story, especially when talking about life back home to writers in the United States, made it up.

Tom actually talked little publicly about his memories of his childhood but years later he offered this glimpse of the young battler.

"My early boyhood can be disposed of in a very few words," he said, always interested primarily in talking about his years in the ring. "I was always happy, was never quarrelsome, and if my schoolmates suspected I could fight they conceded the point without seeking actual demonstrations.

"Like most boys at school, I had a nickname, and the only times I wanted to fight was when some fresh kid hid around a fence and yelled at his companions to come and see 'The Badger'. I do not like to be reminded that my face was covered with white fuzz."

Later the *Dundalk Democrat* tracked down old school friends: "He is spoken of as having been always a quiet lad and indeed there are fellows of his own generation about the town who privately boast that they licked him at the Friary School or the Christian Brothers. They would not offer to repeat the operation just now."

School probably offered little by the way of education for him. It was at the quay that he learned most. It was not just America that people were travelling to. Certainly in the first instance it was Liverpool which would open many people's eyes to the world. From the middle of the 19th Century to the beginning of the twentieth, it was a revolving door. During the 1890s the docks would experience their golden age, becoming England's Ellis Island, the

11 miles of docks seeing the movement of millions of people and thousands of tons of goods in and out of Britain.

Spending so much time at the quay turned his head. If he had never been filled with the sights, sounds and smells of travellers leaving Dundalk, he would almost certainly have ended up in the railway works, where his father and so many of their neighbours in Hill Street worked, or at Manisty's foundry, the boat builders at Soldier's Point, in Carroll's tobacco industry, or at the town's distillery or brewery.

While his father shifted signals to allow people to come and go by train, Tom went to work on the merchant vessels, the *Parside* and *Queen of Oak*, as they set off between the heavy sandbanks of the bay to ply their trade in Liverpool and Scotland.

"The first work I ever did as a boy was aboard a ship," Sharkey said later. "I used to run on small coaling vessels between my hometown and ports in Scotland. I took my turn at the wheel and often went 19 and 20 hours at a stretch without sleep.

"Later I shipped on larger vessels and before coming to New York from Buenos Aires in 1892, I had travelled over the world - to Alaska, through the Indian Ocean and to ports where no white man had ever set foot.

"I could tell a very interesting story of adventures in foreign lands and seas. I was shipwrecked one time and spent many days in an open boat without a drop of water to drink. But this story will keep for some other occasion."

It did, and was told in many different ways over the years, exaggerated not just by Tom but by boxing journalists. Writers in the United States, in particular, loved this period of his life because it allowed them to not only imagine Tom's seaman adventurers and his eventual discovery of his new homeland but also the scraps in the dark ship corners, the dusty ship yards, which would form the germ of the ring career to come.

According to the *Sporting Chronicle*: "After having the experience of being shipwrecked four times and having saved no fewer than three lives from drowning, he settled down in New York, his business being confined to the docks. Whilst gaining a livelihood in this manner Sharkey was several times compelled to defend himself in some rough-and -tumble bouts, with so much success that he decided to increase his exchequer by participating in the ring."

According to *Sports History*: "When twelve years old, he ran away from home, shipping as a tramp sailor."

In a tribute for *The Ring* following Sharkey's death, Jersey Jones wrote that Tom had been just 10 when he "shipped out to sea as a cabin boy". Jones went on: "For nearly a decade he sailed the Seven Seas, from London to Cape Town, Hong Kong to Sydney, San Francisco to the China coast and into the frigid wastes of the Arctic. He had his share of dramatic struggles with the typhoons of the Indian Ocean and the hurricanes of the Caribbean. Four times he was shipwrecked, and his experiences read like something out of 'Sinbad, the Sailor'."

Dundalk historian Jack McQuillan wrote: "[Sharkey] wanted to see the world and made voyages to China and then Australia, where he settled for a time. It was here, with the famous ship and star tattoo on his chest, he developed his passion for physical fitness and boxing. Within a short period he was engaging the best of Australia's 'big boys' and became well known across the continent as he defeated them all, mostly by the knock-out route."

According to an article in the *Brooklyn Daily Eagle*, published in 1896 as Sharkey's celebrity started to grow: "After he had served his apprenticeship a love for sea asserted itself and he shipped in a British merchant vessel. He liked America too well to stay on the other side long and soon became one of Uncle Sam's sailors."

The newspaper said that in the navy a "fondness for boxing was encouraged among the seamen by the officers". There, it said, "Sharkey first became known as a fighter."

Sharkey's life on the seas became distorted after he reached America. The newspapers there were competitive and, as now, were interested in creating characters in which readers were interested: boxers, with their tall tales and bragging were ideal. In addition, Sharkey himself would have been keen to play up his background, for although many including himself said he preferred fighting to talking about it, he had to play the game. It was part of the picture for title contenders as it remains today. It helped him, the promoters and the newspapers to create more exciting myths.

However, Tom was more likely to speak truth at home, with his father at his side and with people around who would know when he was embellishing the truth about his past.

In 1897, during a triumphant visit home from the United States, he told what was probably the nearest to the truth. The newspapers then revealed Sharkey had *permanently* left County Louth only a few years previously, aged around 18.

This version was later confirmed by his father who stated: "He left school when but a lad of 13 and went to work on a Dundalk sailing vessel called the *Irish Girl*… He was first engaged as cook and remained on her two years. Then he shipped for a trip to India, returning to London where he went aboard an American steamer and made six round trips."

Before he left Dundalk, as *The Irish News and Belfast Morning News* noted, there had been plenty to inspire him with "celebrated pugilists" of the early 19th Century, Donnelly, Joe Coburn, and George and Jack Rooke, all hailing from the town.

Indeed, many rumours still persist that it was in Ireland Sharkey threw his first punches, even travelling up to Derry docks for one illegal fight.

Some of Sharkey's interesting stories were told in his dotage and recorded by journalist George T Pardy.[9] In the early days, Tom's role as a teenage cabin boy set him up for some fistic battles. Tom had not liked kids in school who had poked fun at the fuzz on his face and he would not now like a role which, according to tradition, gave him the status of a "human football who could be kicked around with impunity by any member of a crew who had a grouch to work off". Pardy noted: "Some lived through this ordeal to become big enough to turn the tables on their tormentors, others died or deserted and sought the friendly haven of the shore with their romantic notions of the sea thoroughly eliminated."

But Sharkey would never back down and never give up. He could take the clouts around the ear from the mates and the captain as it came with the job. However he would take nothing from the "sea bullies" among the lowly crew like himself. His fists, even at this age, were like iron, and his frame was as if compacted of "whalebone and steel". Mix that with a hot temper and genuine love of fighting for fighting's sake, set it up against a bunch of shipmates who had no intention of backing down on an argument either, and life on board was going to be a mix of back-breaking hard work and aggression. "So it followed," wrote Pardy, "that for a time life was just one mix-up after another for Thomas J". There were no rules in these brawls, of course. Fighters kicked, head-butted and bit each other as they rolled around deck or battered each other in the confined spaces below. And no opponent "ever escaped scot-free and unmarked from a tussle with young Tom" and the young Irishman "never stayed licked".

Some would have their fill of the fight, but Tom would only get harder and stronger. These fights were not for the championship of the world, they were about something more: survival. Confined on board ship, tempers got frayed and scores needed settling. Tom intended to get by, building a reputation every bit as strong as that given to the wearer of a championship crown. He wanted all-comers to know that if they mixed with the short, hard-as-nails boy from Dundalk, they were going to get hurt. "He never had to learn to fight," noted a leading boxing writer later. "That came naturally."[10]

On a ship called *Martha Daly*, he made his third voyage around Cape Horn. On board was a Swede who had taken against Sharkey from the moment he had joined the crew. Their mutual dislike exploded into violence one night at the crew's quarters on the forecastle. Tom had ignored the huge man's bullying for several days but now the Scandinavian was determined to provoke a fight. He hurled abuse at Sharkey and then gave him a back-handed slap that sent the Irishman staggering backward.

"The next instant the big man must have thought that he had stepped into the teeth of a whizzing buzz saw," wrote Pardy. "The youngster was upon him fighting with a speed and fury that completely bewildered his slow-thinking antagonist."

The Swede swung his long heavy arms clumsily. But Sharkey

took some blows, ducked others and sent his own punches in. "Youth and grim determination did the rest and scarcely two minutes had elapsed before the Swede was lying prostrate, his features a mere bloody pool, and yelling for mercy."

The affair created a stir among Sharkey's shipmates who had seen the Swede as too big, too powerful and too mean to take on. When the news of Sharkey's exploit reached the first mate, he immediately ran along to the captain.

The captain listened and then snorted. "Licked that bullhead Swede, did he? Well, if the kid did that, he's man enough for real work. Put him in your watch, Mister!"

According to Pardy, "few men have seen more of the world in a comparatively short period than did Sharkey in those early days of seafaring before the mast". He visited China, Japan and Africa, and was shipwrecked four times.

Pardy describes one of the occasions that Sharkey was shipwrecked, saying that the ship was sailing from Hong Kong when it was disabled in a typhoon.

"She was an ancient none too seaworthy craft, and the following morning her battered bulk developed a leak that no amount of pumping could overcome," wrote Pardy. "She was sinking so rapidly that the crew had to take to the small boats without waiting to take as much as an ounce of fresh water or a ship biscuit with them. From a Monday morning at four o clock until the next Wednesday night when they were picked up by a British steamer, the castaways had neither food nor drink."

Sharkey always said the weather "was so flaming hot there in the tropics that three of the sailors went clean out of their minds in our boat, drew knives and went for the rest of us".

The men "were knocked on the head with boat stretchers and the Old Man ordered them chucked overboard for fear they'd start another killing rampage if they came to". Over the men went, "into the sharks".

On the third day, said Sharkey, a big Finn went crazy and "jumped the Old Man". The captain drew a gun and shot the man through the heart.

"When he was about to be thrown over the side I hollered out, 'Hold on there, Captain, let's eat him'.

"The Old Man sort of hesitated a moment but then shook his head and a few seconds later the sharks were having a full meal. And don't you know, I kind of envied them. Sounds tough I suppose but just try drifting around the Pacific for days and nights with an empty stomach and see if it won't rub civilization off of you."

CHAPTER TWO

Master at Arms

In September 1892, when Tom Sharkey arrived in New Orleans, the city was buzzing.

Stepping off the merchant ship, he quickly picked up the excitement. He may not have yet turned 19, but he had already had his full quota of brawls about ship and in port.

He and his crewmates liked to fight and they liked to watch – and bet on – others fighting too.

They had hit New Orleans at exactly the right moment and quickly made sure they had tickets for the event that not only the Big Easy but the whole of the United States sporting community was talking about: the battle between the fistic great, John L Sullivan, and an impudent young dude named James J Corbett.

Massachusetts-born Sullivan was a star. They called him "The Champion of Champions".

According to Gilbert Odd, of the *Boxing News*, his chief asset was "his ability to put the fear of God into his opponents long before the starting bell of a contest". He had taken Paddy Ryan's crown in a bare-knuckle fight to a finish in February 1882 and for 10 years had met all comers in the heavyweight division "except Negroes". While he upheld the colour barrier which cut through boxing at the time, few other "laws" concerned him. To avoid interference from the authorities in France in 1887, he had fought Englishman Charlie Mitchell in the grounds of a private estate. The fight was called a draw after the 39th round and about 190 minutes. Soon after, Richard K Fox, owner of the influential Police Gazette, organized a fight between Sullivan and Jake Kilrain, with the fighters agreeing on a side bet of $10,000. The fight took place in the clearing of a wood at Richburg, Mississippi.[1]

This would be the last heavyweight fight under London Prize rules so the punches would keep going until there was only one man left standing. The battle went on for 75 rounds and in the end Sullivan took the spoils.

However, prize-fighting was evolving. The sheer brutality of the spectacle in the Richburg woods helped set the stage, according to the great boxing journalist Nat Fleischer, for a "new and more civilized fistic game – boxing". While writer Dale Webb has noted: "The events of that day would mark a passing of one age to another; the birth of a sport from the death of an age-old tradition."[2]

Part of that new age was Gentleman Jim Corbett.

Born in San Francisco, California, on September 1, 1866, (with Irish parents, like Sullivan), he had ditched the life of a bank clerk to achieve "fame and fortune" in the ring. He had come to national prominence just two years earlier when he, too, had beaten Kilrain and then drawn with the great Peter Jackson.

He had earned the right to have a crack at Sullivan's crown and returned to New Orleans, the scene of the Kilrain fight, to do it.

Sullivan may have been the fight fans' favourite but he had not donned a pair of gloves in more than three years, except for exhibition matches. He was overweight and bloated from idleness, overeating and drinking. His reputation alone could be no match for Corbett's speed and skill, and the younger man not only walked off with the $25,000 purse but also cleaned up on an outside bet of $10,000.

The sailors got drunk. One slapped Sharkey on the shoulder,

and shouted above the din in the saloon: "Sullivan looked so bad tonight I'll bet Tom here, could have taken him."

Another nodded.

"Hell, he could have taken Corbett too," he said. "Couldn't you, Tom?"

Tom Sharkey shook his massive head and spoke, his accent then still thick with the green hills of Dundalk.

"I don't know," he said. "Sullivan is still tough. Still great. And anyway, fighting him would be like spitting in church. But Corbett now…" His blue eyes narrowed "…Corbett I will fight, someday."[3]

His shipmates believed him. Tom may have been shorter than them but his huge bull-chest, his heavy jaw and square chin made him stand out and he demonstrated the power he could pack between his fists in the brawls they had already witnessed at sea.

All the same, even in their drunken state, they could not have believed what was to come.

Heading off into the night in the early hours, Sharkey still idolised Sullivan. Tom, himself was just a brawler and fan. But the champion had been vanquished and he knew what he wanted now: to get into the ring and seize back the heavyweight championship of the world from Corbett. Amazingly, the next time he would see John L Sullivan and James J Corbett it would be to shake hands on arrangements to fight them both. The face in the crowd would become the man in the ring.

Firstly, though, there would be a major change in Sharkey's circumstances. Now on American soil, he had made a decision to swap the life of a merchant seaman for that of a sailor in the United States Navy. One leading writer said the Sullivan fight had a direct influence on Sharkey's career change. "The fight thrilled him," he said. "It also broke him and being penniless, and since there wasn't a merchant ship in New Orleans in need of a husky youngster, he joined the Navy."[4]

His opportunity to sign up came soon after the visit to New Orleans when his ship called in at New York. Quitting his own ship, he hiked to the Brooklyn Navy Yard and enlisted in the United States Navy.

Sharkey enlisted on November 28, 1892, two days after his 19th birthday.

He made no attempt to hide the fact that he was Irish-born but he did lie about his age, recording his date of birth as January 1, 1871.

Sharkey's status as a foreign-born recruit would have made him far from unusual. In 1890 only 47 per cent of people serving in the US Navy were native-born.[5] And the fact that he was 19 would not have been an issue with the authorities. The Navy at that time had enlisted apprentices as young as 14 and "boys" who were younger still. It would not be until 1904 that the minimum age of enlistment would be raised to 17 with parents' consent or 18 without it. It seems likely in Sharkey's case that he worried about what he thought might be the enlistment age. It is possible that he did not know his exact birthdate or that he was hiding from home, as he once later claimed. Consequently, perhaps, he stated his home was Park Street, Dundalk.

Sharkey was given a medical. His height was given then as a fraction over five feet seven inches and his weight 183 pounds. His eyes were blue, his hair brown and his complexion ruddy. A note was made of the tattoo of a ship and a star on his chest.

He was enlisted onto the receiving ship, *Vermont*, as an ordinary seaman, signing up for three years to "the utmost of my power and ability discharge my several services and duties, and be in everything conformable and obedient to the several requirings and lawful commands of the officers who may from time to time be placed over me".

For his service, the mariner would receive payment of $19 a month.

Friends said he was an adventurous young man who talked in "quick short sentences". He probably could not yet read or write very well, but he would learn, although not to a very high standard.[6]

Tom was transferred from The Vermont to the cruiser USS Philadelphia on June 19, 1893, when his health was described as good (By the time he left the navy in October 26, the medical officer was describing it as "excellent").

And, within a short time, the cruiser was in the Hawaiian Islands, helping to protect American interests when royalists loyal to the former Queen Liliuokalani, who had lost her throne after trying to abolish American influence in the government, rose up.

But Sharkey had his own battles to fight and had started to get a little exercise while on board ship. He began to spar with gloves now, joining hundreds of other sailors every evening, from seven to nine, as boxing bouts took place on deck, with officers acting as referees.

Sharkey later described these days. "I liked to box and it was not long before I was putting on the gloves and trading punches with the other sailors," he said. "These bouts, however, were all of a friendly nature, between fellows who never expected to shine in the ring, and it was not until I was riled up one day that my mates learned I might fight if forced into it."

The guy who first riled the man who would fight for the heavyweight championship of the world was a navy tough guy named "Reddy" O'Neill.

Sharkey knew the Bostonian did not like him and they started arguing one morning below deck as they bumped together while lashing their hammocks.

"Get away from here," O'Neill told the Irishman, "or I'll swing for you."

"What's that you'll do?" Sharkey hit back.

"I'll break your jaw."

Both men wandered off scowling. Then Sharkey saw "Reddy" on the spar deck.

"You're going to break my jaw," said the Irishman, looking around. "Here's your chance to do it."

According to Sharkey, the hard man came towards him, saw Sharkey put up his fists and then turned on his heel. "He was never regarded as a tough guy after that," the Irishman said, revealing the confidence that the run-in with "Reddy" gave him.

"I knew that he wasn't exactly a coward," Sharkey said. "He had engaged in a number of fist fights on shore and had built up a reputation as a bad man to mix with. I figured that if 'Reddy', who should know a fighter, was afraid of me, he must have seen something about my work with the boxing gloves which caused him to hesitate about hitting me.

"I boxed more than ever. I put on the gloves every chance I had – tackled five or six men one after another."

In fact, in that first year in the navy, Sharkey knocked out fellows named Jack Gardner (in four rounds on March 17, 1893), J Pickett (in two on April 7), Jack Langley (four on May 3), Jim Harvey (also two on May 27) and Jack Walsh (August 21) and J Barrington (September 10), both in the first.[7]

Sharkey later forgot in which order he knocked down these early opponents as his memories were stronger of some fights than others.

Gardner, he said, had arrived in Honolulu on board an English man o' war and was considered a "heavyweight champion of the British Navy". "I deprived him of his title by stopping him in four rounds."

Pickett he remembered little of, not even a first name. "He was easy. They packed him out in two rounds."

The first Langley fight – they would fight again on April 7, 1894 when Sharkey knocked him out with a huge right hand in the eighth [8] – was fought for "$100 a side, winner take all the gate receipts". It was fought near the beach at Waikiki.

Sharkey remembered nothing about Harvey or Walsh and was now "thinking pretty well of myself".

"I asked them to get me a real man, one who could take a wallop," Sharkey said. "The Honolulans dug up Jim Barrington. He was no better than either Langley or Pickett and lasted about as long."

Cries of "foul" and claims that Sharkey was not the best of the two guys in the ring would taunt Sharkey's career in the most notorious boxing scandals of the period. The first sign of trouble came after a bout with a guy named "Rough" Thompson on May 14, 1894.

They fought for a $500 side bet and the sailor put "Rough" down in two rounds. However, Thompson's friends claimed Sharkey had won with "an accidental punch".

Sharkey stepped into the ring again with him 12 days later. This time he knocked him out in the first round. [9]

There was a lot of money on these fights. In fact Sharkey later claimed that he made $12,000 from the ring in Honolulu. [10] One day he was called to the captain's cabin and was asked how long it had been since he had written home.

"I've never written," replied Sharkey.

"Do you recognise the writing on that envelope?" asked the captain.

"Sure it's my father's writing."

The captain gave Tom the letter. He discovered it had been written to the captain and was asking if the fighter whom Mr Sharkey had been reading about in the Dublin newspapers could be his son. [11]

Tom said he talked to the captain and decided to write to his mother, enclosing $5,000 of his fight money. Tom claimed now that he had always been afraid that if he let his family know where he was, his father would have him taken out of the navy, because he was not of age. Later, letters to the ship informed Tom that his mother had "believed him to be dead".

Word had spread around Honolulu so much that Sharkey was considered a champion pugilist in the area.

Tom James was chief steward on the steamer, *Australia*, which was in port at the same time as the *Philadelphia*. James was not only a big fight fan, he was also the man who had brought heavyweight champion contender, Bob Fitzsimmons, and many other noted fighters from Australia to America. [12]

On the steamer with James was a professional fighter named Nick Burley, who had met Peter Maher and other famous heavyweights.

James wanted Burley to meet Sharkey in the ring. He sent word to the sailors of *Philadelphia*, who were crowing about their "champion", that he would take the keenest delight in having Burley shut them up.

"My shipmates were up against it," said Sharkey. "They didn't want to be bluffed, and knowing that I had never engaged in a professional fight they did not like to ask me to tackle a seasoned man like Burley."

Some sailors approached their Irish friend, unsure what to say.

"Tom," said one at last. "There's a man over on the *Australia* who has a fighter he thinks can whip you. The fellow wants you to fight as a professional."

"Well," said Sharkey, "what of it?"

"Nothing," said his shipmate, "only it isn't fair for him to be wanting you to tackle such a tough game."

Sharkey puffed out his chest. "Tough game! Who told you this fellow was tough?"

The sailor stepped back.

"Will you fight him?"

"Fight him?" said Sharkey. "I'll fight anybody."

The Burley fight probably took place in June 1894 in Honolulu. This, Sharkey recalled later, was just "several nights" after the initial discussions. Sharkey counted this as his "first professional fight".

Looking back after his career, Sharkey said: "I have heard fighters tell, and good fighters too, how frightened and nervous they were in their first fight. But I must stick to the truth and state that I was neither frightened nor at all nervous when I crawled through the ropes to meet Nick Burley. Perhaps I didn't have sense enough to be. But, anyhow, I wasn't.

"Burley gave me a good taste that night of what I might expect if I kept at the fight game.

"In the second round, I believe it was, he whirled on the balls of his feet and pasted me squarely on the face with a La Blanche swing. The blow broke my nose and covered me with blood.

"But it also did something else. It woke me up. It made me want to kill the fellow. I rushed in and began swinging punches as fast as I could.

"I could hear my shipmates around the ring yelling like crazy Indians. I couldn't stop. Between rounds they had to drag me to my corner. The end came in the eighth round.

"I felt my fist collide with Burley's jaw and I saw him drop in to the floor."

Sharkey's shipmates had their hero again.

"Next thing I knew I was being carried out of the building on the shoulders of a bunch of yelling, wildly excited sailors," remembered Sharkey. "That night there was a great jollification on the good ship *Philadelphia*."

Sharkey's recollection of his tangle with Burley might not be entirely accurate. Firstly, it seems there were two fights against Burley, sometimes referred to as Nick Barrowich, in 1894.

The *Daily Bulletin* (Honolulu) records a hard fought draw between Sharkey and Barrowich having been fought on May 24. It describes Sharkey as the more attacking boxer, coming close to winning in the third and fifth rounds: "The call of time saved Barrowich from a defeat," it noted of the fifth. Sharkey pushed home his advantage during the sixth, seventh and eighth, and "the ninth and final round, in the opinion of those present, was in favour of Sharkey, but the referee decided it a draw. Both men shook hands and were the same friends they were before the match." A moral victory for Tom, then, which perhaps grew in his mind by the time he came to write of it.

The same newspaper also records Sharkey and Barrowich fighting three friendly rounds "during an entertainment" on June 21, 1894.[13]

A local black boxing instructor named George Washington had noted Sharkey's lack of technique and offered to show him how to box.

Sharkey went to see him and they put on their gloves.

Immediately Washington started to tell Sharkey that he did not know how to "put up my hands". Sharkey's pride rose, the red mist descended.

"I know just as much about holding up my hands as you do," Sharkey bit back.

Washington told him he had a "swelled head". He almost certainly did. Sharkey admitted as much later.

But now he wanted to offer Washington a fight.

"Look here," the trainer said. "I got nothing against you. Get along now before I disfigure you."

But they both wanted to show each other a thing or two. Sharkey said later: "I am satisfied now, when I come to think how quickly that Negro jumped at the chance offered to meet me in a fight, that he actually thought he would chop me to pieces."

They fought, according to some sources, on July 4, 1894.[14] Sharkey recalled the venue to be a small hall. The ring was on a stage and had ropes on three sides only. An unfamiliar looking venue but another typical story: Sharkey's brawn and guts, against an opponent's skill.

And in the opening round, Washington made Sharkey look foolish.

"I just couldn't hit him," said Sharkey. "When I rushed he slipped aside and made me bump the ropes. And when I stood in the centre of the ring and dared him to come on and fight he poked my head and hopped away."

The anger was rising though, and the anger always seemed to be Sharkey's friend in the ring.

There are no official written records of the Washington fight – just Sharkey's extremely colourful description of what happened next. It's true that Washington was knocked out and almost certainly right that Sharkey's anger gave him extra strength.

But as for Sharkey's recollection of the detail of events, it might contain some of the hyperbole usually more closely associated with a fisherman's tale rather than a boxer's.

"I was furious when I went to my corner," Sharkey said. "I had been thinking I could fight and here was a boxing instructor - not a regular fighter, just a plain every day instructor - showing me that I didn't know a thing about it.

"I wouldn't even sit down. During the minute rest, I kept digging my toes into the canvas in my anxiety for the bell to ring.

"When it finally did ring, I jumped 10 feet and landed in the centre of the ring on the dead run.

"The Negro saw me coming and tried to side step. I struck him with my arm and shoulder and slammed him against the wall. As he bounced back, I swung and landed on his chest. He went plumb through a window in the back of the stage."

SAILOR TOM

And life got better back on board too as Sharkey experienced a kind of celebrity or, as he put it, he became "quite a man" on board. "Even the officers, who had scarcely noticed me before, seemed anxious to give me a pleasant word," he said.

There was little of what modern fighters – or even the brightest of the day – would call "technique" in Sharkey's boxing.

He, himself, later admitted that he was just brawling, winning only as he could dish out a little more punishment than he was taking. The fights may have been short, the opponents may have been crashing down but Sharkey was taking hits too, as he only knew how to attack.

"The way I fought I had to take punches," he said. "I didn't know then that there was such a thing as a side step, a feint or an uppercut, and the idea that a man could guard himself by holding up an arm never entered my head."

Sharkey's time at Honolulu was drawing to a close. On July 18, he fought Bill Tate and knocked him out in the second round. It was a fairly insignificant bout but Tate was a friend of "Spider" Kelly in San Francisco, a man who was to have a big influence on Sharkey in the next few years.

Tate stayed on his feet twice as long as first round knock-outs Jim Dunn (July 21) and Jack McAuley (July 28), and as Jack Marks (August 11) and Charles "Sailor" Brown (August 21), two fighters Sharkey met when the *Philadelphia* docked at Vallejo in California.

Sharkey later claimed the Dunn and Brown fights took place in Vallejo, at the Armory Hall, at the corner of Georgia and Sutter Street. Boxing records show otherwise and it may be that the early fights later became mixed up in the boxer's mind. To further confuse his memory, Sharkey did later fight Brown at Vallejo (on April 7, 1896). According to the records, Sharkey won that in the first too.

He said the Dunn fight was organized by a sailor on the *Olympic*.

"Jim was as big a man as Jess Willard, 6 foot four, a fine looking big fellow," recalled Sharkey. "His friends wanted to bet $1,000 on him."

Sharkey's backer was the *Philadelphia*'s chief boatswain's mate, Paul Herman. He would put up his own money and collect what the other sailors wanted to bet. They would throw in up to $20 dollars each, about a month's wages for many of them.

Herman collected $1,000 to match that laid down by Dunn's friends.

"Several fighters claim the world's record for quick finishes. But that affair of mine with Dunn was pretty near the limit for brevity. It lasted 26 seconds flat.

"When the bell tapped I took a hop, step and jump. A right-hand overhead swing which I started from my corner landed flush on the chin. Persons who were holding watches told me that it was exactly 16 seconds from the time the gong sounded until the referee began counting. The other 10 seconds were consumed in counting Dunn out!"

The same guy from the *Olympic* organized the first fight with Brown, according to Sharkey. Brown, Tom was told, was a former heavyweight champion of the American Navy and had once boxed Peter Jackson, a black boxer Sharkey revered.

Brown had been on a long cruise in the Arctic Ocean and was "spoiling for a fight". He jumped at the chance to take on the big man on the *Philadelphia*.

Sharkey's recollection of Brown probably referred to a mix of the August 1894 and April 1896 easy single-round knockouts: "Brown didn't give me much trouble. I busted him so hard in the first round that I thought he would snap the ropes. In the second round I gave him a few cuffs and it was all over."

Today, the city of Vallejo has more than 112,000 inhabitants who work in a variety of fields including the high-tech and engineering industries. Back in the 1890s Vallejo's development had been largely down to its connections with the United States Navy. The partnership had began in 1853 when the US government bought Mare Island, a stretch of land about three-and-a-half miles long and a mile wide on the western edge of Vallejo. Here, about 30 miles northeast of San Francisco, the government built the first Navy Yard on the West Coast.

The Navy would be Vallejo's saviour. When it had first been founded in 1850 on land donated by General Mariano G Vallejo, it had been designed as the state capital of California. That honour, though, later switched to Benicia and then Sacramento, 60 miles away.

But the navy stayed and the yard grew becoming a major centre for shipbuilding. The first new vessel to leave there was the paddle-wheeled gunboat *USS Saginaw*, which was launched before the American Civil War in 1859.[15] During the civil war, the Navy Yard's first commandant, David Glasgow Farragut, gained undying fame when, at the Battle of Mobile Bay, he cried: "Damn the torpedoes – Full speed ahead!"

To some extent, the navy was Vallejo – and Vallejo maintained a draw for old seamen. Many of the thousands of servicemen who were based at Vallejo throughout the years returned to live when their sea-going days where done.

The yard's original dry dock was a large floating structure, built in New York, knocked down, and reassembled at the yard following a journey around Cape Horn. Three years before Sharkey arrived, a second dry dock which had taken 19 years to build, was completed. It was 508 feet long and rested on a rock foundation of cut granite blocks, and by 1894 would have been busy with construction, overhaul and repair work on the pride of the US Navy.

Because of Tom's strength and courage, he was quickly made up to master-at-arms on the *Philadelphia*. This role gave him plenty of opportunity to flex his muscles. "He was a 'Jimmy-Legs', assigned to the task of keeping the boys from manhandling one another," explained one historian. "It was a tough job, for which he was fitted."[16]

By the time Sharkey reached California, he was a big man on the boat and talk must have been spreading through a navy in which crews liked nothing better than boasting about and laying bets on their favourite prize-fighters. As Sharkey himself said: "It was some trick for a green sailor like I was to knock out so many men right off the reel."

Sharkey admitted later he had his moments of being "badly puffed up - a victim of the swelled head". But he said a conversation with Tom James had got him thinking and kept him focused.

He had bumped into James shortly before leaving Honolulu.

"Tom," said James, "you've been doing some good fighting."

Sharkey smiled, agreed he had, and expected him to go on to predict the Irish sailor would be a champion some day.

"Let me give you a word of advice, Tom," he said instead. "You think you've done very well in the ring and, to be truthful, you have. But, Tom, all you don't know about fighting would make a cargo for a ship.

"You've been meeting bums. The only man you whipped worthy of mention is Nick Burley, and he doesn't figure one, two, three with the champions.

"You are a big man in Honolulu. In California, they've never heard of you. And they have real fighters there.

"Go see some of them fight. Then, if you're still game, go to it. The champions need strong, husky fellows like you to practise on. If you can stand the gaff we may hear something of you in a few years."

They were powerful words for Sharkey and came from a man he respected. They had stayed in his mind throughout the voyage to California.

When he hit the mainland, Sharkey planned to heed James' advice and see some of California's great fighters in action before he tried his hand.

It did not work out like that because word was spreading about the sailor in San Francisco.

One of those who heard about the new pretender was a man from Hayward, California, called Martin Mulverhill (Sharkey referred to him later as Mulvihill). Mulverhill fancied himself as a future champ and, like Sharkey, always let it be known he was ready to take on all comers. Sharkey, someone told Mulverhill, was unsure about going against men of reputation, and so he would have to trick the sailor into a fight.

One day a crowd from the *Philadelphia* was standing in Tim Sheehan's saloon when the door opened and in walked a man in a blue shirt and overalls. Sharkey later described him as looking "like a rube just out of the hay field". Whether he looked like a country bumpkin or not, he was looking for trouble.

"Say," Mulverhill said to one of the sailors, "you from the *Philadelphia*?"

The sailor said he was.

"Well, my name is Mulverhill – Martin Mulverhill – and I can lick anything on two legs."

The other sailors turned slowly to Sharkey, knowing the boast would come like a slap in the face to him.

"I understand," Mulverhill went on, "that you've got a duffer named Sharkey on that tub o' yours. He's my meat. Trot him out and watch me maul him up."

Sharkey stepped forward. "Look here, my friend, my name is Sharkey, but this is no time to have trouble. If you are a fighter we can meet and have it out in the ring."

"That's my idea exactly," roared Mulverhill. "But I don't think you're game to meet me in the ring or any other place. Sailors are a lot of bluffs. Never saw one of 'em yet who could fight. They're all full of soup and potatoes."

The insult was almost too much for Sharkey's crewmates. They all wanted to take on Mulverhill there and then. But he left having set a date with Sharkey in the ring.

Sharkey turned up at the Armory Hall on November 24, intent on convincing the big talking Mulverhill that he was no champion. He found himself facing a fighter with a similar style to his own.

"Mulverhill was a scrapper of the barroom order, covering his face with one arm and lashing out with the other when he got in close," said Sharkey. "I had to beat him down by main force, slamming him on the back and trading punches with him when I could."

Sharkey knocked him out in the ninth, making it his longest fight to date, but he changed Mulverhill's mind about what all sailors were full of.

Several of Mulverhill's friends who had bet on him did not have money to pay their fares back to San Francisco. They had to walk around the bay to get home.

But things were moving again for Sharkey. His prestige was now outgrowing Vallejo and the sailors who backed him with their hard earned dollars and shouted for him ringside wanted him to go after even bigger fighters.

It was his next fight which would take his name to a wider audience and mark the first significant step in his pursuit of the heavyweight crown.

His opponent would be "Australian" Billy Smith, a fighter whom Mulverhill's lot felt would whip Sharkey. Smith had fought Joe Goddard, the Barrier champion, the tough fighter Frank "The Crafty Texan" Childs and Jim Corbett, a couple of years before he had become world champion.

Paul Herman, Sharkey's backer on the *Philadelphia*, got a little nervous. As the final preparations were being made for the fight, he approached his boxer.

"Tom," he said, "don't you think you are going up against a pretty tough game? This 'Australian' Billy Smith, I hear, is about the best heavyweight in San Francisco."

"No!" Sharkey snapped. "I'll fight him if he's the champion."

Sharkey was upset that Herman, who had seen him fight so many times in backstreet bouts, should be getting cold feet now that he was getting a sniff of something approaching the big time. It did not matter to Sharkey whether Herman was worried about the boxer's health or his own cash – his pride was hurt.

He said later: "It made me just a little bit sore that Herman should think I would sidestep any man. I had fought them all, just as they came, and though I been hit, good and hard sometimes, I can truthfully say that I had never been really hurt."

In truth, Sharkey's confidence was growing. "I was beginning to think that I could not be hurt with a sledgehammer," he said.

Sharkey described the venue at Colma as below Barney Farley's place, just across the San Mateo County line.

"I did my training, as usual, on the *Philadelphia*, running around the deck in the morning and in the evening around the Vallejo Navy Yard. The officers on the ship were very kind to me. Many of them were rabid boxing fans and I got all the time I wanted off regular duty to condition myself."

He needed to train too. He had not fought for eight months.

On the morning of the fight, July 25, 1895, he made his way to the venue with Herman and a few personal friends from the ship. Others found another way to get to Colma, on the San Francisco peninsula. Sharkey's friends from Vallejo chartered a steamer which headed out onto the water in the afternoon, loaded down with sailors and a crowd of gamblers. The gamblers delayed the boat as they made additional bets and then spent the hour on the water making more wagers again.

Sharkey recalled the betting in San Francisco being seven to one against him. "If you wished to back me you could almost write your own ticket. Smith was considered the biggest cinch bet that ever came over the pike."

Sharkey's friends were not put off though. They laid down their ten and twenty dollar pieces to match the money on Smith. "If I had lost," said Sharkey, "most of them would have to swim back to the ship."

If Herman was nervous in the days before the fight, he was panicking as the crowd began to gather. His calming words to Sharkey were meant more for his own benefit.

"Now, Tom," he said. "Don't get scared. This Smith may have nothing more than his reputation. Go after him just like you have all the other fellows. If you hit him he'll drop."

Sharkey was silent and gritted his teeth. As he put it later: "It made me sore to have Herman advising me not to get scared when he was the worst scared of the two."

The fight was promoted by either Jim Gibbs or Jim Groom, while the referee was a well-known bookmaker named Alva King, who was a very close friend of Al Herford, the manager of fighter Joe Gans.

According to Sharkey what followed was a battle. Smith was an accurate and strong hitter. Sharkey came in with his head down and his arms swinging. Smith took his measure and planted a right on his chin, a punch which Sharkey said "very nearly lifted me off my feet".

He said: "In later years, when I had learned a little about boxing, that punch would have served me as a warning that it was dangerous business to tear into a man who could hit like that. But in those days, I was young and foolish and strong as a bull. The punch merely made me mad. I wanted to get in close and give him a good one in return."

Head down, Sharkey went in for the Australian and the two men came together in the "finest little slugging bee in the centre of the ring that you ever saw".

Sharkey said: "Smith didn't back an inch and neither did I. We just put our heads together and smashed away while the sailors outside the ring yelled at me like crazy men. One round was very much like another, with the exception that, toward the end I began knocking Smith down."

The end came in the seventh round. "It was a happy bunch of blue jackets that returned to the *Philadelphia*. And not one of them was happier than I."

Sharkey left the *USS Philadelphia* on September 11, 1895 to spend six weeks at the *USS Independence* before being discharged.

Sharkey's service record shows a largely dedicated and able serviceman.

The Navy marked sailors every three months on professional qualifications (proficiency in rating, seamanship, gunnery, marksmanship with the "great guns" and marksmanship with small arms) and conduct, sobriety and obedience. The scale ranged from 0 (bad) and 1 (indifferent), through 2 (fair) and 3 (good), to 4 (very good) and 5 (excellent).

The majority of Sharkey's marks were 4 and 5, with a clean sweep of "excellents" for sobriety and obedience, almost throughout. He dramatically blotted his record during the last few months of 1893 when he returned to the *Philadelphia* "tight" and saw his sobriety rating plunge to 2. Throughout the rest of his service he got top marks for sobriety and was continually rated as good, very good and excellent in all the other disciplines. He only briefly had a crack at firing the great guns but did well.

Other offences during his service included spitting on deck

and not lashing his hammock, committed while he was still a rookie.

In October 1894, he was made up to Master At Arms (third class) and when he left the ship he was listed as desirable for retention as MAA.

All changed during September and October, 1895, though, on board the *Independence*, with thoughts of a life outside the service and, perhaps, of a boxing career beckoning.

His obedience rating dropped to 1 when on September 24, 1895, he stayed away at the end of his leave for 23 hours, was charged with leaving the ship without permission, tried before a summary court martial and spent 20 days in solitary confinement.

It was a miserable end to his navy career but he still received an honourable discharge on October 26, 1895 when he left the *USS Independence* at Mare Island, California.

Sharkey now had other things on his mind, although he would always fondly remember his buddies on the *Philadelphia*, and they would honour him a year later as his fame grew with the presentation of a gold-headed cane.[17]

He later recalled through rose-tinted glasses the last days of his navy career and failed to mention his time in solitary. "The fight with Smith was the last I had as a member of the crew of the *Philadelphia*," he wrote. "My time of service was nearly up and, as the day for leaving drew near, the officers and my pals among the sailors began urging me to re-enlist, to remain with them as their champion.

"But I was beginning to make a little money and couldn't see my way clear to do so.

"Two months after fighting Smith I received my discharge papers and left the ship; and on it I left as good and loyal a set of friends as a seagoing man ever had."

While training for his next fight, Sharkey met someone who was to have an influence on him in and out of the ring. That someone was Tim McGrath. They had met previously in Vallejo when McGrath and a fighter named Vic Lazay visited the Sharkey camp. Lazay, according to Sharkey, was a tall, raw-boned man who had just about convinced McGrath that he was the makings of a good prize-fighter.

"There were several good heavyweights around San Francisco who could have tried Lazay out," said Sharkey. "But Tim wanted something easier. So, having heard that I was nothing more than a rough-and-tumble fighter and that I had gained a little local prominence by whipping "Australian" Billy Smith, he conceived the idea of having Lazay whip me and thus establish a reputation."

They met in one of Sharkey's favourite haunts, Sheehan's saloon, when McGrath walked in with Lazay. McGrath spotted Sharkey in a crowd of his crewmates.

"You're Sharkey, the sailor?" McGrath said.

"Yes, I'm Sharkey."

McGrath looked him up and down, then reached into his pocket, drew out a document and began tearing it into shreds. He turned to Lazay and placed a hand on his shoulder.

"Vic," he said. "You catch the next boat and get back to San Francisco as fast as you can."

"What for?" demanded Lazay. "I've signed to fight this Sharkey."

"I know," McGrath told him, "but you are not going to fight him under any contract you've signed with me. I don't want to be arrested for murder."

McGrath's instant confidence in Sharkey made them immediate friends. McGrath quickly began training Sharkey properly for a fight with John Miller, the Terrible Swede.

McGrath, who was from County Limerick and like Sharkey had come over from Ireland when just a young man, was some character with a most distinctive look. Sharkey, who would describe McGrath as his best friend, said he "looked so funny. He reminded me of a rabbit, with his white hair, fuzzy face and little short bowlegs."

Whatever his appearance, when Sharkey went into training at Henry "Pop" Blanken's gymnasium, McGrath was in complete charge, despite only being about a year older than the sailor. He appointed himself boss and Sharkey began to feel like the hired man, not that he seemed to complain about that. His pride coped with a battering from McGrath when he told Sharkey he "didn't know anything about boxing or training".

The Irishman started to demonstrate his uppercut.

"What are you trying to do?" asked McGrath.

"Uppercut," Sharkey replied.

"Forget it," said McGrath. "You'll never make a fancy boxer if you live to be a thousand! Just wallop – that's all."

For the first time, Sharkey went through something which could be described as a systemized training regime: "so much running, a little wrestling, some slugging with sparring partners and just so much of certain foods to eat".

Sharkey explained: "That was all new to me. On the *Philadelphia* my training was limited to runs around the deck and an occasional bout with whatever sailors I could induce to don the gloves.

"When in port, as at Vallejo, I did a little running on the roads. But I had no idea as to what constituted physical fitness. I knew that running improved the wind. But that is about all I did know."

However, some of McGrath's ideas were strange to say the least. One day, old "Pop" Blacken – who trained a number of top fighters including Gus Ruhlin, who would later trade gloves in three significant fights with Tom - came out of his gym to find McGrath at the head of a bucket brigade throwing water against an outside wall.

Blacken became angry and said the water would warp the wooden boards. McGrath took him aside. "Listen, Pop," he said. "This fellow Sharkey is just off the ocean. Never worked on land before. If we dash water against the walls he'll think he's on a ship and train his head off."

Later, McGrath, who had a saloon called The Tip on Ellis Street, noticed that as Sharkey's reputation grew people wanted to see him train. McGrath began charging 25 cents admission to Pop's gymnasium. One day there was such a big crowd the building could not take anymore and there were still 20 or 30 outside clamouring to get in. McGrath turned on them, and said: "Say, I don't see you fellows trying this hard to get into The Tip."

The build-up to the Miller fight – Sharkey's last in Colma -

was more significant than the nine rounds which followed in the ring. "Miller was a big, good-natured fellow and I felt ashamed of myself when I crawled into the ring to meet him," said Sharkey.

It seems Miller was not too keen on hitting Sharkey either. Sharkey said the November 7, 1895 bout lasted as long as it did because "I didn't know exactly how to get at Miller and he wasn't quite foolish enough to accept my frequent invitations to stop and fight".

Sharkey had a little money and he took a long Christmas break from training while Tim McGrath planned their next move.

Tom Sharkey was resting as 1896 dawned but plans were being hatched for his future. Six months ago he had been languishing in relative obscurity, the Smith fight finally giving him some fame beyond the excited cries of a few sailors. Now though he was fighting his way nearer the top, nearer to names like John L Sullivan, Jim Corbett and to Bob Fitzsimmons, the major new contender to the heavyweight championship of the world.

Before 1896 was out, "Sailor" Tom Sharkey would have fought them all.

CHAPTER THREE
"Sharkey: You're pure gold"

On the verge of the big time after fighting professionals Billy Smith and John Miller, Sharkey had taken a four-month break while waiting for Tim McGrath to sort out his future.

Then in February McGrath came to Sharkey with the name of his next opponent.

"Tom," McGrath asked, "are you ready to fight again?"

"I was ready last November," the Irishman told him.

"Well," he said, "I have matched you for eight rounds with Alec Greggains."

"Good man. He's been pointed out to me around town."

McGrath gave Sharkey a look and dropped a question sure to rile the sailor.

"Not scared of him?" he asked.

"What you talking about?" Sharkey snapped. "Can't a man say another's a good one without being scared of him?"

"I was just asking," said McGrath. "It's always well to be certain of these things. Now let me tell you about this Greggains. He's a clever boxer, the cleverest you've ever been called on to meet.

But he can't hit. He couldn't break an egg if he punched at it for a month."

"If he can't hit, how's he going to lick me?" Sharkey asked.

"Ever hear of a man being outboxed?" said McGrath. "Think every man you'll be called on to meet is a bum? You've never met any clever guys, unless you call that 'Australian' Billy Smith one, and he wasn't clever or he'd never tried to mix with you.

"This Greggains is the real thing. If he gets started on you he'll make you think you fell into a boxing glove factory and are being buried under the stock."

Sharkey met Greggains before a rowdy crowd at the Bush Street Theatre, San Francisco, on March 12, 1896. It was going to be an eventful night as in Greggains' corner was one

Billy Harrison, a man later described with understatement by Sharkey as "a scrappy individual".

"Billy, we soon saw," recalled Sharkey later, "would make trouble if the opportunity offered."

Greggains was as smart a boxer as McGrath indicated. Early in the first, he took the centre of the ring and let go a straight left that jarred Sharkey's head back.

"The punch didn't hurt much, merely surprised me, but it started a rough house," said Sharkey.

Sharkey could hear McGrath yelling from the corner, telling him to "dig in", and he did, head down, fists up and flying, for eight rounds when the fight came to an unusual conclusion.

Sharkey said later: "To this day I do not know just how the fight ended. All I know is that it was a draw. Remember, I hadn't been off the ship very long and was still pretty green, so I let McGrath do all my talking.

"As I went to my corner at the end of the eighth round I heard a commotion and, looking across the ring, I saw Billy Harrison in the act of drawing his gun.

"I didn't stop to investigate. Gun-fighting is not a favourite pastime with me. The moment I saw that gun I ducked."

Sharkey disappeared back to his dressing room. Five minutes later there was a tapping at the door and McGrath slipped quickly inside.

"Where have you been, Tim?" said Sharkey.

"Been?" snorted Tim indignantly. "Where have I been? Somebody's going to get in trouble. What's the use of having fire regulations if they're not enforced!

"Here I been trying to get out of this theatre and couldn't find an exit. Barked my shins and almost cracked my ribs."

"Where's Harrison?" Sharkey asked.

"To the devil with Harrison," said Tim. "I'm not looking for him. What's he think I am – a moving target?"

McGrath and Sharkey avoided Billy Harrison after that, although Sharkey became friends with Alec Greggains, describing him as a "very decent, clever fellow…I always enjoyed his company very much". Much of the time they spent laughing about how the panicked McGrath hurt himself trying to kick his way out of Bush Street Theatre.

The Greggains' fight – and a further one-round victory, his second over Charles Brown on April 7, 1896 - raised Sharkey's stock again and the San Franciscans started looking for a "man who could whip (him)". They hit on an old foe of Jim Corbett's, the clever and swift boxer Joe Choynski, who had seen better days before suffering at the hands of Corbett in 1889. Sharkey was making the conditions now and McGrath telegraphed Choynski's friends to make a deal. The match was settled for April 16, 1896, at the People's Palace, on the corner of Mason and Eddy streets in San Francisco. According to the agreement, Choynski would have to try to knock me out in eight rounds. He obviously relished the challenge. As a veteran of 12 years in the ring, he had an imposing list of knockout victories and was known as a spoiler of the hopes of aspirants to the title.

The building shook with excitement that night, as white navy uniforms and officers' gold braid filled the seats around the ring.

Sharkey had never seen Choynski until he stepped through the ropes. The sight did not scare him. He wrote later: "I knew the minute I saw him that he had bitten off more than he could chew. Choynski, you know, had little thin legs and he wore his hair bushy, like Paderewski [a Polish composer famed for his wild hair].

"I wanted to laugh when I saw him. The idea of a little thin, dude-ish fellow like that stopping me seemed ridiculous to think of. But I didn't laugh. Tim McGrath had told me that I was not to underrate Choynski - that he was one of the hardest hitters in the world."

And Sharkey was not just taking advice from McGrath now. He had a new man in his corner, a celebrated second and tough fighter named "Spider" Kelly. Kelly, aged 24, a couple of months older than McGrath, was from the old country too, having been born James Patrick Curtin in County Kerry and come to America when he was about ten. Sharkey had heard all about Kelly long before the outstanding lightweight fighter had arrived in San Francisco and was pleased to have him on his team.[1]

Now, faced with Choynski's spindly legs, he said to Kelly: "He doesn't look tough. Bet I can break him in two."

"Never mind how he looks," replied Kelly gravely. "You'll find him tough enough. Look out for his left. If he hits you with it on the right spot we'll be taking you home in a hearse."

When the gong sounded Sharkey discovered what Kelly meant. "Choynski had a sure enough left," he said. "I could feel it whizzing past my ears."

Sharkey was learning though, trying to bring some method to his fighting. McGrath and Kelly were experienced men whom he respected and, even as the punches came in during that first round, he thought calmly to apply some science to the battle.

Back in Honolulu, he had done some training with a man named Fred Nealon, who depended on a left-hand punch.

"When he leads," Nealon had told Sharkey, "duck a little to the side and step in with your right. Hold your arm stiff and dig your glove into his ribs."

That's what he did now. Every time Choynski led, Sharkey stepped in and caught him. "I didn't mind his other punches," said Sharkey afterwards. "I caught them on the neck and face. But every time he tried to use his straight left, I beat him to it with my right."

Sharkey blazed away, landing "a flurry of unremitting lefts and rights", which after less than two minutes sent Choynski through the ropes. The final punch, described by Sharkey as "one of my rib roasters", created pandemonium, sending the spectators into a frenzy of excitement.[2]

Said Sharkey: "What followed cannot be easily described. I thought Hades had broken loose and that I was right in the centre of it all. Eddie Graney, who was in the Choynski corner, jumped in through the ropes and claimed a foul. And "Spider" Kelly jumped in through the ropes and started to lead me to my corner."

"Spider" clapped Sharkey on the back: "You've licked him!" he screamed. "Come away! Get out!"

The referee, Alva King, was totally confused and Graney came at him, jumping up and down and yelling: "Foul! Foul!"

King turned to whoever was near asking them what they had seen. Everyone had a view, depending on whose corner they were in or on whose back they had laid their dollars.

Choynski had been dragged to his corner and was trying to recover from the crashing blow. Sharkey saw nothing wrong with the punch and was astonished by the reaction. "It was a terrible mess," he said. "Everybody in the crowd was standing up and yelling. You couldn't hear yourself think."

Graney would not give up the fight. In the press row, just outside the ring, was Moses Gunst, rich cigar merchant and police commissioner. He had an officer at his side.

"Moses!" shouted Graney, "Moses! Choynski has been fouled!"

It was probably that appeal which led to the unusual circumstances which followed. Choynski was allowed between fifteen and twenty minutes to recuperate before resuming. Sharkey's soreness at the decision probably affected his performance. Choynski went for him with a blistering attack and beat Sharkey back sprawling halfway through the ropes. But he could not put Sharkey down and, after eight rounds of "brutal, barbarous brawling, in which all rules of fair play had been cast aside", the referee declared a draw.

Sharkey, according to the agreement, could claim victory, but he felt little satisfaction.

"Graney, as I learned afterwards, laughed over the way he had 'buffaloed' the referee and, in fact, admitted that Choynski had not been fouled," he claimed later. "He explained his action with the statement that it was all a part of the game, and that he thought if a second could fool or bluff a referee it was his business to do so.

"I also learned that Graney, after having the fight stopped in order to get Choynski his rest, was instrumental in getting it started again. He said that the people had paid their money to see a fight and that it wouldn't be right to deprive them of the fun."

Sharkey said: "Now that it's all over I can laugh about what Graney did. But I was a mad sailor at the time. I couldn't understand that Eddie in saving his man, who had actually been knocked out, had accomplished a wonderful piece of work.

"The fact that I held Choynski to an eight-round draw did not help my feelings. Nor did the fact that the papers next day all agreed that Choynski could hardly have gone two rounds more. All I knew was that Choynski had agreed to stop me. That, instead, I had stopped him, and that I had been bamboozled out of the decision."

The crowd treated Sharkey as the victor anyway, following him back to his dressing room. For the first time, he felt an early taste of the big time when a policeman was posted outside his door. As Sharkey was getting a rub down, there was the sound of raised voices outside.

"I am going in, sir," a man said grandly. "Going in, sir! Understand?"

"Spider" Kelly tiptoed to the door and peeked out.

Then, he threw the door open and began berating the police officer: "What do you mean, sir, stopping our friends? Haven't you any sense at all?"

Sharkey watched as Kelly made a low bow and in stepped a man of "very distinguished appearance".

"Tom," said Kelly. "I want you to meet Lord Talbot Clifton. He is one of our most prominent and best known sportsmen."

Lord Clifton was a tall, rangy Englishman, who had come to live in San Francisco and together with a colourful Irishman named Dan "White Hat" McCarty, had created the Tanforan racetrack.

The Englishman reached over and tapped Sharkey on the shoulder and then walked around him as if studying him like a horse.

"And you're Tom Sharkey," he said. "Well, sir, you're quite a stunning boy. Yes sir, a stunning boy."

According to Sharkey, the lord was a "genuine member of royalty and he became one of my best friends" while he was in the city.

Lord Clifton insisted the Sharkey team be guests at his home, Cliff House, and they were glad to accept. "He took Tim McGrath and 'Spider' Kelly and I out in a tallyho [a fast coach driven by four horses], with a big black man in brass buttons handling the ribbons." Sharkey was impressed. "Some class," he said afterwards. "I kept looking around to see if there were any sailors around from the *Philadelphia* to whom I might wave my hand."

Sharkey's next fight showed he was moving up inside the ring as well as out, as he pulled on his gloves at San Francisco's Mechanic's Pavilion, a busy indoor venue with more than 10,000 seats, to be watched by the heavyweight champ, Jim Corbett.[3]

Sharkey's opponent on June 2, 1896, was Jim Williams of Salt Lake City, who had not been beaten and "was reputed to be able to take punishment like a bulldog and to have a great right hand".

The three-round knock-out Sharkey inflicted on Williams, though, was something of a sideshow to the events which really helped shape his future career. From the first, all eyes were on the ringside seat in which local boy and world champion James J Corbett sat enjoying every bit of attention.

Said Sharkey years later: "I can see him still, sitting there, surrounded by admirers, talking and joking while he laughed at the two 'dubs' in the ring."

And Sharkey remembered also that as the two fighters "stood and whaled away at each other" someone in the crowd yelled across the ring: "Jim, how long would it take you to whip either one of these bums?"

"A couple of punches," replied Corbett to roars of laughter. "A couple of punches."

Despite the laughter, Sharkey still felt it a "treat" to hear the champion talk.

Tim McGrath did not. He turned around and glared at Corbett.

"Yah," he sneered, "a couple o' punches. You can't knock him out at all."

After Sharkey had finished Williams, he wandered off to his dressing room with McGrath, the attention outside still on the champ.

Suddenly "Spider" Kelly burst through the door.

"McGrath!" he cried. "Sharkey, come over here!"

Kelly gasped for breath and the men waited for him to speak. He was searching for words as he poked a finger back at the doorway.

"Say, I just come from out there," he said. "Know what they're saying? That Corbett can stop Sharkey in four rounds." He waited for the penny to drop. "Get the idea?"

"Spider" laughed and began a little jig. "What a cinch!" he said. "A cinch!"

Sharkey said hesitantly: "But Corbett is the champion of the world."

"You keep still!" roared Kelly. "You've got nothing to do but fight. Tim and I will fix this and you'll be champion. Stop you in four rounds – he can't do it with a hammer."

Kelly grabbed Tim and ran out, saying he was scared Corbett's backers, who were urging him to show how he could stop Sharkey, would back down.

Sharkey sat alone in his dressing room and "thought the matter over". His mind ran a simple route: "Corbett was the world's champion. He ought to be able to punch my head off."

Three days after the fight with Jim Williams, Sharkey went to a place owned by Corbett's brother Harry on Ellis Street. At his side was a Boston-based businessman named Danny Lynch who had made a lot of money on race horses in California and believed he could make even more with Sharkey. With him were Tom's trainers and pals, Tim McGrath and "Spider Kelly", and Danny Needham, an old-time boxer. They found Corbett sitting in a corner with a drink before him and admirers all around. The scene was meant to intimidate the visitors. As Sharkey said later: "He was telling a funny story when we entered and though he knew what we were there for, as did all the others who were present, he did not seem to notice us until he had finished his story and everybody had laughed."

Having made Sharkey wait, Corbett rose, shook hands with Lynch, McGrath, Kelly, Needham and, finally, Sharkey. "Howdydo?" said the champion.

Lynch did the talking. "I understand that you still think you can stop Sharkey in four rounds."

Corbett laughed and slapped his hand down on Lynch's back.

"Yes," he said, "you have it straight."

"The match is on, then," said Lynch. "It's all right with the promoters."

"Yes," said Corbett. "I've attended to my end of the business with Groom and Gibbs."

"Well," said Lynch, turning to Sharkey, "you get over to Oakland and go into training."

The deal apparently done, Sharkey went to his home in Vallejo to get his things and moved over to Danny Needham's home in Oakland, on the eastern shore of San Francisco Bay. He was to train at the Acme club, where DeWitt Van Court was boxing instructor, and McGrath and Kelly would look after his work. He boxed every day with "Spider" and Needham and went running over the Piedmont hills.

In Corbett's camp, though, all was not well. His manager, Bill Brady, had been working hard to get a big purse for Corbett's proposed fight with Fitzsimmons. Corbett had apparently come to California against Brady's advice and had probably not told him about his match with Sharkey. As Sharkey thought, the champ was just "thinking, of course, that he was picking up some extra money for himself on the side by whipping the 'soft sailor'".

The problems came to Sharkey's attention one day when Lynch came over to Oakland "one afternoon with a face on him a foot long" and interrupted his training.

"Tom," he said. "I'm sorry, but you had better knock off work and go back to Vallejo. Corbett's backed down."

McGrath and Kelly began to argue, but Lynch went on: "Corbett refuses to go through with the proposition of attempting to knock Tom out in four rounds."

Sharkey was calm for the moment. "What will he agree to do?"

"He states," said Lynch, "that he will box you four rounds for a decision."

Now, Sharkey's temper blew. Was he going to miss his big chance? Was the champion backing out on him, messing him around?

"He's a fine champion," Sharkey said sarcastically. "Makes a man a proposition and then backs down cold. Go back and tell him I'll bet him $10,000 that I can stop him in four rounds."

Lynch began to smile.

"Oh," Sharkey said, his pride ruling his brain again, "you needn't think I'm bluffing. I've got the money. I've saved it up."

Lynch laughed out loud.

"Hold your horses, Tom," he said. "I know that you're not bluffing. But let's not make any fool bets. Corbett is the world champion. They'd put us in the asylum if we offered to bet that you or any other man can stop him in four rounds. Let's be sensible."

Lynch had a talk with McGrath and Kelly as Sharkey continued to fume.

"If he won't agree to knock Sharkey out, take him up on any kind of proposition," advised Kelly, realizing they could not let the opportunity slip away. "Man alive! Can't you understand that this Corbett is the world's champion? We're pretty lucky to even get him to talk about meeting a rough sailor. Get him! Tell him he can have the decision to start with. Promise anything – but get him in the ring."

So, Sharkey waited in Oakland while Lynch returned to San Francisco. Late that night he showed up again at Needham's.

"It's all fixed," he said, this time smiling. "Corbett agrees to box for a decision. I'm on to him. He figures that he'll run rings around you and make you look like a sucker. I don't suppose that he'll even try to knock you out."

"That's his business," said Kelly sharply. "He can make his fight and we'll make ours."

The next morning Sharkey was out on the Piedmont hills again. The fight between the rough sailor and the world champion – "the four-round go which made me known to the sporting world" - was back on.

The Corbett fight was fixed for June 24, 1896, at the National Athletic Club, San Francisco. Corbett not only stood to get the decision if Sharkey could not knock him out in four, he would pocket the first $10,000 taken at the box office plus fifty per cent of the rest. The club would pay Sharkey and he could only get a win by knocking out the champ. A reporter from California wrote as the details were announced: "Scarcely anything else is discussed in sporting circles, the clubs and by men about town. At first, the people were inclined to think the affair was all a hoax but when they were assured that Corbett had really consented to meet the local man, they commenced speculating on the outcome."

The writer went on: "Although Corbett does not claim that he will put out the marine in the specified time, he admits that he will administer a terrific beating to him. He says the real reason for accepting the proposition is his desire to prove to his friends that the stories of his degeneration are out of joint."

Corbett was delaying a trip to Europe – as well as risking Brady's wrath – in order to prove a point with Sharkey. He went into light training at the Olympic. He had no worries about the upcoming bout. As he later wrote in his autobiography, *The Roar of the Crowd*, he believed Sharkey "was a fellow capable of taking a lot of punishment, but good only in a 'rough-house' fight". Consequently, he claimed he did little preparation for the bout "for I had never seen the time when, even though out of condition, I couldn't box four fast rounds, certainly fast enough to beat such an awkward fellow; and I had made up my mind not to exert myself by trying to knock him out, but merely to make a fool out of him for the short period, by my superior skill. That would give the audience enough show for its money."

Meanwhile, Sharkey – who had no more contact with Corbett until they stepped into the ring – was sounding very confident that he would last the four rounds.

"I do not think there is a man living who can put me out in that space of time," he said in an interview quoted in the *Brooklyn*

Daily Eagle. "There is a great deal of difference in a man fighting a man who wants to fight back and going after a man who knows that all he has to do is to keep away for a short period of time. Of course, I do not for a moment place myself on a par with Corbett so far as science is concerned, but I am positive that he will never punch me out in four rounds."

In another interview, Sharkey said: "If I win the battle, I will be ready to stop any and all challengers for the title. I believe it is the pugilist's business to fight, not talk and it is men who monopolize the columns of the newspapers and fight shy of the ring, who have debased the manly art in this country."

"I candidly admit that Corbett is more scientific than I am. He is a shifty fighter and a good ring general. But I am going to surprise some of the people who think I have no show with him.

"Twenty-three men have donned the gloves with me and they went down. One blow did the business for most of them. Several of the fights were won in less than a minute each. Corbett can't keep me from hitting him once during four rounds and when I hit him, he will go the same as the rest".

On the afternoon of the fight, Sharkey, Kelly and McGrath crossed over from Oakland and went to the old Windsor Hotel, on the corner of Fifth and Market streets. Inside there seemed to be the whole of Vallejo. All Sharkey's old friends had come to see the fight. Mrs Gillren, the hotel's owner, took charge of the man of the moment.

"Ah, Tom, me boy," she said. "There's nothin' to it. Listen, I've sent $20 to the poolroom so that you'll knock the stuff out of this Corbett."

Mrs Gillren then took the three men to the dining room and made them sit down to dinner. Then they headed to the Mechanic's Pavilion to be there at a good time, and found it already filled to the rafters.

Danny Lynch was busy at the box office and did not have time to chat to Sharkey, who went straight to his dressing room and stayed there with McGrath and "Spider" until a man stuck his head in the door and announced that it was time.

The Vallejo contingent cheered as Sharkey entered the ring

but then had to wait twenty minutes before Corbett appeared. "He figured that by keeping me waiting he would make me nervous," said Sharkey, admitting that, "When Corbett finally did show up I thought the crowd would tear the roof off the place with their cheers."

Corbett took off his bathrobe, folded it very carefully and then walked to the centre of the ring, where Sharkey was waiting to pose for a picture. According to the Irishman, Corbett then came up very close to him, reached over quickly and, grabbing his hand, attempted to jerk Sharkey toward him.

"Stand over here," he growled.

Wise old "Spider" Kelly had warned Sharkey that Corbett would attempt to wind him up so when Corbett tried to jerk him Sharkey stood firm.

"No," he said, "stand over here," and jerked back hard on Corbett's grip so that he "almost yanked his arm out".

Corbett had arrived in the ring with no towels or buckets. He did not think he would need such things. His second-in-chief was George Green, later boxing instructor of the Olympic Club.

Master of ceremonies Billy Jordan introduced Corbett as "a native son of California and champion of the world", and the crowd cheered again. Sharkey was introduced as the "pride of the American navy" and received a few hand claps from the sailors, drowned out by the Corbett fans who dominated the 10,000 capacity crowd.

Local man Frank Carr was the referee and he told both men there should be no hitting in the clinches and, said Sharkey, "we both understood that when we went to our corners".

The Irishman then said the champ played foul. "No sooner did we go into the first clinch than Corbett, ignoring the referee's instructions, let go a punch that landed flush on my eye. That punch gave me the only black eye I ever had in my entire ring career.

"Naturally I expected that Carr would at least say something to Corbett about having disregarded his order and, when he didn't, it made me so mad that I forgot all about Corbett's being the world's champion.

"I put my head down and sailed in, not caring how or where I landed, nor how many times Corbett landed on me. All I knew was that I had been struck an unfair punch and that I ought to clean the fellow who struck me.

The first three rounds were pretty much alike – me digging in all the time and Corbett doing his best to avoid me and at the same time making a pretence of boxing cleverly."

By the time Sharkey returned to his corner at the end of the third round, McGrath and Kelly were going "crazy".

"You've got him, Tom," screamed McGrath. "You've got him."

"You're the champion of the world," screamed Kelly above the din. "You're the champion."

They pounced on Sharkey, sat him on the stool and rubbed him down ready for the final onslaught.

"Now," said McGrath as they breathed life into Sharkey's aching muscles, "when the bell rings you run out there and beat him down. Don't stop for anything – just sail in, and punch."

"Spider" Kelly kept telling him he had won the championship, he just had to keep on. When the bell sounded for the final three minutes of the contest, Sharkey was filled with renewed confidence and ran at his rival.

"I met Corbett coming out of his corner, and pumped punches into him so fast that he staggered back, and the crowd came to its feet as one man," remembered Sharkey later. "Then something funny happened. When I began getting Corbett good and hard, when he was actually groggy, Frank Carr, the referee, got to holding me back. On the slightest pretext, he took hold of my arms and tried to keep me from hitting Corbett."

One onlooker noted the punishment Corbett was taking, despite his superior height and reach. "The blows rained thick and fast on the champion's head. Twice the sailor tripped him to the floor. Twice he fought him to the ropes, while Corbett, in return, failed to deliver the looked for knockout blows."

Sharkey became angry at the referee: "I became so furious at the evident favouritism being shown Corbett that I finally rushed in with all my might, not only taking Corbett to the floor

SAILOR TOM

with me, but the referee as well."

There was a danger the contest, goaded by a baying crowd, could have descended into farce. The fight was stopped and declared a draw with some saying Corbett had asked the authorities to step in. Sharkey later brought that up, perhaps to clear Corbett, but maybe to remind people of the allegation.

"[I] wish to say something in the spirit of fairness," he said years later. "It has been said that when [the men went to the floor] Corbett called on the police to save him his championship. I did not hear Corbett call. I don't believe he did utter a sound with his mouth. But persons around the ringside, a score of them, told me that they saw him nod to Captain Wittman. And whether he did or not, there is no question as to the fight being stopped and being declared a draw.

"And neither will anyone who saw the fight argue that Corbett could have gone another round. There was a lot of money bet that Corbett would knock me out. And you could have written your own ticket at any old odds if you thought Corbett would not get the decision.

"The action of the police, in stopping the fight when they did, saved a great deal of money.

We still had a minute to go and Corbett was a very wobbly man when he went to his corner. Much might have happened even in that one minute had we been permitted to go on."

Certainly, one reporter whose copy was printed next day across America, described how Corbett was almost "knocked out". The writer stated: "Champion Jim Corbett climbed down last night from his pedestal of pugilistic greatness and at the same time husky Tom Sharkey, who was eight months ago a mere blue jacket at the Mare Island navy yard, mounted to the top notch in the sporting calendar."

He added that at the end of the fight the massive crowd saw "an undefeated world's champion hanging around his opponent's neck, weak, listless, panting and leaning against the ropes to prevent himself from falling". The fight was declared a draw, he said, but "had it lasted a few rounds more there might have been a different story to tell – a story that would make pugilistic history. There are those in San Francisco today and their number is legion, who say that twelve more minutes of fighting last night would have made a new world's champion."

He said Corbett went into the ring smiling and confident, and "came out of it trembling and crestfallen, having "narrowly escaped being a whipped man".

Most onlookers dismissed the fight as a disappointment with more clinching than punching, making it a "wrestling match".

But the *Brooklyn Daily Eagle* reported: "Round after round the champion's admirers cheered and goaded [him] on to the victory he could not win."

It said part of Corbett's failure, as the journalist viewed it, was down to "overconfidence." But, "probably Tom Sharkey was himself really the cause of it, for Sharkey is a wonderful fighter. Corbett is magnanimous enough to declare that the sailor is the best wrestler he ever met." It was, though, a back-handed compliment from the champ.

Corbett's statement after the fight said: "When I say that Sharkey is a good, strong man, I tell the whole story. He is a bull, but he is no fighter. The people are mistaken if they think he landed a serious blow on me. My face is now without a mark or bruise. My shoulders are a little red from the effects of his blows, but that is all.

"In the second round I had him going and would have put him out if the round had lasted ten seconds longer. The referee stopped us when I had Sharkey in his corner, rattled, in the second round and offered to give me the decision, but I would not accept it.

"I had no difficulty in hitting Sharkey, but he can stand more punishment than the ordinary man. I could have blinded him by continuing to hit him on the eye, which I nearly closed in the second round but it would have done no good to hurt the poor fellow that much, so I refrained from hitting his right eye after the first blow.

"The people seemed to think that I was doing all the hugging in the last round, but that is a pardonable mistake. Those who simply saw it could not realize what was being done as the participants could. Sharkey hugged me as often and as long as he could and I had a hard time of it keeping him from crushing in the top of my head with his arm. He aimed blow after blow at my cranium while we were clinched and if one of them had landed I would have had a crushed skull.

"If my seconds had made the claim I would have secured the decision on fouls. Sharkey was continually giving me the shoulder and cross buttock. But my seconds had instructions to claim no fouls."

Reporters saw the champion's final ignominy after the "crestfallen world beater" went to his corner for the last time, as the sailor challenged him to a $10,000 finish fight for the championship and "Corbett, in the hope of recovering his laurels, accepted."

Corbett said in his statement: "I am ready for Sharkey at once. Let him cover the money and all arrangements will be made at once for the affair. I am going to leave the city in a few days, so he must act quickly. Finish fights are what I desire and not four-round battles, in which a man cannot fight scientifically but must slug and wrestle."

Corbett, in his 1925 memoir, tries to make a joke out of the fight and his excuses with the pen come quicker and faster than his punches did on the night. Describing the moment he went to the floor, he wrote: "It happened that just before the fight I had eaten one of the French dinners for which San Francisco was noted in those days, and when the referee landed on my stomach I realised how many courses I had tried – shrimp salad, Swiss Gruyère, vanilla ice-cream, *vin rouge*, etc, etc, and instead of protesting to the referee, all I thought of doing was calling for the steward, as one does on shipboard on high seas."

Corbett described the end of the fight: "As I stood up with my arms around [Sharkey's] neck, with a minute to go, I knew that if ever he threw me down again the champion of the world would not get up. Realizing the danger, I couldn't understand why Delaney, usually a quick thinker, did not jump in and claim 'Foul!' He had every justification. So I looked at him over Sharkey's shoulder and gave an appealing nod, trying to tell him to come to the rescue, when suddenly the Chief of Police jumped in the ring and stopped the fight, partly because of the extremely rough and foul tactics of Sharkey, more because he thought the great disorder of the audience would turn into a riot."

Corbett then makes a claim described by his own biographer as "ludicrous": "[The police chief] allowed the referee to give his decision, which he gave all right – a draw – and yet I had not been hit once in the whole fight!"

Five decades later, in a piece written after Sharkey's death, writer Jersey Jones delivered *The Ring*'s verdict on the fight: "It was lucky for Corbett the meeting wasn't scheduled for longer (than four rounds). Sharkey nearly wrecked him. With his fancy boxing and snappy punching, the champion did well enough for two rounds, but he began to tire in the third from the fast pace and Sharkey's roughhouse tactics. Tom swarmed all over Corbett in the fourth round and a weary champion slumped on his stool at the end of the round. Referee Frank Carr called the bout a draw, but the verdict met with noisy disapproval from the crowd. Almost unanimously it was conceded that Sharkey had won."

And in his biography of Corbett, Patrick Myler states: "The round was almost over when the chief of police, believing the fight had turned into a brawl which could incite a section of the crowd, jumped into the ring and called a halt. The referee declared it a draw much to the disgust of spectators, who felt Sharkey had deserved to win."

The next day the papers were giving a six-month deadline in which the fight would be fought with the five-figure sum listed as the largest purse offered by any club. Nothing had been signed yet but Paul Herman, ship flag signal quartermaster on the *USS Philadelphia*, who claimed to have taught Sharkey how to read and write and to have given him his first lessons in boxing, said he was ready to back his protégé to the tune of $10,000. Another offer came in too, from Parson Davies in Chicago, who was looking after Choynski and wanted a rematch. He posted $1,000 as an "earnest of his willingness" to match Choynski against Sharkey for $5,000 a side in a finish fight. "If Sharkey does not desire a finish, Davies will back Choynski to stop Sharkey in eight rounds," an

Illinois reporter wrote. "He also offers to back Choynski against Corbett, the latter to stop Choynski in eight rounds, the entire gate receipts to go to the winner."

Sharkey was big news and he certainly was not finished with Corbett, whom he readily claimed to have "virtually defeated…in four rounds". He was, he admitted, "the man of the hour".

"I won't attempt to be modest because I wish to stick to the truth," he said, writing about the event later. "The papers the day after the fight agreed that Corbett could not have lasted another round. That helped out. People followed me on the streets and pointed me out to their friends."

Two days later, Sharkey said, he met with Corbett at Ellis Street.

"I could see that Corbett was feeling badly and that he was doing his best to appear cheerful and unconcerned," said Sharkey. "He clearly indicated how he felt by his eagerness to engage me in conversation."

Corbett told him: "Well, you did pretty well."

Sharkey told him he did as well as could be expected "considering the conditions".

"Yes," said Corbett with an air of superiority. "You are a very strong man. You ought to make a good wrestler. You'll never make a fighter."

Sharkey blasted him with a response he later would not repeat and then repeated his offer to fight Corbett at "any time, any place, for any amount of money and for any number of rounds".

"And when I finish with you," Sharkey said, "you will have found out whether I will ever make a good fighter."

Sharkey claimed an agreement was made between the two fighters, confirming a fight to the finish for a side bet of $10,000 and with each putting up $2,500 to bind the match.

One sporting celeb, who said he "no longer placed a bet on the horses, for the reason that his judgment in picking them had cost him $100,000 in the last six years" said he had "still $5,000 left with which to bet that Corbett will defeat Sharkey". John L Sullivan backed Corbett too, saying he would win "in a walk". The former champ was not backward in delivering his view of the four-rounder: "To knock a powerful young man out in four rounds requires a tremendous hitter. Corbett is not that kind of fighter. The first two rounds the other night proved that, for he hit Sharkey where and when he liked and failed to knock him down. When he had expended all his best hitting powers Sharkey was still there and was strong – probably stronger than Corbett. In short, it was simply a case of Corbett not being a hard enough hitter to knock the strong young fellow out. If the same two men were to fight to a finish and Corbett was properly trained, he would simply butcher Sharkey. I have no doubt on this point at all. I have met men similar to Sharkey in my time, and I know that in a finish fight Corbett would either close up his eyes tight or knock his wind out gradually and then knock him out very easily".

Sharkey was now finally making the news back home.

On July 11, 1896, the *Dundalk Democrat* reported the plans for the big Corbett fight, stating: "The coming battle is now looked forward to with intense interest in America, and Corbett, after a brief training, will be different from what he was when competing in the combat which ended in a draw."

The paper then stated indignantly that American papers refer to Sharkey as "of Irish-American" parentage.

"This is quite wrong," it stated. "Sharkey first saw the light in Hill Street, Dundalk, and went to American only a few years ago."

It added of the local hero: "He is a Sandow in appearance and development."[4]

A week later, still following the situation in America keenly, the newspaper reported that Corbett's failure to knock out the Dundalk hardman had "occasioned the greatest excitement throughout America".

However, there was still talk that Corbett, through his manager, had already signed up to fight Fitzsimmons, speculation as to when that would go ahead and counter-speculation that Fitzsimmons "did not care to fight anymore".

For some time, the Sharkey-Corbett prospect enchanted everyone, but they would not meet again for more than two years and it would be in one of the most baffling encounters of both fighters' careers.

Describing Corbett's intentions over the planned 1896 rematch, Sharkey said: "Corbett, as foxy a man as ever drew on a glove, had no idea of going through with that match. This we ascertained later, when it developed that, in the articles we signed, he caused to be inserted a clause which prohibited either of us before we met again in the ring from participating in a contest with any other opponent. This clause resulted eventually in the match falling through, though it hung fire and was written about for several months."

Sharkey always smarted at the disrespect he felt Corbett showed him. Almost 40 years after the fight, he wrote in an article in *Liberty* magazine: "When I fought James J Corbett, the champion of the world, in San Francisco, I was trained to the minute. Corbett was not. If the police hadn't interfered I would have licked Corbett. Corbett was not caught out of condition again. Because I kept in top condition I could throw just as many punches in the twenty-fifth round as the first."

At the end of July 1896, Sharkey was spotted in the lobby of the Victoria Hotel, Chicago, where he told people: "Jim Corbett could not whip me in a thousand years." A city newspaperman gave locals a description of Sharkey: "[He] looks like a fighter. He has immense shoulders and a huge neck, while even the lines of his face indicate great muscular strength. Then, too, Sharkey suggests the fighter in his talk more than the average big pugilist. He talks…with quick short sentences."

Sharkey told people in Chicago that he was on his way east to "look around a bit" having done so much training that he needed a rest. It would not be a case of putting his feet up, though, as there was always the opportunity to pick up a few dollars by refereeing and giving sparring exhibitions with his trainer, Danny Needham.

In August 1896, Sharkey was due to referee a three-fight card in the Olympic rink, Fiftieth Street and Third Avenue, Brooklyn. The bill included Dick O'Brien and "Scaldy" Bill Quinn but, the *Brooklyn Daily Eagle* reported, Sharkey "will be an added attraction, as it is the first opportunity of viewing the man who made matters so interesting for Corbett."[5]

But as Sharkey later noted the "additional publicity" given him through the Corbett fight meant that Lynch was able to arrange a special highlight for Sharkey's first eastern tour – an exhibition bout with Sharkey's inspiration, the former master John L Sullivan.

The event, on August 31, was announced two weeks ahead of time, and fans wanting to see the "new pugilistic star" promised to fill Madison Square Garden. Newspapers reported: "While many persons are in doubt as to the merit of Tom Sharkey's performance against Corbett, yet there is a unanimous desire to see the man who came out of a four-round affair with the former champion and showed nothing worse than a puffed eye."

Sharkey knew his opponent was now "old and fat", but said: "It was quite a treat for me to put on the gloves with a man whom I had looked on through my boyhood as the greatest fighter that ever lived."

The *Brooklyn Daily Eagle* explained – at length - why Sharkey, who was still not 23, was not being pitted against a younger and quicker man. The explanation went back to the planned Corbett rematch: "Sharkey is matched to fight Corbett to a finish next December and his contract with Corbett calls for his keeping out of all manner of boxing bouts till after the big fight, the spirit of which seems to be that if Sharkey should happen to be bested by anyone, enough to lose any prestige, Corbett might deem the contract broken and probably lay claim to forfeit the money, while if he went on with people and bested them or broke even, there would probably be no objection. It will be seen, therefore, if Sharkey meets anyone in the East, he is doing so at his own peril."

Sharkey, the paper pointed out, obviously accurately, does not believe that Sullivan "can do any harm" but, it warned, the "great John L may bustle the new aspirant for the championship more than he anticipates".

The Ring later explained that Sharkey, who met Sullivan in New York's Jimmy Wakeley's saloon, a popular hangout for sporting celebrities, had another reason for fighting his hero. "The old champion was pretty much down on his luck," explained the magazine, and the bout would be a benefit for him. Writer AD Phillips joined a group of Irish fans who accompanied Sharkey that day. "Tom, with chest out, eyes front and a big 'rock' pinned to his shirt, walked proudly along the Bowery to Jim Wakeley's saloon where he was introduced to the 'mob' - the sportsmen," wrote Phillips.

On the way, fearing a thief might take a liking to the six-carat diamond that Tom wore on his chest, he fastened the pin to some cardboard under his shirt and, throughout the journey to Wakeley's, "he never kept his eye off the valuable 'shiner'".

In the bar, John L walked over to the Sailor, grasped his hands and patted him on the back.

"Young fellow, you're pure gold," he said. "They come no better than you. I hope you some day hold the world's title and with it, get a heap of coin."

Sharkey swelled with pride and was almost struck speechless. Finally, he told his hero: "Anybody ought to be tickled to get a chance to fight at your benefit."

Sullivan's manager, Parson Davies, commissioned Tom O'Rourke – who would become an important new figure in Sharkey's life - to make all the arrangements in New York, where fight fans were quickly buzzing.

According to journalists in the West, Sharkey was now being called the new John L Sullivan so the bout, although just a three-round exhibition, was being billed by some as a contest between the "original strong boy from Boston and the new Hercules of the ring".

The heavy-drinking Bostonian, according to Davies, had "walked a straight line for some months past with the result that he is in very good physical condition". In addition, he was arriving in a city where he had "thousands of friends" itching to "see the old gladiator put up his hands". A has-been, perhaps, but, wrote the reporters, "it is questionable if the man who held the heavyweight championship against all comers for twelve years will not prove as great an attraction as Sharkey".

Sharkey, on the other hand, was being billed as the boxer who gained an international reputation quicker, or least as quick, as any other.

"Prior to the night he had a brief set to with James J Corbett, he was practically unknown except to the few who follow the fistic game with regularity," said the *Brooklyn Daily Eagle*. "He went on the stage with Corbett that night with all the confidence possible in a man in his position and justified all the good things his friends had said about him by more than holding his own with the man who was thought to have only one or two rivals for the championship of the world.

"When the sailor boy woke the next morning he found himself a noted character." Following the "remarkable feat" against Corbett, the paper started, Sharkey thought he was the "best man in the world and is anxious to prove it".

Its boxing writer introduced the new star to New Yorkers: "The sailor is not a particularly handsome man but he has all the earmarks of a great athlete.

"Many will think it was a bad thing for him to come before the people so suddenly, arguing the tendency to become inflated with his own importance. There is nothing at all boastful about him, nor does he impress one with being in the least susceptible to flattery. His great breadth of shoulders and the rapid manner of moving are the principal things that attract an onlooker to him."

Another writer noted: "Physically, Sharkey is admitted to be the most remarkable specimen that ever stepped into the ring and Corbett is quoted as saying that New Yorkers will see an astonishing example of muscular development."

It was not just the fans whose mouths watered at the prospect of the old master taking on the young pretender. Corbett, Fitzsimmons, Peter Maher, Frank "Paddy" Slavin and Steve O'Donnell pledged to be there as spectators, making the "gathering of heavyweights…the most notable in ring history".

Corbett – whose manager, Brady, was still reportedly meeting with Lynch to discuss a fight - used his arrival in New York to have another dig at the man who had so hurt his pride: "Yes, he gave me a hard fight in 'Frisco but if I had been in better shape I think he would not have lasted the four rounds. As it was, the referee gave the decision to me no less than three times but as

Sharkey kept on fighting all the time there was nothing left for me to do but to continue. Had my opponent been a man who could have beaten me, I would have claimed the fight, but I figured that I could not afford to do so with a man like Sharkey.

"He is a strong fellow, but one who will need a lot of watching in the ring, as he is apt to go foul at the first chance. From what I am told, Sharkey easily bested Choynski and the latter acknowledged that two of his ribs were broken by one of Sharkey's blows."

A few days later, neither Sharkey nor Corbett appeared to want to meet each other face to face in suits, let alone only in shorts inside the ring, as neither turned up to discuss their rematch in a meeting at the New York offices of the *Police Gazette*. But the fact that Corbett had reportedly separated from Brady was made clear at the meeting, which heard that the National Athletic Club of San Francisco had made a bid of $20,000 for the fight. The boxers' representatives made reference to Fitzsimmons and a clause was added to their agreement that the Corbett-Sharkey battle be "for the heavyweight championship of the world, and the belt emblematic of the same".

Within a year of becoming professional then, "Sailor" Tom Sharkey was being given a glimpse of the world heavyweight title. Although again, as with a couple of years previously, when Corbett, reluctant to fight, had offered the title on a plate to Maher it remained questionable as to whether it was his to give —without acknowledging Fitzsimmons.

Corbett missed the meeting as he was spending a few days in Baltimore with his brother, Joe, a pitcher with the local baseball team. There, he was asked if he would release Sharkey to fight Fitzsimmons first and so make the Corbett-Sharkey or Corbett-Fitzsimmons fight a genuine title decider.

He reacted angrily. "I positively refuse to consider any such proposition," he said. "Until I meet Sharkey no one else shall. If Fitzsimmons wants to fight, I am ready to meet him in three weeks or less. After he has met me, he can get on all the bouts he wants with the San Francisco man."

Meanwhile, Sharkey had set up training camp at Mount

Clemens, Michigan, and was "enjoying the baths and scenery". Boxer Fred Hallen checked him out and declared: "He is a man of wonderful physical power and, unlike most strong men, is not in the slightest degree shoulder-bound. I took particular notice of that. There is a great flexibility of movement of arms and shoulders and he strikes freely with right or left. I watched him punch the bag and I never saw such thumps. While in the matter of science, I should rate him a novice as compared to Corbett, yet it seems to me if Sharkey ever lands one of his terrible blows on an opponent, somebody will ring for an ambulance."

Sharkey arrived back in New York with Danny Needham late on August 30, 1896, the night before the fight. They went straight to the Hotel Warwick on Broadway, where Lynch had rented them rooms. A number of fight fans greeted him at the hotel and he talked happily about his fight with Corbett. He was asked whether he had fouled Corbett and said, on the contrary, the champion had been guilty of the "most flagrant breaches of boxing etiquette himself". Sharkey also repeated the claim that had the police not stopped the bout, in another round Corbett would have been in a very bad condition. Sharkey admitted that some of Corbett's blows had landed but argued that the champion's denials that he had been hit to be "untrue in the extreme". He punished Corbett's body badly, he said, and was confident of defeating Corbett in the coming battle. If first class physical condition counts for anything, he told onlookers, he would do so.

Despite the now familiar boasts from both boxers, they again failed to pull off a second meeting to discuss their fight. Sharkey was there – even though it was only hours before he was due to trade blows with Sullivan – and so was Lynch, who became angry when Corbett failed to show, saying a big offer, much larger than the $20,000 offered by the National Club of San Francisco, had come in from British Columbia. Lynch wanted articles signed for a fight to take place within four weeks. "If Corbett demurs, I will arrange another meeting and, if he shows the white feather again, I will throw him aside and take on Fitzsimmons or Maher or the next best man on the list," he said. "But mind you, we won't let

Corbett rest. Every time Sharkey meets Corbett on the street, he will try and lick him there and then. It will be a case of rough-and-tumble scrap every time they meet and Sharkey will keep this up until Jim comes to time, won't you, Tom?"

Sharkey, who had been listening to Lynch's rant, lifted his head and nodded. He then made his own statement for reporters, saying "anything my manager says goes". He added: "I am not in the business for my health but I am going to take it out of Corbett if he throws me down. He knows I can lick him and he has no reason to treat me in the manner he has done. I'm tired of being fouled and I don't want to be used as a football. I'm not a talker, but I must express my mind. Talking and no fighting will kill pugilism but if such a thing comes to pass it won't be through me. I want to fight, and that's all I have to say."

Lynch and Sharkey put down a second deposit on the $10,000 side bet to attempt to rattle Corbett's cage, and then Sharkey hurried to Madison Square Garden.

For all Sharkey's talk about Corbett, he knew the champion was a great fighter, probably the smartest ever to step into a ring. He knew the fight they were planning, wherever and whenever it finally turned out to be, would be a bruiser. The Sullivan fight that night, however, was something quite different.

The night started with high excitement as 4,000 people squeezed into their seats early on to watch the supporting bouts.[6]

Sullivan arrived, noted one observer, looking "very much over the 220 mark" and was joined in the dressing room shortly after eight o'clock by Sharkey and the two men shook hands "cordially", a gentle greeting which anticipated what was to come.

Sullivan took the ring to his usual New York reception but everyone commented on his weight. Some said he looked a full fifty pounds heavier than Sharkey, who fought that night at 190 pounds. Sharkey, five feet eight-and-a-half inches tall with a forty-four inch chest, seventeen-inch neck, two ten-inch fists and a thirty-five-inch reach was shorter and smaller than Sullivan and most of his rivals. But he looked at his peak with his "wonderfully broad shoulders and a deep chest and well developed muscles".

I FOUGHT THEM ALL

The old fighter was asked to make a speech and recognized the gulf in fitness between him and the man who faced him. "It is scarcely necessary for me to say anything," he told the growing crowd. "This is only a friendly bout. I would not have come here otherwise... I'm too old and fat and I'm glad to see this clever young fellow, to whom I wish all sorts of success."

The friendliness – Sharkey was still fond of Sullivan in the way people are for old boyhood heroes – continued on the bell as the boxers, according to one headline writer, chose to "exchange love taps". One writer ringside wrote: "In the first round, Sullivan and Sharkey landed light lefts on the body. They sparred around a bit and each succeeded well in stopping each other's leads. The second round was like the first, of one minute's duration only, and the men merely exchanged love taps. During the third and last round, Sharkey worked his left very cleverly but there was really little work to do, for neither man had his fighting clothes on. The crowd which had gathered had but little opportunity given them to judge the man who expects to meet Corbett. There were merely straight leads and few of them."

At the end of the exhibition, Sullivan went to the centre of the ring and shook Sharkey's hand.

"Tom," he told him, "I'm pleased to have met and sparred with you. You are strong and rugged and game. If you keep on, you'll be the champion of the world. You'll whip them all."

Sharkey said later: "I never had a higher compliment paid me than that. When I had dressed and left the building I must have been a couple of inches bigger around the chest."

Later that evening, they all went to Wakeley's to see John L presented with the money. When it was counted out and turned over to Sullivan, he threw the entire amount on the bar, grasped Sharkey by one hand, pulled him close to his side and said: "My boy, you drew that crowd. Take your share of the money."

Sharkey shook his head.

"Mr. Sullivan, the show was for you. I was glad to help you. The money is yours. I shan't touch a copper."

John L, the fellow who had whipped dozens of men by merely

scowling at them, wiped the tears from his eyes with his big red handkerchief and slowly said: "Tom, my boy, I admire you. I hope you'll soon take the place which I so long held and make your fortune."

But Sharkey's meeting with the Champion of Champions proved nothing and hardly set the world alight. Questions over Sharkey's merit as a world championship contender remained. But Sharkey's altruistic motives for fighting John L appear to have been justified with the exhibition netting much needed cash – around $10,000 according to *The Ring* – for the troubled Bostonian.

Sullivan obviously never forgot the kindness either and, according to Sharkey, the two men became "very friendly and when we happened to meet on the street and in other places, he gave me pieces of advice which I was very thankful for". Sullivan also liked Sharkey because he was made more in his mould than in Corbett's. Once, he told the sailor that he was fond of him because he "had walloped Corbett".

"He's a parlour fighter, that Corbett," Sullivan said. "And he never would have whipped me, old as I was, had he dared to stand up and trade punches with me. In my younger days, I would have caught and beaten him down."

One thing that early journey to New York did do was get Tom familiar with a restaurant he would come to frequent, Sherry's. His first visit would also provide one of the many classic tales about the boxer.[7]

Tom was very hungry when he arrived at Sherry's and, as soon as the party got seated, he called: "Hey, waiter, bring me a dozen lobsters!"

None of Tom's companions had considered what they were eating yet so they all turned to look at him. The waiter was confused too.

"Why, sire, have you a party?" he asked.

"I am the whole darned party," Tom said laughing. Then he shooed the waiter away as his friends told him to wait for them.

Eventually, Tom's lobster arrived. He looked at it with a mixture of confusion and disgust: it had a claw missing.

The waiter felt a tug at his arm. "What's the matter with that lobster?" asked the ravenous boxer. "His claw is missing, and that's the best part of him."

"Nothing, sir," replied the waiter patiently. "I suppose he was in a fight and the other lobster chewed his claw off."

"Well, that being the case," shot back Sharkey, "then bring on the winner."

Meanwhile, Sharkey had bigger things on his mind. Not Corbett. But Fitzsimmons.

"That trip east did me much good," he said later from California. "It gave me the opportunity to meet many prominent sporting men whom I had heard of and to see many things which I did not even know existed.

"We remained in the East several months" – fighting three exhibitions in New York and one in Philadelphia, all with his friend Danny Needham – "the fact that I was then supposed to be matched with Corbett making me a live theatrical card. But all good things must end, so in September we began working toward the Pacific Coast.

"We arrived in San Francisco in November, ascertained that the match with Corbett had fallen through and then…I was matched with 'Ruby' Bob Fitzsimmons."

The fight would be one of the most controversial in Sharkey's career, contain one of the strangest and hotly contested decisions in boxing history, and cast a dark cloud over one of the legends of the American Wild West.

CHAPTER FOUR
The fight he won flat on his back

Bob Fitzsimmons was a great fighter, crafty with two hard fists. Now aged thirty-three, the Cornishman, who took first Australian, then American citizenship, had been well-known since 1891 when he took the middleweight crown from Jack "Nonpareil" Dempsey, giving him a savage beating before knocking him out in the thirteenth round.

While Tom Sharkey had been enjoying the attention of the exhibition fights which followed the Sullivan bout, Fitzsimmons had been trying to pin Corbett down on a date for their contest. They met at a room at New York's Hotel Bartholdi, slowly turning ice cold in the atmosphere of the men's mutual dislike, and it was agreed that they would fight sixty days after Corbett's fight with Sharkey – for which there was no firm date anyway – or no later than March 1, 1897. Both men agreed to put down $5,000 which would be lost to he who failed to honour the deal, and then Fitzsimmons surprisingly insisted – like Sullivan had done once before him – that he would not accept the *Police Gazette* Championship Diamond Belt if he won. That risked upsetting one of the most influential sports figures in the US, Belfast-born Richard Kyle Fox, who had arrived in New York penniless, worked his way up to buy the cops-and-robbers scandal sheet *Police Gazette*, added a thriving sports section created primarily around boxing, and made himself a millionaire.

Corbett, on the other hand, would happily accept the belt, which was encrusted with 200 ounces of silver and gold and decorated with a diamond-encircled boxing ring. But in signing the agreement to defend his title against Fitzsimmons, he appeared to be slapping Tom Sharkey in the face.

However, Fitzsimmons now agreed to fight the Dundalk sailor as he wanted to get a decent fight in as part of his preparation for the heavyweight title fight with "Gentleman Jim". Both men were clamouring for a crack at Corbett and the title so it seemed natural that they take on each other.

Because of the confusion caused by Corbett's earlier apparent withdrawal from boxing, and his attempt to hand the title to Maher, who was then beaten by Fitzsimmons, some newspapers called the Cornish fighter the champ (others labelled him the great pretender) and so billed the Fitzsimmons-Sharkey fight as a world championship. It was also lauded as the most important sporting event ever to be held on the West Coast.

Sharkey was immediately and characteristically confident. He was back in San Francisco, this time at Cliff House, Ocean Beach, and would fight at the Mechanic's Pavilion where he had enjoyed what he saw as the glory of his four-round fight with Corbett. "I was never better in my life, and after five weeks work I am confident of winning sure," he said from his training camp, where not only Danny Needham was sparring with him now but also George Allen and "Australian" Billy Smith, the fighter he had defeated in July 1895. "You may smile and say all fighters talk that way before a contest. All who think different can bet against me and that will leave some nice people pasteboards to show after the fight." The date was set for December 2, he said, and then "everyone will know who is the best man".

The bookmakers were in no doubt who was the best man; only sadly they disagreed with Sharkey. The day before they were giving even money that Sharkey would not stay six rounds. Thousands of dollars had been wagered on Fitzsimmons, with some laying down up to $100 on him.

However, a day before the fight, a problem remained. Who would referee? There was stalemate between the two camps and the decision was being put to the National Athletic Club. Martin Julian – Fitzsimmons' manager – and Lynch each suggested a number of names. "But not one proved satisfactory to both sides," said an insider.

The club made its decision. They chose a man who had worn a marshal's star in the Kansas cattle towns and in Tombstone, who fifteen years earlier had stood with his brothers and Doc Holliday in a 30-second gunfight which had already assumed mythical proportions across the West, who had tracked down and blasted to death with a shotgun the murderer of his brother. The referee was the larger-than-life character from the gunfight at the OK Corral, Wyatt Earp.

Who was the real Wyatt Earp and how did he come to be the referee? Wyatt was born in Illinois on March 19, 1848, the fourth son of Nicholas and Virginia Earp. He grew up mainly in Iowa with his brothers James, Virgil, Morgan and Warren, and half-brother Newton. Shortly before his 22nd birthday, he found work as a constable at a little town in Missouri, but his reputation was dogged by unproven allegations of fraud and horse thieving, and he settled into the life of a wanderer and buffalo hunter, meeting another future lawman and boxing official, Bat Masterson. Eventually settling in the busy cowtown of Wichita, he was chosen as deputy, probably during 1874 or 1875, dealing with drunken, gun-happy drovers. Here, he became admired for honesty, restraint and effectiveness, and he moved up in the world when he became assistant marshal at the "Queen of the Cowtowns", a thriving but lawless place called Dodge City, which had grown up on the banks of Arkansas River after two liquor dealers had built a tent store for thirsty railroad men and hunters. He stayed there for only a short time, but shooting someone who made an attempt on his life, gave him a fame which began to extend to the

East. Even so, in 1879, he had left the life of the lawman and gone to the silver-mining boomtown of Tombstone to make his living as a stage-coach owner. When he got there, he found there were already two well-established stage lines, so he tried a number of jobs before being offered the role of Tombstone's deputy sheriff – and a legend was born. Always a gambler, Earp also bought a money-spinning concession at a saloon, but he would play for the biggest stakes when he faced down the new troublemakers in the area, the crooked ranchers who backed so much criminality by buying stolen cattle and giving sanctuary to thieves.

On October 26, 1881, three Earp brothers and Holliday strode through the streets of the town to meet the Clanton brothers, the McLaurys and Billy Claibourne and to settle a long-standing feud. Thirty shots were fired in as many seconds. As the gunsmoke settled, Frank and Tom McLaury and Billy Clanton lay dying; while Virgil and Morgan Earp, and Holliday were wounded. Only Wyatt was unscathed in the gunfight which took its name from the land off an alleyway linking Fremont Street and Allen Street, the OK Corral. As Casey Tefertiller records in his comprehensive study, *Wyatt Earp: The Life Behind The Legend*: "After seven years, off and on, as a lawman in Kansas and Tombstone, Wyatt Earp had fought a stand-up gunfight. He had found a way to avoid killing the Dodge City troublemakers and the Tombstone toughs, but once the shooting began, there was to be no escape."

Tombstone was a "town on the edge", and the anger spilled over into further violence when the Earps' enemies found out the brothers would not face trial for their actions. An attempt was made on Virgil's life and then Morgan was shot in the back as he played pool. Wyatt Earp bent over him as he lay dying and Morgan asked Wyatt if he knew who did it. "Yes," said Wyatt, "and I'll get them."

"That's all I ask," whispered Morgan with his last breath.

A classic, bloody, western tale of revenge then began, in which Earp shot dead one man with a shotgun at close range in Tucson. The man was begging for his life as Earp pulled the trigger. The lawman had turned killer, and reaction to the killing divided

Arizona between those who defended Earp for taking the life of a villain and those who felt the US marshal was now out of control.

More blood flowed and eventually Earp wound up in Idaho, as a lawman again, before settling in 1887 in San Diego to run a string of saloons. By the time he reached San Francisco, he had lain down his tin star, but had earned a fair reputation as a referee after watching over more than thirty fights in San Diego and Tijuana. He began hanging out with the sporting crowd, stopping for drinks after the races and eating at Pup Rotisserie on Stockton Street or at the Café Zinkand. He, as horse-loving Sharkey must have, often went to the Oakland track.

The fight game existed for people to gamble. In San Francisco, the police and courts were turning a blind eye to fighting, seeing as it had taken a short step up the ladder of respectability. All the same, something seemed awry when the morning before the fight a wordy note arrived at the offices of the *San Francisco Evening Bulletin* saying that "opinion prevails, and belief in its truth is growing, that the police have been instructed to protect the interests of their official superior, Moses Gunst, who wagers on Fitz, by stopping before the final round the mill between Sharkey and Fitzsimmons, contingent upon the apparency of Sharkey winning".

Gunst – who eight months earlier had apparently controversially stepped in to help Choynski out when Sharkey smashed him through the ropes - reacted angrily to the accusation, vehemently denying that he had bet on the fight and saying "I couldn't stop the fight if I wished. San Francisco is not like New York, where the commissioners have the say".

The omens here were bad. For Earp – who had probably never refereed a fight under the Marquis of Queensberry rules - and the fighters, too. The scandal which followed would rock not only Earp but would affect Sharkey until his last breath.

An estimated 10,000 packed into the Mechanic's Pavilion that night, including the elite of San Francisco who occupied the $10 seats near the front and, for the first time at a major fight, women from the city. Chinese fans, it was reported, were "sitting in common brotherhood with the whites…and they all yelled just the same"[1] The $2 and $3 gallery seats were so tightly packed the fans could hardly breathe. The tills in the box office rang to the tune of something close to $40,000 that night. Fitzsimmons entered the ring at 10.10pm, followed by Sharkey who, weighing about 182 pounds, was around five pounds heavier than his opponent but a little over three inches shorter. Sharkey had Smith, Needham and Allen in his corner.

The master of ceremonies, Billy Jordan, called for Wyatt Earp. The controversy began immediately. According to Tefertiller, Julian spoke to Lynch and, overheard by a ringside *San Francisco Evening Bulletin* reporter, said that he objected to Earp. He said he had heard enough around town to convince him that the referee had been fixed. Lynch refused to allow a change, saying the club had the right to choose who they wished and the decision had been made. Julian said: "Take anybody in the house, we don't care whom; but spare us from Earp."

When Lynch again refused the change, a self-righteous Fitzsimmons stood up and said: "I'll do as I've always done before. I give in."

However, according to James Gibbs, of the club, Earp then asked to be taken out of the ring, but Gibbs told him he was to officiate the fight. Earp stayed.

But there was to be another ring drama, even before the bell had started the fight. Police captain Charles W. Whitman apparently noticed a bulge in the referee's pocket.

"Have you got a gun?" the police officer asked.

"Yep."

"You'd better let me have it."

"All right."

Earp divided the press. Some newspapers, quite simply, hated him. This, without doubt, would affect the presentation of what was to come and the way Sharkey's part in it would be perceived. The *San Francisco Evening Bulletin* did not record the gun incident, but the *San Francisco Examiner* called it an "event" of the evening. It stated: "So, for the first time in the history of the prizering in California it was necessary to disarm the referee." The *San*

Francisco Call said Earp had shown "the 'yellow dog' in him by going into the ring with a Colt's Navy revolver in his pocket, indicating that he feared trouble over the decision that he would give if opportunity offered." The same paper said it was only "after repeated orders from the big police officer that Earp gave up his weapon on which he depends for a living".

Eventually, the fighters took centre stage. From the outset it appeared Sharkey struggled with Fitzsimmons' speed and agility as "Ruby Bob" broke away promptly from clinches, kept away cunningly from Sharkey's mad rushes and poked his long left into Sharkey's face whenever he got too near. Sharkey's height and reach again put him at a disadvantage. He could not get inside of the reach of Fitzsimmons' long, thin arm, which when straightened out was "like a bar of steel". It was a fast moving fight, with both men fighting aggressively and Sharkey being kept on the move throughout.

Sharkey's battle to contain his opponent meant that, according to the *San Francisco Evening Bulletin*, he kept straying outside the rules, particularly hitting in the clinches (a point of debate as the Queensberry rules allowed fighters to fight themselves free of clinches). "Fitzsimmons played with the sailor from start to finish," said the newspaper's writer. "Sharkey fouled him frequently, but the Cornishman never lost his temper."

In the first round, a right from Fitzsimmons caught Sharkey on the jaw and sent him to the floor. It made the sailor more cautious and during the next four rounds he tried to keep out of reach.

The *San Francisco Evening Bulletin* admitted that Fitzsimmons "did show a little surprise at the clever way Sharkey ducked to avoid his swings. Sharkey countered well, too, more than once, and Fitz got it, strictly, in the neck."

In the fourth, according to one local reporter who seemed to favour Fitzsimmons, "Sharkey pushed Fitzsimmons over on the floor and before Bob could get up made a couple of vicious swipes at him. Fitz cleverly clinched and avoided damage, but it was a clear case of foul on Sharkey's part. No claim was made, however, and the fight went on."

The reporter, filing for the *Brooklyn Daily Eagle*, said Sharkey continued in the fifth to do "more mean work, grabbing Fitz around the legs and trying to throw him. Fitz began to warm up and went after the sturdy sailor like a cyclone."

He said Sharkey took a "poke on the nose and a left swing on the jaw", went down and "rolled under the ropes". This most partisan of writers added that Sharkey "would have gone off the platform had Bob not courteously hauled him back. It looked as if Sharkey was done for, but the gong sounded and he was given a minute in which to recuperate".

The *San Francisco Evening Bulletin* also reported that Sharkey was saved by the gong twice during the fight. "But," it added, "he stayed the six and seven rounds required to win a host of bets, and was deservedly cheered for his performance. The people were willing to have it go at that; let Sharkey get the credit for staying his rounds, and now let Fitz knock him out and have done with it, a thing which appeared to come to pass in the very next round."

In the sixth, Sharkey had struggled but survived. He looked "decidedly groggy but was on his feet" and a "joyous shout went up from the many sports who had bet even money that he would last six rounds".

In the seventh, too, Fitzsimmons had tried to end the fight but Sharkey either withstood the blows or escaped them. The *Brooklyn Daily Eagle* acknowledged that at the end of the round, while Sharkey was "on the wane", "Bob himself was none too strong and seemed to be a bit tired".

However, the eighth started with a flurry of punches from Fitzsimmons, smothering him with lefts and rights, working "like a demon". Sharkey stood, though, even as Fitzsimmons' long arms came out and banged his head back again and again.

Fitz came in close, a right half-arm jolt under the chin sending the Irishman's head to one side and a left hook sending him backwards.

Then, Fitzsimmons punched toward the gut. Sharkey fell.

All hell broke loose.

According to the *San Francisco Examiner*, Sharkey put his hand down to his groin and began to grimace and groan, as Danny Needham leapt into the ring and cried foul. Fitzsimmons, it said, laughed as the police followed him in.

Tefertiller writes: "Quietly, Wyatt Earp walked over to Sharkey's corner and told his seconds that their man had won the fight. Sharkey's staff lifted him into a chair, where he sat with his head sunk on his chest, seeming to take no interest in Earp's decision."

According to the report filed for the *Brooklyn Daily Eagle*: "While the marine was falling, the referee claims that Fitz struck him in the groin with his knee, thus committing a foul."

It said: "Sharkey was undoubtedly badly hurt. He was unable to move his legs, though he clutched spasmodically at the groin with his gloved hand. His seconds rushed into the ring and raised him up, but he fainted away and was borne from the ring unconscious."

There was confusion amongst the crowd until Needham waved a towel over his head to signify that Sharkey had been named the winner. "Hardly anyone among the spectators saw the foul and the decision was received with hisses and groans."

Julian ran to Earp as the gunman ducked through the ropes. Earp confirmed his decision and left. Fitzsimmons tried to speak above the din but could not be heard and Sharkey – the victor – was carried from the ring.

Sharkey certainly seemed in pain. The *San Francisco Examiner* reported he "was making grimaces and placing his hand on his groin. And, if he were not in agony, all I can say is that he must be a consummate actor and must have rehearsed that particular scene many a time and often."

Tefertiller writes that Earp "called the foul for a low blow into the centre of the groin and awarded the fight and the championship to Sharkey. Such a decision is solely the responsibility of the referee, who has no one to ask for help. Earp made the decision in a split second…"

Now the crowd began to realize the result. According to the *Brooklyn Daily Eagle* some let out a "howl of indignation" and "hisses, curses, groans and hoots split the air". Most of the smart money had been on Fitzsimmons. Neither Fitzsimmons nor

Julian could make themselves heard as they jumped about angrily in the ring, but their expressions of "dismay and disgust" reached supporters. There was no foul, said some. If there was, it was no way intentional. Fitzsimmons continued to gesticulate and cry out that he had not fouled Sharkey, that the fight had been taken from him.

"I have been robbed," he claimed afterwards. "I have always fought fairly and I did not foul Sharkey. If he was hurt, it was done without my knowledge and was an unavoidable accident."

The *Brooklyn Daily Eagle* very definitely backed Fitzsimmons.

"The feeling that exists today as a result of referee Earp's decision is great," it reported next morning. "Sharkey is in the position of a man who has been knocked out but ostensibly has a championship title. Fitzsimmons is credited with the victory by everybody but the stigma of the decision remains."

According to the newspaper, Sharkey "recovered consciousness about half an hour" after the controversial blow. "He was apparently badly injured, his groin being swollen. He says he had Fitzsimmons going until the eighth round when the foul occurred. Wyatt Earp, the referee, says the foul was deliberate. Fitzsimmons, just before striking his left hook that apparently knocked Sharkey out, hit the sailor below the belt with his fist."

It also reported Earp had spotted a Fitzsimmons foul earlier on. "Earlier in the fight in a breakaway, Earp says Fitzsimmons deliberately struck Sharkey over the eye with his elbow making a bad cut. Earp was tempted to give Sharkey the fight then and there but the sailor made no claim and he allowed the contest to proceed."

According to Tefertiller, Sharkey rested for about half an hour in his dressing room. A *San Francisco Chronicle* reporter met him and was greeted with a weak handshake from the tough ex-sailor. "I'd have licked him if he hadn't hit me that way," Sharkey said, who claimed he had felt stronger and more confident as the fight went on. Now, he said, he was feeling "awful bad". He added: "I am certain that Fitzsimmons fouled me deliberately. He did it to save himself from defeat. It was getting plain to him that I was growing in strength, while he was going down hill, so to speak, and rather than be knocked out, he thought he would lose on a foul. Had he not delivered that nasty blow which crippled me, I would certainly have finished him in that round. I was, for a moment, paralysed when I received that blow, and was wholly unable to protect myself. I felt myself sinking to the floor and I was doubled up in such a way, that I could not guard myself from the last upper-cut which he sent in – I suppose on a finisher. I am sorry that the question of supremacy was not settled on its merits, rather than in this way."

Now, there occurred a fresh twist to the tale; one which would later only cause suspicion to deepen. Dr Daniel D Lustig, the official medical examiner for the National Athletic Club, arrived at Sharkey's dressing room door with four other physicians. They were refused entry. Lustig, as the man whose job it was to determine the severity of the injury, protested but to no avail. He was barred from examining Sharkey. As Tefertiller notes, in analysing Earp's part in that night: "It was a deliberate act – or a mistake – that would make Fitzsimmons' claims seem far more plausible."

Sharkey was eventually lifted onto a stretcher by his seconds and carried to the Windsor Hotel. The news reporters buzzed around the stricken fighter.

At the hotel, Sharkey was seen by a doctor, Dr Benjamin Lee. He checked the Irishman over and certified the injury, stating that, "Mr Sharkey is without doubt in great pain from the result of a blow in the region of the groin. He is badly swollen and may have to remain in bed for two or three days."

Now, the accusations flew like punches.

Fitzsimmons and Julian accused the National Athletic Club and Earp of fraud. Fitzsimmons spoke to the press, saying he had been warned before he stepped into the ring that Earp had been part of a plot to fix the fight. He had gone on with the fight, he said, to protect his reputation as champion as "if I had refused to fight, the whole country would have said that I was afraid to meet the man who nearly put Corbett out." He grumbled: "No pugilist can get a square deal from the thieves who handle fighting in this city and it is a safe bet that the last big fight San Francisco will ever see was pulled off tonight."[2]

William Randolph Hurst's *San Francisco Examiner* devoted six pages to the fight, taking in all opinions. It printed fifty-four spectator statements, with twenty-eight saying no foul had been committed, seventeen viewing a foul, and nine saying they could not clearly see and were uncertain. The opinions probably best reflected where their money had been laid, rather than any sense of fair play or indeed whether they had really seen anything clearly at all.

Earp told the newspaper: "When I decided this contest in favour of Sharkey I did so because I believed Fitzsimmons had deliberately fouled him, and under the rules, the sailor was entitled to the decision. I would have been willing to allow half-fouls – that is, fouls that might be considered partly accidental – to pass by with only a reprimand, but in such a case as this I could only do my duty.

"Julian approached me before the contest and said he had heard stories to the effect that I favoured Sharkey. We talked a few moments and he went away, apparently satisfied that everything was on the square. Any talk to the effect that I was influenced in any way to decide wrongly against Fitzsimmons is rubbish. I saw Sharkey but once before in my life, and that was when he boxed with Corbett. I had no reason to favour him. If I had allowed my feelings to govern me, my decision would have been the other way.

"I am a pretty close observer and under most conditions, I think I am cool. I went into the ring as referee to give a square decision and, so far as my conscience speaks, I have done so…

"I feel that I did what was right and honourable and feeling so, I care nothing for the opinion of anybody. I saw the foul blow struck as plainly as I see you, and that is all there is to the story…

"No man, until now, has ever questioned my honour. I have been in many places and in peculiar situations but no one ever said, until tonight, that I was guilty of a dishonourable act. And I will repeat that I decided in all fairness and with a judgement that was as true as my eyesight. I saw the foul blow."

In the *San Francisco Chronicle*, Earp said he had been introduced to Fitzsimmons by Masterson, "the best friend I have on earth. If I had any leanings they would have been toward Fitzsimmons, for I know that Bat Masterson, who is in Denver tonight, had every dollar he could raise on Fitzsimmons."

The day after the fight, the *San Francisco Call* was unequivocal in its coverage, under the headlines "Fitzsimmons was robbed" and "Referee Earp gave a raw decision". It was rumoured in the city that the *Call*'s editor had bet heavily on Fitzsimmons. The paper certainly always welcomed the opportunity to attack the controversial Earp.

After meeting with Sharkey in his hotel room the day after the fight, the *San Francisco Evening Bulletin* took a different approach.

"No one who saw the doughty sailor rolling on the platform gasping with agony, could doubt that he was badly hurt in some tender spot. And all doubts on this point are forever set at rest by Sharkey's condition this morning.

"Tom Sharkey passed a sleepless night. It was almost noon today before he shut his eyes for a slumber. Dr Benjamin Lee, who was called in immediately after the fight, remained at his bedside all night and administered to his injury. About 10 o'clock this morning Dr Rottanzi and Dr Ragan called at the Windsor and examined the disabled pugilist. There is no gainsaying the fact but what [sic] Sharkey is horribly crippled. There was an immense swelling in his groin about 5 o'clock. Then, it perhaps reached a climax. By means of leeches and hot applications, the swelling was reduced almost one-half. Hot cloths were continuously applied for twelve hours; the leeches were not used until daybreak. Accompanying the swollenness there is, of course, more or less inflammation, but this was nearly allayed before Sharkey went to sleep."

On examining the bruised groin, the *Evening Bulletin* reporter added: "People who saw the fight and who entertain doubts about the Cornishman striking below the belt should visit the sailor's room and make a personal examination. Should they do so they will be convinced that there was a foul blow struck by none other than Mr Robert Fitzsimmons."

Earp called at the hotel room during the newspaperman's visit but stayed only a "few seconds". "The swollen groin satisfied Mr Earp that he did not err in giving the prize to Sharkey," said the newspaper.

Earp fixed the group with his steel blue eyes and said: "It was the most deliberate foul I ever saw struck. Fitz hit him squarely below the belt. I can understand how many could not see where the blow landed. It was an up-swoop, which to many not near the ring looked as if Fitzsimmons struck him in the stomach, when in reality it was clear below the belt. Of course, Fitz was the favourite in the betting and he carried more money. You know how it is at the racetrack when they tip over a favourite well played. Won't a roar go up to the clouds especially if the judges disqualify the favourite for fouling?"

The roar of which Earp spoke was rising.

Dr Lustig, the man refused entry to examine Sharkey immediately after the fight, raised the temperature with an angry letter to the *San Francisco Examiner* (on the Thursday). Lustig claimed he did not get to see Sharkey until late the next afternoon when asked by Groom to check the boxer's condition. Lustig and several others examined Sharkey and then adjourned to another room to discuss their diagnosis. They agreed there was swelling and discolouration in the groin but did not give a cause. Lustig said Dr DF Ragan had told him that the swelling had increased in the fourteen hours since he had first seen it. Lustig was still stung by the slight done to him outside Sharkey's dressing room. "In my judgement, had it been due to a blow such as [Sharkey] complains of having received I think the swelling and discolouration would be far greater than it is at present…

"I am unable to understand why, if Sharkey was suffering such severe pains as were attributed to him, none of the physicians at the Pavilion were called upon to attend him or even permitted to see him."

The police commissioner, Gunst, who was possibly out-of-pocket for the second time due to Sharkey, spoke to the *Examiner* too. He also waded in against Earp and Sharkey.

"Fitzsimmons was robbed by an unjust decision and honest sport in this city has been struck a blow from which it will not recover for a long time. The decision of Earp was deliberate robbery, and I have reason to believe that I was rightly informed when I was told before the fight that the referee had been 'fixed' and that the fight would be given to Sharkey. I expected such a decision much earlier in the contest.

"I am not at liberty to tell my informant's name, but he is thoroughly reliable and, as events proved, quite as well informed. I was sitting in the Baldwin restaurant shortly after six o'clock when my friend approached me and asked me if I had bet anything on the fight. I told him that I had not.

"My friend surprised me and I asked him why he had asked such a question. He replied that the fight had been 'fixed' and that a 'crooked' decision would be given in Sharkey's favour. This information was given positively without rumour or insinuation."

Earp had been "tired and depressed" when he returned home to his wife, Sadie, after the fight. She knew at once "something was seriously wrong". She asked him why he had not removed the gun before entering the ring and he said he had forgotten it was there; the gunman said he was "no more conscious of its being there than of my coat or my vest". Despite his apparent regret about being involved in the fight, Earp left for the Ingleside racetrack on Thursday morning, apparently unaware that he was supposed to appear in court on charges of carrying a concealed weapon. He was later picked up by police and bailed to appear in court the next day. After the adjourned hearing, an *Evening Bulletin* reporter spoke to Earp and later joked about the furore over the former US Marshall's gun, writing that not once during their conversation did Earp's hand wander "toward his hip pocket". Earp, however, now drew the line at talking about the fight. "I've said enough, and have been reported to have said more than I have. My attorney, Mr [Frank] Kelly [of the Southern Pacific Railroad], advises me that the less I say the better. So I'll await results." Earp said this was the first time he was ever arrested on such a charge, although he had carried weapons practically all his life.

Earp went to trial on December 10 and when the police produced his foot-long gun said he needed it as released convicts all over the West wanted him dead. The judge ruled he had committed a "technical violation" of the law and fined him $50. The threat of jail gone, now Earp only had to deal with the damage to his reputation as drinkers and gamblers still only had one topic of conversation: the fight.

Earp, though, was not involved with the legal proceedings which began the morning after the fight when lawyers for Julian and Fitzsimmons filed a formal complaint against Sharkey and his ringmen and the National Athletic Club.

A San Francisco reporter for the *New York World* explained: "Tom Sharkey will have to fight in court for the $10,000 cheque presented to him by referee Wyatt Earp, at the conclusion of the sailor's fight with Bob Fitzsimmons last night. The Anglo-Californian Bank has declined to cash the cheque, which was drawn by the National Athletic Club and certified. After the Bank opened next morning, Sharkey's manager, Daniel Lynch, presented the cheque, then Paying Teller Stimson informed them that he had been instructed not to pay it and referred them to Manager Lilienthal, who said that the bank had been formally enjoined and would hold the money pending a court decision as to who was entitled to it."

However, back home in Ireland, the *Dundalk Democrat* picked up the *World* writer's support for Sharkey. "Doubt as to Sharkey's having received injuries below the belt during the mill is vanishing," the newsman stated. "That he was hit in the groin, and hit hard, is the opinion of three medical men who have examined him, and their declaration is borne out by the appearance of the sailor."

It added: "There was no denying that Sharkey was badly, though not permanently crippled."

The doctors had told him he "should keep to his bed for some days", it said.

"I was just going to finish him up," said Sharkey in describing the alleged foul. "I made a couple of passes, and I think one landed. Then, he came back at me. He struck me three times in rapid succession. The first blow I got on the chest, the next on the face, and then he swung low, making a sort of upper cut, and took me right in the groin I fell in a faint, and that's all I remember until they brought me to the hotel. I did not know whether Fitz had won or I had won, or a mob had stopped the fight. I did not realize what really had occurred."

I would have "whipped him", said Tom Sharkey. "Didn't I have him started? Was not I stronger than he in the eighth round?"

One of the reasons that the sports pages in the States backed Fitzsimmons was that most of its readers would have had their money on the favourite. In Ireland and among the Irish of America, the favouritism worked the other way. The Dundalk Democrat reported: "Louthmen in the States are naturally almost unanimous believers in Sharkey and several of them have kept us posted on the progress of affairs in connection with the fight. One old Dundalk man writing this week says, 'There is no doubt in my mind that Fitzsimmons fouled Sharkey when he saw he was going to lose the fight. That is the view taken by all impartial men, and all this great talk of Sharkey not being the real victor is only the wild vaporing of disappointed spats who put their money on the Australian, not knowing the true stuff in the Dundalk man. He will get his ten thousand dollars all right as he has right and the law on his side and is not lacking friends in San Francisco.'"

The *Dundalk Democrat* printed a statement from Earp. "I saw the foul struck as plainly as a man could see anything. Fitzsimmons hit Sharkey on the shoulder and then struck him below the belt with a left uppercut. Sharkey was leaning over and was felled by the blow. So palpable was the foul, that I awarded the fight to Sharkey without a moment's hesitation. I should have given Sharkey the fight earlier in the contest, when Fitzsimmons cut his eye open with the point of his elbow. I was not influenced in any way to decide against Fitz. I was not acquainted with Sharkey until I entered the ring, while some of my best friends were the hottest backers of Fitzsimmons."

The Irish paper also raised an issue which was to become key in the upcoming court case. "Fitzsimmons' injunction restraining the bank from cashing the cheque raises a new and unique question in the courts. Prize-fighting under the laws of California is made a felony. Boxing contests are permitted and it was under this law that Sharkey and Fitzsimmons were granted a permit by the supervisors. Should Superior Judge Sanderson reverse the decision of Earp, it would place him in the position of acting as an arbiter on a wager, which is forbidden under the statutes."

Julian railed against Earp, whom he heard was looking for him a couple of days after the fight, giving him a thinly veiled threat. "He ought to have little trouble [finding] me," said Julian. "Everybody knows where I am stopping. Mr Earp may be an expert with a gun, but there are others."[3]

The fires were stoked further when an accusation was made that the day before the fight Sharkey's man, Danny Needham, who sent a telegram to a guy in the East saying: "Place all your money on Sharkey. Will explain further." The trainer denied sending it and an *Evening Bulletin* reporter hurried to the offices of the Postal Telegraph Company, where manager LW Storror told him: "We sent no such dispatch. The printed dispatch is a fake upon the face for there is no destination mentioned. We are not in the habit of sending messages without having the destination expressly in the 'head'."

The newspaper war between the *Call* and the *Examiner* turned the heat up further and the continuing bashing of Earp did not help Sharkey's reputation. However the outcry from fans and gamblers appeared to have died down.

A telegram from a San Franciscan hack in the New York papers on December 5 stated: "The excitement over the Sharkey-Fitzsimmons fight is subsiding. Earp's decision in favour of the sailor has been accepted by the poolrooms and bets to the extent of $20,000 were paid off this afternoon. Sharkey is still in bed nursing his injuries, actual and alleged. Fitzsimmons was about as usual today and was the hero of the street. [The "street" had had its money on him]. $10,000 purse still remains unpaid."

The hearing began on Monday, December 7. Fitzsimmons wore a silk-lined overcoat and a top hat. Tom Sharkey remained in bed and Earp failed to show too, despite being subpoenaed to testify. A warrant was issued for Earp. Only Lynch, Groom and Gibbs were there and gave evidence.

The following day, before court began, Julian told Groom: "I am going to show Needham, Lynch and Earp up in such a light that if they have a spark of manhood in them they will fly the country and seek parts unknown. If ever there were three men caught with goods on them, they are the people. I have positive, indisputable proof that they concocted the fraud and the National Club is not clear of it, either." Julian, overheard by an *Evening Bulletin* reporter, then said Gibbs knew of the plot and had confessed his knowledge to Groom.

Groom was angered. "I have nothing to confess," he said. "I don't know what you mean by your insinuations. My record is absolutely clean."

"No matter," Julian replied, adding mysteriously, "you know very well what I allude to."

The altercation over, the court opened and Earp took the stand. The forgetful ex-lawman was first made to apologise for failing to respond to the subpoena. Earp said he had accompanied Lynch to two banks to try to cash the winner's cheque but both times they were informed payment had been stopped.

However, there were none of the fireworks threatened by Julian. The drama would wait another day.

On the Wednesday, in front of Judge Austin A Sanderson, the court eagerly awaited Julian's arrival. When he was late, Lynch said confidently that he knew the whole case had been a "bluff from beginning to end". The courtroom crowd stamped its feet. It was getting impatient.

Then, to maximum effect, Julian's attorney, Henry I Kowalsky, burst into the room, with Fitzsimmons, Julian and a group of others at his heels.

Among the group was Australian trainer, Billy Smith, one of Sharkey's ringmen.

For a man about to make damaging allegations against a friend, Smith was remarkably calm as he began to describe conversations with Sharkey three weeks before the fight in which the Irishman vetoed all possible referees. Smith claimed Lynch said he also planned to reject every suggested referee until the choice fell to the National Athletic Club. Smith said Lynch felt the club would then point the "kind of man we want" and would pay him $2,500 for awarding the contest to Sharkey on a foul. Smith added: "He told me they had the referee that they wanted, and he would suit – Referee Earp, the racehorse man – and that was to [win] on a foul in the first round, and Referee Earp was to give him the decision – give Sharkey the decision… He said the first time that Fitzsimmons was to hit him in the body, Needham was to jump in and claim a foul."

Smith said he did not see the blow that felled Sharkey but he claimed he heard Lynch telling the apparently stricken fighter: "Put your hand on your groin and pretend to be in great pain." Sharkey said, "All right", and was then taken to his dressing room as the uproar began. Out of sight of the crowd, Smith said, trainer George Allen did something to Sharkey but Smith did not know what.

Smith said he was with Sharkey until Monday after the fight and that when strangers called he would be in great pain but the rest of the time he would move around and smoke cigars.

Smith then told a strange story about 48-year-old Earp's visit to the hotel the day after the fight. "I was sitting on a trunk. He… looked at me and said, 'Sharkey, how do you feel?' I said, 'I am not Sharkey. There is Sharkey in bed over there.' He said, 'You look a bit like Sharkey; I thought it was he'."

Earp, according to the *San Francisco Examiner*, responded: "Smith's allegations to the effect that I entered into any kind of a conspiracy with Mr Lynch, Sharkey and anybody else are positively untrue and absurd on their face. I did not agree to give the decision in favour of Sharkey on a foul in the first or any other round as he says. I have always been honourable in my dealings, and defy anybody to prove otherwise. When I accepted the National Club's offer to referee the recent contest, the only promise I made was that I would decide the match on its merits. I was offered no money by Lynch or anybody else to give an unfair decision. I would not have listened to a proposition of that kind to begin with and everybody who knows me will not doubt my word."

Groom defended Earp's honour and said if a fix did happen it must have come after the referee was selected and not before.

Lynch threatened to prosecute Smith for perjury.

On Thursday, the trouble deepened when George Allen appeared to corroborate parts of Smith's story. Allen, also an Australian, said he had been charged with watching every blow, but he did not see a foul. He claimed Sharkey showed no sign of injury in the dressing room after the fight and that he did not complain in private but screamed in pain when he was carried out in sight of the crowd.

Why was the Australian giving this evidence now? Because, Allen said, Sharkey's camp had not paid him for his services and he had had to argue for a $150 cut.

The court adjourned for the weekend. On the Monday morning, a week after the hearing started, Sharkey attended for the first time.

He watched Julian's lawyer, Kowalsky, call Dr Lustig, the man still smarting from his rebuff at Sharkey's dressing room door.

The *San Francisco Examiner* reported the exchange between the two men.[4]

"Could those injuries," said Kowalsky, "have been caused by artificial means?"

"Yes, sir."

"By the injection of fluid?"

"Yes."

"What fluid?"

"Any acidulated water."

Lustig repeated his belief that an injury to the groin from Fitzsimmons would have caused greater swelling and discolouration.

Sharkey's opponent himself then took the stand. Not surprisingly, he insisted there was no foul: "I have never made a mistake of that kind yet. If I had been in a dazed or groggy condition, it might have been possible for me to have made a mistake. But I was as cool then as I am now. Sharkey was not fouled at all. I have been through an experience of that kind and know just how an injured man acts," he added, recalling the time he was struck in the groin by a cricket ball.

Julian then told of a meeting with Moses Gunst in which he was told, "Don't you under any circumstances stand for Wyatt Earp to referee that fight."

Julian claimed another man had overheard Earp talking with a horseman named Joe Harvey in which Earp had said: "You rely on me."

This was the level of hearsay being offered to the court.

Earp's evidence was "peculiar" and "startling in some particulars", according to the hostile *San Francisco Chronicle*, which reported: "He swore more than once that Sharkey had never fouled Fitzsimmons, that the sailor had never caught his opponent by the legs, that Fitzsimmons was fouling all the time throughout the fight and that Martin Julian never made any announcement of any kind in the ring on the night of the fight about the referee being 'fixed'; all of which evidence astounded nobody more than General Barnes [Earp's lawyer] himself."

Earp said Julian's accusations of his participation in a conspiracy with the former sailor were false. "I will say now that what he testified to, the other day, was a pack of falsehoods in every respect."

Kowalsky moved to have the statement struck from the record.

"I am on the stand now," said Earp, "and have got my right hand up, and I say it is a pack of falsehoods."

Judge Sanderson told Earp he was just to answer the questions. Earp snapped: "I am not like him, going around and shutting people's mouths."

"Mr Earp," said the judge, losing patience, "I instruct you to only answer the questions."

The allegations against Earp got wilder. Kowalsky – perhaps sensing a troubled witness - claimed that once while separating the fighters, Earp had poked his fingers into Fitzsimmons' eye.

Earp was shocked and angry. "I never did it," he said. "I emphatically say I did not do it on any occasion – and I don't believe Fitzsimmons will say that I did it."

On Thursday, December 17, when everyone returned for the judge's decision, the case ended with a whimper and not a bang. Sharkey's legal team moved to dissolve the injunction, arguing that the case was unworthy as it was nothing more than an argument over the purse from a prize-fight. Fitzsimmons' lawyers repeated their conspiracy theory and then it was left to Sanderson, who firstly had to consider a point of law: that prize-fighting was still technically illegal in San Francisco.

"In my opinion, under the statute standing as it does now, they can no more legalize a fight in this city than they can legalize a duel," he said. "There is no doubt… that these men were fighting, must have been fighting if this complaint is true. For, if they were boxing they were fighting. They were committing an offence against the law; and it is elementary law, and no lawyer will challenge it, that no court, either of law or equity will take cognizance of a suit of this character the moment it is challenged… I understand that these exhibitions are given; and they are given because the people and the police wink at them. But no court will recognize any such proceeding. And there is no doubt in my mind that this injunction should be dissolved and it would have been dissolved if the motion had been made immediately upon the heels of issuing it, as the court, in fact, expected. The order to dissolve the injunction will be granted."[5]

The legal fall-out of the case was then formally brought to an end when the grand jury "decided to bring no indictments against Sharkey, Fitzsimmons or their backers for infringement of the state law against prize-fighting, believing no convictions could be obtained."[6]

At last, the prize money could be collected. Although, on arriving at the Anglo-California Bank, Sharkey and Lynch discovered there were to be $1,500 charges on it. "All right," said Tom, "Give me the balance."

The pair walked out with $8,500. Lynch was apparently carrying the money.

Sharkey, according to the *New York Times*, walked away "jubilantly", but the court verdict had been inconclusive. There was to be no decision of guilt or innocence on the accusation that there was a conspiracy, that Sharkey had faked the foul. Furthermore, the Irishman's legal team could have spared themselves the embarrassment of the hearing by moving to have the injunction dissolved right at the start.

The judge simply could not rule on the prize money because the law did not regard the fight itself as legal.

Now, then, more than a century later, we must review the evidence left to us again.

Had Sharkey and Lynch conspired to "rob" Fitzsimmons by faking a foul, with or without Earp's help? Or had there really been a foul and the judgement was correctly made by the referee?

Despite Dr Lustig's speculation, there was much to suggest the foul was genuine. Sharkey fought from a crouch. Did he come up straight after the blow at the head which proceeded Fitzsimmons' low blow?

Newspaper reports about the way Sharkey looked on the canvas and after the fight did not doubt the agony he was suffering. One reporter has said he had to have been a "consummate actor" to fake the grimaces he was making while lying in the ring – Sharkey's later brief career on the stage and in the cinema appear to prove he was anything but that.

In agony or not, Sharkey probably was not going to get up and say he was not fouled. He had been beaten by the count, he was out.

Would Sharkey, for instance, have fought eight rounds to see if he could win on his own merits before realizing he was going to lose and going down crying "foul!"? He was a fighter who prided himself on taking endless onslaughts on his body. He was not a "scientific" fighter, but he never gave up the ship. This was the biggest fight of his life so far – and he wanted to be sure of winning it.

Allen and Smith claimed Sharkey's groin injury seemed to have disappeared by the time he got to the dressing room and Smith said he had heard Lynch tell Sharkey to fake it. Their testimony seemed to suggest a conspiracy between Sharkey and Lynch to fool Earp. But how trustworthy were the two Australian trainers? They survived on the generosity of the fighters and both had issues over payments from Lynch. Julian would not have to offer much of the $10,000 his side would gain on winning the case in order to get them to testify. They may even have decided on switching sides themselves realizing Sharkey's case was looking shaky. Whatever, some might say their testimonies appear too well tailored to suit Julian and Fitzsimmons' case.

At the height of the controversy, Tom heard from Jim Corbett, the real owner of the world title, and John L Sullivan, who both simply challenged him as the "winner". Now Tom received the backing of two men who had faced him in the ring.

Jim Williams, the middleweight of the Pacific coast, told the *Illustrated News*, New York, that Sharkey was a "tough customer". The man, who had fought Sharkey and was soon to do battle with him again, added: "I do not think any men in the world can knock him out. Fitzsimmons must have fouled him."

Another fighter, Joe Choynski, who had fought a vicious eight-rounder with Sharkey only eight months earlier, backed Tom too, although as he was still wanting his say on the fracas which had ended their fight. "Give a dog a bad name and it will stick to him," he said.[7] "Sharkey has the name of being a foul fighter, and everyone seems to have the impression that he can't fight a fair round. I want to say however that Sharkey is one of the fairest fighters I have ever stepped into the ring with. He is an awkward, rough and ready sort of a fellow, always coming with a rush, but I must give him credit for fighting fair, and I do this in spite of the fact that he did foul me accidentally so badly that the fight was stopped twenty minutes to allow me to recover from the blow he gave me...

"When I read about people who say that Fitzsimmons did not foul Sharkey because they did not see it, although they were in a position to see, I am reminded of the fact that my seconds did not see Sharkey foul me, although they were in a splendid position to see, and it was a part of their duty to look out for fouls.

"I see it is claimed on behalf of Fitzsimmons that Referee Earp is a novice in the ring. I have known Earp for a long time and I believe he knows just as much about boxing contests as I do. I have seen Earp referee fights and I know he has acted scores of times in that capacity. He refereed a contest in Los Angeles in which Solly Smith was one of the principals, Earp may have a record but he knows all about boxing and is well known on the coast as a champion of fair play.

"Fitzsimmons is always in trouble and a great deal of his trouble is of his own making. When Jim Hall knocked him out in Australia, he said it was a fake admitting that he deliberately laid down for a consideration. A man that will do what he said he did should not do much yelling for fair play. When he fought me in Boston, I had him practically knocked out and but for the interference of the police, I would have finished him. After the bout, he said he had agreed with me to go light, and that I crossed him when I got a chance. There is not a word of truth in the statement of his. The go was on its merits and because he got the worst of it, made that lame excuse. All this talk about a job in San Francisco is nonsense, Fitz hit Sharkey foul and properly lost the fight."

Earp's character has always been at the centre of the question.

At the time of the fight, he would have been certainly a candidate for a con. He was unfamiliar with the Marquis of Queensberry rules and might take extra care to avoid the fight descending into a brawl. His inexperience would make him easier to dupe.

However, he would have also been easy to bring into the plan, and had plenty of reason to have been one of its instigators. He desperately needed money and admitted during the hearing which followed the fight that he was poverty-stricken and that the horses which ran in his name were leased from a woman in Santa Rosa. Terfertiller points out: "[Earp] was a gambler and his fortunes rose and fell like those of any gambler." In addition, Earp was not of the pure character often depicted in the movies: as well as being quick to use his gun, he was not always honest. In 1911, for instance, he was arrested for his part in a faro game con and only escaped jail on a technicality.[8]

For some time, as the Earp legend grew, and became part of the great Wild West story, articles appeared which, on their way to depicting Earp the hero, sought to exonerate the former marshall at anybody's expense.

Sometime in 1915, according to Tefertiller, Sharkey met the author, Eugene Cunningham, who asked him about the incident. Cunningham related his response to Robert Mullin for an article he later produced with William D McVey for *The Chicago Brand Book of Westerners* (1949) called "Wyatt Earp: Frontier Peace Officer". According to Cunningham: "Tom looked down at his feet and up at the ceiling and seemed honestly embarrassed. Finally, he muttered something about there being 'more to it than folks knew about' and 'no use talking about it'." These quotes are third hand and there was more than 30 years between Cunningham's apparent conversation with Sharkey and the publication of Mullin's article.

In another article in a volume of the same *Chicago Brand Book* in 1951, Charles Fernald recalled his own meeting with Earp while they were passengers on a steamer to Alaska. Fernald wrote: "He claimed that there was a lot of money bet on this fight, and he told me that to make the foul stick, somebody injected iodine into Sharkey's groin. I always understood Wyatt Earp was on the square in his decision, but he did not know about this iodine business until sometime afterwards."

Both articles might be true, but by this time Earp was a hero who had been depicted on television and in film. He was not the kind of man to be shown as a con artist, a cheat or a fake. Perhaps, the conversation on the steamer did take place but Earp would have known of Lustig's contention that a substance could have been injected into Sharkey's groin to fake the injury so it is conceivable he had turned that into the true version of events, as it was the one which cleared him of blame. Why, as Earp seems to suggest, would one of the small group of conspirators – only Sharkey, Lynch and Needham needed to take part in the "iodine" conspiracy – tell him about it much later?

In 1912, an article entitled "Real Story of the Sharkey-Fitz Fight: Why Gun Fighter Earp was Selected as Referee and Why His Kind are No Longer Wanted" was syndicated to a number of newspapers in the United States.

Written by Robert Edgren, the former sports editor of the *New York Evening World*, it was extremely hostile to Sharkey. "The ins and outs of that fight and the much discussed decision are known to few men, and not one of those who know the true story has ever given the facts to the public," he wrote, before claiming to have become an "intimate acquaintance" of Earp's long before the bout.

Edgren painted a picture of a fight in which Sharkey continually fouled, and then wrote: "There had been much money bet on the seventh round. The betting, hours before the fight, had been even money that the sailor wouldn't last the seven. Just before the fight began, betting commissioners had flooded the Mechanics' Pavilion and circulated about among the 15,000 spectators offering rolls of gold coin on Sharkey to last seven rounds at even money, and to win the fight at 1-to-3. The money didn't appear until Wyatt Earp was in the ring."

The knock-out punch, Edgren said, came from a "left fist under the sailor's chin with the crushing impact of a mallet".

He claimed it was the "opinion of nearly every man in that great pavilion…that Fitzsimmons had been 'robbed in the most cold-blooded manner'".

Edgren is nothing if not partisan and it is hard to know what weight to give this piece which was written 15 years after the fight. After all, he goes on to claim that cries were later heard from Sharkey's dressing room and to say that even in the days after the fight the "evidence of a foul blow was never given out", although we know in court that Dr Lustig and others were at least allowed to examine him in his hotel room.

He goes on, however, to make even greater claims in a detail which "has never appeared in print". This scoop is based on a third party, an unnamed San Francisco man who was "intimately connected with sporting matters".

Edgren claims he walked unannounced into this man's office (whether he was a "doctor, a lawyer, a saloonkeeper or simply a sport" Edgren refuses to say) the day after the fight.

The man was sitting in a revolving chair with his back to the door. In front of him, hands behind his back and head bent forward, was Wyatt Earp. Earp, according to Edgren, was striding up and down the room in evident excitement.

"My God!" Earp exclaimed suddenly. "The *Call* has got the whole damned story."

Earp, we can assume if we give Edgren's story weight, must have been looking at the *San Francisco Call*, the anti-Earp newspaper which called him a "yellow dog" for carrying a gun.

The mysterious gentleman in the chair leaned forward and calmly told Earp: "Now, Wyatt, don't get excited. Let them print whatever they want to. They can't prove anything."

Edgren concludes: "You can form your own conclusions about this little detail. I formed mine on the instant and, stepping back, closed the door after me quietly and went away from there. But it is a significant thing that from that day to this no gunfighter has been asked to referee a fight in San Francisco, and as long as the Sharkey-Fitzsimmons fight is remembered none ever will be."

One fact that Edgren and others through the years have agreed on is the way Earp was chosen to referee the fight. According to Tefertiller, Earp was chosen by the National Athletic Club almost by accident. Earp, he said, had happened into Lucky Baldwin's hotel the day of the fight and been spotted by James Groom and James Gibbs, of the club, as they desperately searched for a man to stand in the middle. It was normal for the club hosting the fight to chose the referee if the two sides could not agree. They had said it would be an honour to have him and after a little thought, Earp agreed as he thought the "two best men in the world are coming together now". Edgren agreed that Earp's selection as man in the middle was "last moment".

Tefertiller also contests that the referee could not win. "Had Earp not called the foul with Sharkey rolling around in the ring, the referee would have faced an outcry from Sharkey's bettors nearly equal to the one he faced from Fitzsimmons' backers."

However, there is a version of events, reported by an exemplary source, which states that not only could Earp not *lose* but that the story that Earp was a last minute choice was a carefully put about deception at the heart of an elaborate con.

For many decades boxing fans have gone to *The Ring* magazine for their history lessons. In 1961, in its 'Ring Detective' feature, the magazine analysed the Sharkey-Fitzsimmons fight again.[9] The writer came with a conclusion that the fight was rigged but that just about the only two people who were not in on the con were the two fighters themselves. The analysis is remarkable and would perhaps sound too far-fetched were it not the work of Dan Daniel.

Daniel had helped Nat Fleischer start up *The Ring* and by the time he wrote that 'Detective' piece he had been a sports journalist for more than half-a-century. He had won honour after honour during a journalistic career which would continue until he was well into his eighties.

"This fight, one of the oddest, strangest and most suspicious appearing in the history of boxing, ended in the eighth round," Daniel told a new generation of fight fans. "Much has been written about this fight. Much in the way of innuendo, of suspicion, of veiled accusation. The time has come to say the final word, and to lay this meeting away among the most aggravated cases of skulduggery in the annals of the ring."

The Ring was taking the issue up because of readers' new-found interest: not in Fitzsimmons and Sharkey, on this occasion, but the referee. Earp was famous again, having been played by Hugh O'Brian on television.

"In the television production, we hear Wyatt Earp lauded as one of the untarnished greats of the Southwest in Tombstone, and later in Dodge City," wrote Daniel. "We are told that Wyatt Earp is famous in song and story. True all true.

"Famous: and then he got himself into the Fitzsimmons–Sharkey mess, which now comes under the unbiased eye of the Ring Detective and the errorless view of *The Ring* spyglass.

"What prompted Wyatt Earp to give that fight to Sharkey on a foul? Was he right, was he wrong? If he was wrong what was in it for the former Sheriff of Dodge? What was his financial status in 1896?"

Daniel also noted that Earp was "nearly broke" at the time. "In

November 1896, Earp was racing a few of his selling platers in the area, possibly at the old Tanforan Track. Then, he was approached to become the referee of the impending elimination between Fitz and Sharkey."

Sharkey, *The Ring* said, was on the up. The Corbett fight had taken the Irishman's "stock to the 1896 IBM level". However, the clever, hard-hitting Fitzsimmons remained 3-to-1 favourite. "Mark this down with a circle around it," noted Daniel emphatically. "Fitz 3-to-1."

Now Daniel came to the moment Earp was appointed referee. The organizers, he said, had the option of going to a number of "eminently qualified referees in the Bay area".

"Eddie Graney for one. 'Honest' John Kelly was available. Greggains, too, was eligible. But Gibbs, who composed the National Athletic Club, passed them up. Why?"

The club, Daniel claimed, played up the notion that Julian and Lynch could not agree on the third man, and then met with Earp.

"The story goes that Earp wasn't keen for the job. He is alleged to have said that if on the day of the fight no other referee had been approved by Lynch and Julian he would undertake to go into the ring…

"The caper was not to announce the identity of the referee until both fighters entered the ring."

Then, claimed Daniel, Julian would make a complaint. "When Julian saw Earp in the ring he hollered vehement protests," he stated. "It was a great show. But then, Julian had been with circuses and was something of a ham actor."

Fitzsimmons, of course, told Julian to stop protesting and announced that who happened to be the official did not matter: Fitz planned to finish the fight quickly.

And, as we know, he very nearly did, fighting like a demon.

When Sharkey was floored, Daniel said, Earp had to call foul for them all to get a share of the loot.

The source of Daniel's discovery was Bat Masterson, Earp's loyal friend. The writer claimed to have overheard Masterson discuss the fight one night in the "old car barn offices of the

New York Morning Telegraph, opposite the site of the present Garden". Masterson, by then, had spent many years as a sports writer and boxing promoter. He would know what he spoke of. He died in 1921, by which time Daniel had been in the newspaper business for 12 years, having started as a 19-year-old on the *New York Herald*.

There is, then, no reason to believe Daniel's conclusions were not based on what he had actually heard (although Masterson was no longer around to refute it).

"Sharkey and Earp were close friends," Masterson had apparently said. "Lynch, Sharkey's manager, had no part in the original deal. It was a transaction between Earp and Julian.

"Earp had the check for $10,000 which was to go to the winner – and it was winner take all.

"This $10,000 was placed on Sharkey to win, making a pot of $40,000. This was a four way spilt, and nobody could lose. The odds were 3 to 1.

"Neither Sharkey nor Fitzsimmons was in on the plot.

"Sharkey, Earp's winner on a foul, got $10,000. Fitz, Earp's loser on a foul, but actually winner by a knock-out got $10,000.

"Earp, who made Sharkey winner on a foul, got $10,000 and Julian, who cooked it all up, got his $10,000."

Dan Daniel concluded colourfully: "Fitz said that he had won with his solar plexus punch, the one with which he stopped Corbett.

"Sharkey said: 'It must have been a foul or I wouldna won.'

"The fans said: 'This stunk to high heaven.'

"The scandal killed the National Athletic Club and ruined boxing in San Francisco for many years.

"*The Ring* Detective finds that Masterson's verdict against his old pal must be posted in the books for all time.

"The foul was not Fitz's, but Wyatt Earp's."

There is no doubt there was a sense of outcry among sporting fans over the outcome of the fight. But that was very much the nature of the sport at the time. More often than not, and very probably in this case, much of the clamour had less to do with a sense of injustice than with the amount of betting money lost that

SAILOR TOM

night. There were regularly rumours of fights being fixed, of fighters faking; and there were plenty of calls of "foul" – and denials too. Adding to the mix this time was the huge hype, the claims that this was the championship of the world and the larger-than-life figure of Wyatt Earp.

Sharkey could have been celebrating the world title. But the claims that this was a title fight were spurious and would not survive if Corbett – the rightful title-holder – did honour his challenge and agree to return to the ring.

It appears also that Tom Sharkey got conned twice. While the court cleared the way for him to collect his winners, it was Danny Lynch who carried the money from the bank, as noted earlier.

So, while the pro-Earp Edgren noted that – financially – the former lawman certainly did all right out of the fight, suddenly developing "an appearance of sudden affluence", he discovered that there was quite a different outcome for Sharkey.

Edgren claims that Tom told him later that Lynch "didn't show up for several days after the fight, and then, afraid to appear, wrote a letter".

The Bostonian with the eye for racehorses had apparently taken every penny Tom had made from this incredible episode and lost it at the track.

The furore over the Fitzsimmons fight had short-term professional consequences for Tom and long-term private ones.

Even though he was the official winner of what was an elimination bout, public outcry ensured that it was the spindly-legged Fitzsimmons who would face "Gentleman" Jim Corbett for the title in Carson City, Nevada, on March 17, 1897.

That immediate disappointment would be surmounted: there would be another championship fight for Sharkey, an even bigger one.

But nothing would soothe the hurt pride.

Decades later, as he lay dying, he received a visit from a fellow Irishman named Patrick Kerley.[10] Kerley had heard about his stricken countryman, lying thousands of miles from home and fading fast.

Despite his predicament, that night in San Francisco was still at the front of his mind.

"Go back and tell everyone in Dundalk," Sharkey begged of Kerley. "I had nothing to do with the fixing of the fight. That was all down to Earp."

CHAPTER FIVE
A Celebrity Homecoming

As 1897 began Tom Sharkey was back at his home at 319 York Street, Vallejo. The local directory for the year describes him as a "champion pugilist" but the titles were all left behind in the navy.

The Fitzsimmons fight may have billed as a heavyweight championship of the world contest, but it was not. Fitzsimmons and Sharkey were just fighting out a sideshow.

Corbett still claimed moral victory over Sharkey in their June 1896 encounter but was facing growing public pressure to get back into the ring.

Corbett did want to have to fight Sharkey and then Fitzsimmons so he heard the calls and agreed to fight Fitzsimmons.

Sharkey claimed Corbett had forfeited his title by refusing to face him, following his victory over Fitzsimmons. But to win the title in the eyes of sports fans, Sharkey would have had to take Corbett in the ring.

In the meantime, "Gentleman" Jim taunted Sharkey over the fall-out of the Fitzsimmons fight. Sharkey responded by suggesting the accusations of funny business which surrounded that fight could easily be turned on the champion too.

"I will teach Corbett a lesson that he will not soon forget," said Sharkey. "I have something up my sleeve, and it is in my power to turn Corbett's face to the wall in every city in the country. If 'Gentleman' Jim does not keep his mouth shut I will show him up in his true colours."

Reporters in San Francisco, asked Sharkey what he meant. "I mean that I have a letter from Corbett, over his own signature, that would brand him as a fakir all over the world," answered Sharkey. "I received this letter previous to my four round go with Corbett, and its publication would create a sensation. I was too honest to enter into his scheme and our contest was on its merits."

Sharkey was asked to put his accusations in writing over his own signature but the naval champion stated that for $500 he had refused to sign any papers until after March 17 when Corbett would take on Fitzsimmons.

He was asked his opinion of the up-coming title fight.

"If it is on the square, why Fitzsimmons will put Corbett out of business," he said. "He is not in the same class with Fitzsimmons. That is my honest opinion although I made believe yesterday that Corbett would win, but I had reasons for declaring myself. But you bet money that Corbett will try and square the whole business. He does not believe in taking any chances and when I catch him in Carson, I will make him eat his words or slap his face."

On March 17, 1897, four months after Sharkey's controversial victory over Fitzsimmons, the latter finally got Corbett into the ring. The fight took place at Carson City in the first open-air arena built especially for boxing.

In the fourteenth round, "Freckled" Bob shot several lefts to the face, then feinted with a right for the jaw. As Corbett raised his arm to protect himself, Fitzsimmons quickly shifted his right foot forward and shot a right to the heart and a left that landed with paralysing force into the pit of Corbett's stomach. This 'solar plexus' blow astounded onlookers. Henry Cooper wrote later: "It was the first time the punch had been demonstrated. And it paralysed Corbett. He couldn't move. Not until after the count,

A CELEBRITY HOMECOMING

when he tore across to get at Fitzsimmons in anger and frustration. 'Pompadour' Jim had to be restrained by seconds and officials inside the ring."

A new champion was crowned.

There was confusion over who would be Sharkey's next opponent as the contest among the contenders continued. A fight was planned with Maher, who had turned down a bout with Choynski in order to meet his fellow Irishman. But then it appeared to be off. "The contest between Peter Maher and Tom Sharkey is off," said Warren Lewis, president of the Greater New York Athletic Club. "Lynch, Sharkey's manager, has intimated that the sailor is not prepared to come east just yet and if Maher wants to meet him this winter he will have to go to California."

The stalling was down to Lynch and had started before the Corbett-Fitzsimmons championship fight. Lynch had been holding out for more money from promoter Dan Stuart, in order to match Sharkey-Maher as a second bill attraction to fight in Carson City. Lynch believed Sharkey was "as big a drawing card as either Fitz or Corbett".

Maher had fallen into Sharkey's sights as the "next best man on the list" – beneath Corbett – to be beaten after the Fitzsimmons bout.

Sharkey deposited a $2,500 forfeit for a Maher fight with negotiations now in place for a purse worth $10,000. On March 19, Maher accepted Sharkey's challenge when his manager John J Quinn telegraphed the *Police Gazette*: "Maher accepts Sharkey's challenge. Let him transfer his money to your office and I will cover it and sign articles whenever it suits Sharkey." The *Brooklyn Daily Eagle* reported that: "New Yorkers will welcome an opportunity to witness a meeting between the two heavyweights, especially as Sharkey now asserts himself as a claimant for championship honours."

Within a fortnight it had been confirmed the fight would take place at a location – as yet undecided - in Coney Island, with the initial date set for the night of Monday, May 31, following the running of the Brooklyn Handicap at Gravesend racetrack. It would last 20 or 25 rounds. Maher arrived in New York eager to get training at Westchester.

Sharkey meanwhile fought Jim Williams at Salt Lake City, Utah, on April 5, (drawn over eight rounds) and then five four-round exhibitions with Jake Holtman in St Louis (two on April 11, and one each on the 12th, 13th and 14th).

The exhibition tour was slowly winding its way to New York, where Sharkey wanted to be in place to carry out a month's training before taking on Maher.

That April, Coney Island was alive with boxers in training. Dan Creedon, George 'Kid' Lavigne and Tommy White, of Chicago, and their trainers and assistants were all encamped at Van Buren's Hotel on Ocean Parkway, at the corner of Sea Breeze Avenue. And the huge interest in the sport had proved good for Lewis and the Greater New York Club, which was building a "well-equipped gymnasium and a running track". Fighting had now well and truly moved out of the shipyards and the wooded clearings.

But what about the law? The *Brooklyn Daily Eagle* reported an inspection of the club at Coney Island by the city authorities – including the police - and explained that the improvements were to meet the Horton Law, which governed boxing in New York state between 1896 and 1900 and allowed fights with no limit to the number of rounds, decisions by referees and the posting of forfeits and side-bets. It explained: "The Horton Law stipulates that legal permission to hold a boxing contest shall not be given to any organisation unless its plant and equipment is that of an athletic club. Accordingly the Greater New York's clubhouse has been fitted out with a gymnasium, while later it will contain a well-constructed tan bark running track. The former is furnished with all sorts of gymnastic appliances and is being regularly used by the pugilists who are now training at Coney Island."

The gymnasium, it was reported, was fitted with two punching-bag platforms, horizontal bars, Mexican rings, dumb bells, Indian clubs, a trapeze flying rings and an aerial ladder, as well as lockers and shower baths. A police report of the inspection then went to Mayor Wurster, who had the power to grant or refuse a licence.

A CELEBRITY HOMECOMING

Tom and Lynch had already been to the clubhouse and said they were really pleased with it. Lewis also introduced Sharkey to Coney Island, giving the boxer a guided tour of the resort and area which would come to play a major part in his life over the next few years. And while riding on a carriage, Sharkey was spotted by his upcoming opponent, who was staying in Sheepshead Bay. Maher ran out from the pavement and "greeted Sharkey cordially" with both men pumping the other's hand, fondly and respectfully.

Both men took their training for the bout very seriously. Maher lived quietly at Westchester, near the Morris Park race track, running on the local roads and bathing at Long Island Sound. Sharkey based himself at New Dorp, Staten Island, with Tim McGrath and Jim Hall, his sparring partner, and worked on bringing himself down from 184 pounds to a fighting weight of 175. "The sailor is confident and has gone about his work with vim and spirit," reported the *Brooklyn Daily Eagle*.

Describing his training regime, Tom later said: "After rising at 6am. I take a sherry and egg mixture, and then turn out for a walk of a mile or so prior to breakfasting at 7:30. An hour later finds me on the road doing a spin of eight to ten miles, which is followed by a salt water bath. Stepping from the tub, I undergo a brisk rub down from my trainers, using alcohol to harden the muscles. Lunch at noon means a rest for 2 and a half hours, when I resume training, this time going in for eleven rounds at the punching ball, about eight rounds of boxing, some skipping-rope practice, a game or two of handball, finishing up the business of the day with another bath and rub down. I have always three trainers in attendance."[1]

He also said: "When I trained to fight the heavyweight champions of the world I hit the highways for ten to fifteen miles of road work every day for three months. I also boxed ten rounds or more daily with my sparring partners and several times a day punched a heavy bag. So, it was only natural for me to run the hundred barefoot in eleven seconds."[2]

As the boxers trained, the managers negotiated. Corbett's backer, William A Brady, of the Palace Athletic Club, at 107th Street and Lexington Avenue, New York, wanted to host the 25-round fight. A new – and final - date was fixed for June 9.

On May 10, the Californian, Joe Choynski, won on a foul against "Denver" Ed Smith, who "was hooted out of the ring of the Broadway Athletic Club, New York…a shamed, disgraced and discredited pugilist, who will never be permitted to don a glove in any respectable club in the East again". Smith was "so badly and so thoroughly trounced in the first round that he resorted to all sorts of disgraceful ring tactics". After a fourth round incident, in which "he threw his arms around Choynski's shoulders and butted him with his head like a goat and knocked out one of Joe's teeth", the referee awarded Choynski the fight and Smith left to the hisses of the 3,500 spectators.

In the crowd was "Gentleman" Jim Corbett, dressed up in a "natty Scotch tweed". Interestingly, Corbett – the man who had so dismissed Sharkey's efforts in their four-rounder just under a year earlier, despite onlookers' praises of the Irishman – now appeared to be dismissing Fitzsimmons' hammering of him in Carson City. He told the *Brooklyn Daily Eagle*: "You can say for me that when I fight again it will be Fitzsimmons and for the championship of the world. I still consider myself the champion. Everybody admits that I had Fitzsimmons whipped at Carson and, until I get another chance at him and get whipped again, I am not coming down to the class of such third-rate fighters as Choynski. I have $5,000 posted in support of my challenge to Fitzsimmons."

However, Choynski was now in that group of contenders which included Sharkey and the Australian, Joe Goddard. He wanted Fitzsimmons, so did Goddard, but there was hostility towards fighters from "Down Under" fighting for the world title. Sharkey, of course, could claim a moral victory against Choynski and an "Earp" one against Fitzsimmons.

Sharkey was in Choynski's corner the night of the Smith fight and was cheered by the crowd as he posed against the ropes. "Big" Bob Armstrong was there too. The three had been fighting exhibitions together during May. Sharkey had traded gloves with Armstrong twice, Choynski, Tim McGrath and Tom Lansing, all at Southfield, New York. McGrath wrote later in *The Ring*: "Sharkey, because of the fact that he was a fighter and not a boxer, was very hard on his sparring partners. One of my hardest jobs was to get men to come to his training quarters to box with him. I used to get a bunch of them, good and bad, and line them up like a lot of steers waiting to be killed."

Tom would come out, remembered McGrath, and say, "How many you got?"

"Five or six."

The "steers" would go in for a slaughter and after a little time, Sharkey would come out again. "How many's left?"

If there were none to go in, that would be the end of the boxing part of the training and McGrath would go off to hire more sparring partners.

"For the fight with Peter Maher, however," wrote McGrath, "I figured that I ought to get the best help obtainable, men who could really make Tom extend himself and, at enormous expense, as they say, I engaged Joe Choynski and Bob Armstrong, the coloured heavyweight. These two clever, hard-hitting fellows gave Tom some wonderful workouts, and the night of the fight with Maher he was fit as a fiddle."

Despite the Earp fight and certain writers' obvious dislike of the upstart Sharkey, the New York newspapers became extremely excited about his upcoming bout with Maher. The *Brooklyn Daily Eagle* billed it as "one of the most promising sparring contests that has ever taken place in New York". "New Yorkers have never had the opportunity of seeing two such prominent exponents of the manly art perform. Sharkey has never been seen here in competition. Ever since his memorable engagement with Fitzsimmons, Easterners have had great desire to see him. No better man could have been secured to meet Sharkey than Peter Maher. Notwithstanding Maher's two defeats by Fitzsimmons, there are many who hold the opinion that he is still in line for the championship. Both Sharkey and Maher have been in constant training for the past month and are in grand shape."

It added that "if physical condition can be taken as a criterion the twenty-five round bout...should be a fine exhibition". Both were in the best possible shape with Choynski being a great help to 173-pound Sharkey, who was "all brawn and muscle". "Maher has a great many admirers who will be on hand... and, in addition to these, a big delegation will also come over from Pittsburgh to encourage the Irishman. Sharkey is not without supporters and has many friends who are willing to back him to almost any extent."

As the fight approached, sporting men from "all the prominent cities in the East" arrived in New York. Four hundred men will be represented by delegations of sporting men. Five hundred arrived from Boston, led by Jimmy Colville, who had been chosen to referee, and four hundred from Philadelphia; and another referee, Jeremiah "Yank" Sullivan, brought in a large party from Syracuse. Betting was slow but Maher was the favourite helped by New Yorker, Dick Ryan, who wagered $500 to $250 that the Irish champion would defeat Sharkey. The purse was now fixed at $12,000.[3]

Maher was said to be so confident that he had told friends the fight would be all over in ten rounds. In Maher's mind, he had the edge over Sharkey for two reasons: he was more intelligent and he could hit harder. (Boxing historian Tracy Callis agrees with Maher's assessment of himself, believing him to be not only technically proficient but also "the most devastating puncher of the pre-1900 years".) Maher reckoned he would put Sharkey down when he came in close. The sailor, of course, was also confident, believing he could end the contest even quicker, in the sixth. Victory over Maher, Tom believed, would allow him to revisit Fitzsimmons, over turn the doubt about his December 1896 victory and take the now legitimate title off "Ruby" Bob.

There was all that and a great deal of Irish pride on the fight.

Everything seemed settled. Then, the day before the fight, a portent. The massive interest from the public meant that the police was keeping a close eye and looking for a "scientific affair" with "no slugging". Police chief Conlin said he would be sending Inspector McLaughlin, Captain Creedon and possibly even Deputy Chief Cartright to see that "everything goes off smoothly". At the first indication of slugging or brutality, he said, both fighters would be arrested.

On the night of the fight, a crowd pushed through the doors of the athletic club of a size and excitement which was unseen in the city outside of Madison Square Garden. Those unable to get tickets stood around in the blocks outside. This was the fight which would decide who should have a crack at the champion. With the fight now hours away, the betting remained 10/7 in Maher's favour.

These were men at the top of their sport. They had fought the best: Choynski, Corbett and Fitzsimmons. But, would they be allowed to slug it out and prove who was better?

Corbett made his usual ostentatious arrival ringside but the big cheers were kept for John L Sullivan. The crowd settled down to a preliminary bout but it was the scores of police officers which surrounded the ring which caught the eye. Conlin was obviously serious in his threats and the officers waited keenly for the main bout.

Sharkey appeared first, with Joe Choynski, Tim McGrath, Tom Lansing and Solly Smith. He looked strong and fit as he pulled the pale blue bath robe around him and stepped through the ropes. He enjoyed a warm reception from the crowd but Maher got the louder applause. In his corner were Buck Connolly, Pete Lowry, Pat Scully, Jack Quinn and Jack Cattanach.

Both men met in the centre of the ring under the glare of the electric lights. Once again, the brave sailor was facing someone who was taller and with a longer reach. The referee Colville issued his instructions: the fighters had agreed to break clean at his call but hitting with one hand free was allowed.

McGrath, the showman, later laughed when he remembered the last moments before the bell. He said "every Irishman in New York" was there to see the 3/1 favourite Maher throw off his bathrobe and reveal a "bright green pair of trunks". Unlike Tom, Maher had started his a career in Ireland and was already fairly well-known when he arrived in the United States in 1891. To the fans, he was a champion from the "Old Country".

McGrath explained: "Maher, being an imported Irishman, was considered more Irish than Sharkey; Tom was born in Ireland, all right, but the New Yorkers looked upon him as 'one of those native son Irishmen from California' and, as a matter of fact, most the New Yorkers didn't know that Tom was born in Ireland."

"PETER MAHER!" screamed the announcer as the patriotic shorts were flashed. "Champion of Ireland - from Dublin!"

The club shook as the crowd went wild. The cheering went on for five minutes. Looking around at the reaction, McGrath went over and shouted in the announcer's ear.

The announcer nodded, the crowd died down. Now, he shouted: "TOM SHARKEY…! From Dundalk, IRELAND!"

McGrath yanked off Tom's bathrobe and showed a pair of trunks "still brighter green than Maher's". The crowd was a little surprised, "stunned" was how McGrath described it. They had come to see one Irishman lick a fighter from the West Coast. "It didn't know what to do," said McGrath. "If it rooted for one Irishman alone it would be taking sides against another Irishman. So, when the crowd collected its wits, it cheered Sharkey as long as it did Maher, and then it settled back to root for both of them.

"With the championship of Ireland at stake, Maher and Sharkey were both on pins and needles, and when the gong sounded they flew at each other and met with a crash in the centre of the ring."

Sharkey was the least cautious. Maher, not usually restrained, held back. Sharkey moved well, though, and led at Maher with his left. At one time, according to a ringside reporter, "the sailor hummed audibly a popular Negro melody". Sharkey struck at Maher's body but without inflicting damage, his lack of reach already showing itself to be a handicap.

It was Sharkey's size which made him incautious. He wanted to get in and finish but, in attacking, he left himself unguarded. He remained courageous and steadfast as ever though. In the second when Maher landed a light left on the jaw, the sailor responded with a right swing on the head, and when Maher led short for the body, he got a stiff left hand punch in the mouth.

Maher's probing in the third and fourth simply stimulated Sharkey and neither was clear of the other according to sports ringside.

The first move which seemed to jolt Maher out of his steady confidence came in the sixth when, after a short exchange,

A CELEBRITY HOMECOMING

Sharkey's right fist caught Maher on the head and off-balance the fighter stumbled against the ropes. Sharkey waited close while Maher rested on one knee.

The gong went and the fighters returned to their corners, still little between them. However, all hell was to break loose in the seventh round. According to McGrath, Sharkey was more affected by Maher's precise probing punches than he appeared. One right to the jaw had made Sharkey "dazed and foggy" so much so that, in his corner, he had muttered to McGrath: "I'll lick the three of 'em.".

McGrath, as he told it, replied: "That's all right, Tom. Go back and pick the one in the middle."

When Sharkey put Maher down on his knee though, McGrath said the "tide of battle turned". This, according to the trainer, was reason for some around the ring to get twitchy.

The seventh started with a Sharkey left to Maher's chin. Maher responded by cutting loose, landing a light left on the sailor's body and a harder left to his head.

Sharkey hit Maher in the face and stomach, but every strike from both boxers only met with a more vicious response in turn. Maher flashed his left to Sharkey's neck and then pilled a mighty right into Sharkey's head, a punch which "sent Sharkey over as if he had been a paper man".

The sailor showed no sign of having been hurt though. He began to get up and as he did so Maher whacked him again, just – as the *Brooklyn Daily Eagle* reported – the gong sounded to close the round.

Maher, of course, should not have struck Sharkey as he rose. The referee should have kept Maher back until the sailor was on his feet. Whether Sharkey heard the gong or whether it sounded just as he was struck, it is impossible to tell. McGrath doubted that and backed Sharkey over what happened next – although, as a friend as well as a colleague, would do. The referee also backed Sharkey and, on the face of it, had no reason to.

Sharkey rose from the second blow like a "wild bull", clinched with Maher and inflicted three right hand blows into his opponent's head.

According to the *Brooklyn Daily Eagle*, this was now "several seconds after the round closed". Maher struck back but his seconds ran into the ring to claim a foul. "There was a wild scene. The fighters were separated with difficulty and when they broke away Sharkey hit one of Maher's seconds on the head. At this point, the police swarmed into the ring and Inspector McLaughlin declared the principals and their seconds under arrest. The crowd viewed this outcome of the contest with open dissatisfaction. But there was nothing to do except get out. The referee declared the bout a draw."

A *Police Gazette* cable from New York to Irish newspapers reported that while Maher floored Sharkey "no real opportunity was afforded the ten thousand spectators of judging actually who was the better man". The London *Daily Mail*'s New York correspondent wrote: "Over eight thousand people paid five dollars admission on Wednesday night to witness the twenty-five round boxing contest between Peter Maher, the Irish Champion and Tom Sharkey, the American, at the Palace Athletic Club. At the end of the seventh round, the referee declared the fight a draw, but both men continued fighting savagely until the police entered the ring and separated them. The principals and seconds were arrested for breaking the New York law against prize-fighting…"

But at least one newspaper recognised how Sharkey was adding some technique to his undoubted courage.

The *Chicago Chronicle* called his stand against Maher the "pugilistic surprise of the season". He had learnt something about the art of defence and the necessity for it. Where previously he had rushed head first at "an antagonist leaving himself open to all sorts of blows", against Maher he "adopted new tactics and tried to save himself as much as possible". It added that "none of the men in the first class have been able to put an undisputed quietus on the sailor man."

According to McGrath: "Jimmy Colville, the referee, refused to allow the claim [of foul], and as there was a general mix up in the ring, with all the seconds of the two fighters taking part, Colville threw up his arms and called the fight a draw."

A riot was threatened, said McGrath, who seemed relieved that

A CELEBRITY HOMECOMING

they were all arrested and taken to the Harlem jail away from the baying masses.

The newspaper reported: "Inspector McLaughlin said that he sent his men into the ring because it was clear to him that the fighters intended to rough it in violation of their promise to him…On Sharkey's behalf, it was asserted by his friends that in the excitement of the moment he did not hear the bell."

Maher said next morning: "I think that if I had another round I would have knocked Sharkey out. There was no blood shed and no violation of the law. I did not hear the gong sound in the seventh round and when I was told of it started for my corner. Sharkey struck me in the back and I turned to protect myself. Then the police jumped in."

If Maher did not hear the gong while on his feet, would Sharkey have, having taken a blow as it was struck. He said not. "I did not hear the gong sound. When the people jumped into the ring, you must admit it was an unusual thing, I may have lost my head for the moment and struck out."

Boston-based Jimmy Colville, the referee, added: "I don't think either man heard the gong sound. Maher was the first to try to get to his corner and Sharkey struck at him. The men had been clinched in a moment before. There was no violation of the law."

All involved were not in jail long, having help from one of the most powerful men in America, the state senator and Tammany Hall boss. McGrath explained: "We didn't remain in long, though, for that grand man, Big Tim Sullivan, came to our rescue and bailed us out."

That influence may have been reflected in what happened the morning after the fight when crowds thronged to the court to see the men's appearance before Magistrate Cornell at Harlem Police Court. The fighters and their parties arrived by train at the 125th Street station of the Third Avenue Elevated Road, to be met by a crowd of 500. The first to come down the stairway was the Maher party. With the fighter were Buck Connolly, his manager, and his seconds Peter Lowry, Pat Scully, Jack Quinn and Peter Burns. Colville and JJ Quinn were there too. Next, as if coming from the dressing room to ringside, came Sharkey with Choynski, McGrath, Lansing and Lynch.

The crowds dashed for the entrance to the court room but were kept back by police, who had to barricade the door.

"Maher and Sharkey did not seem to pay much attention to each other and later, when they were arraigned at the bar so that their elbows touched, they did not exchange a word," wrote a court reporter. "There was not, however the slightest evidence of ill feeling. On the contrary, all appeared in the best of humour."

As the clock ticked towards 10am, the case began. Cornell said to Inspector McLaughlin: "Now, inspector, tell me all about this case."

"I believe the law was offended by these men last night," announced McLaughlin. "I believe they were engaged in a genuine prize-fight. There was slugging and knocking down. I believed it was my duty to stop them. The law against prize-fighting was clearly violated."

"A good many things happen at a performance of this kind," commented the magistrate, "that would not look well at a five o'clock tea."

McLaughlin insisted: "There was slugging. There was brutal pounding and knocking down. If that does not constitute a prize-fight, I do not know what does."

Cornell flicked his papers. "I read the account of the fight," he said, "and while I believe you were perfectly right in separating and arresting them, I don't think we can strictly hold them as having taken part in a prize-fight."

Sharkey's lawyer, Daniel O'Reilly, now outlined his case: "We claim that there was no prize-fight and that the law was in no way offended. Section 458 of the penal code was in every respect observed. There was no violation so far as the sparring contest went and there would have been none to the end."

Emmanuel Friend, counsel for Maher, added: "Assemblyman Horton was at the contest himself last night and he said the performance was perfectly legal up to the seventh round."

McLaughlin interjected: "Oh, that's only hearsay evidence."

"In a case of this kind inspector," said Magistrate Cornell, "the newspapers are pretty sure to be right."

If McLaughlin was feeling a little isolated in the court room, he did not show it. "I went to the dressing rooms of these men before they went into the ring," he said. "I read the law to them there and told them there must be no slugging. I insist again that there was slugging and that I did right in causing the arrest."

"I think you did right," agreed the magistrate, "in as much as the men were disorderly. But you must understand that they received much encouragement. The public had apparently expressed great interest in what they were about to do. They were very much interested themselves. They are big, powerful men and presumably high-tempered men. It is not to be wondered at if they lost their heads. On that ground an arrest was warranted, if they acted disorderly. I am glad they were locked up, and would have been glad if they had been forced to stay all night in the jail. But I will not entertain a complaint of prize-fighting against them. I think they were within the law."

Cornell then turned to the boxers, who faced him, side by side: "Maher and Sharkey, you are discharged."

There was immediate bustling in the room, as everyone moved toward the door. "Every person present seemed to be a friend or an admirer of the pugilists. A crowd escorted them as they went to Third Avenue and boarded the cable cars." The reporter added: "It was noticed that, as far as the appearance of the men went, there had been no slugging. One of Maher's eyes was somewhat bloodshot but his friends said that it is a constitutional affection [sic]. There was a little scratch behind Sharkey's left ear but that, his seconds said, was there a week ago."

So, the Sharkey-Maher contest had been inconclusive in boxing terms, disorderly in legal terms but there had been no violation of the Horton Law.

McGrath's later recollection of the court case before the "Irish judge" might not have been as factually accurate as the court reporter's contemporaneous account, but it might not have been too wide of the mark in spirit.

According to McGrath, the judge first called up Maher.

"Peter," he said, "where were you born?"

"In Ireland, Your Honor," replied Maher.

"And you, Buck Cornelius?"

"Ireland."

"John Quinn?"

"Ireland."

"Peter Lowry?"

"Ireland."

"Peter Burns?"

"Ireland."

"Tom Sharkey?"

"Ireland."

"Tim McGrath?"

"Ireland."

"That's enough," said the judge. "I can't see any case here. Defendants dismissed."

Off the legal hook but Sharkey was not happy, vowing that no money would ever induce him to get back in a ring in New York again. He still had the world championship in his sights though. A week after the brawling end to the Maher contest he made another challenge to Fitzsimmons, demanding a contest within six months at "Nevada or any other place where it is possible to hold it without interference". Tom added: "If Fitzsimmons does not accept within 30 days, the same offer is open to Maher or Corbett. I am satisfied that I can defeat either of them and I will risk my own money in an effort to win the championship title."

It had been an amazing couple of years for Sharkey. Since July 1895, when he beat "Australian" Billy Smith in his first fight with a genuine boxer and his last fight as a United States seaman, he had knocked out Miller, Brown and Williams, claimed wins over Choynski and Corbett (in a four-rounder) which were supported by many who saw the fights, gone three rounds in an exhibition with Sullivan, beaten Fitzsimmons in one of the most controversial fistic encounters ever and seen the police drag him apart from an Irish hero, Peter Maher.

A CELEBRITY HOMECOMING

Within two years of turning professional, he had made quite a name for himself against ring champions who had been around considerably longer.

Now, in the summer of 1897, there seemed only one thing to do in order to enjoy that success: head home, to the country he had not seen for years, to the family who knew him only through reports in the local newspapers and a few scrawled letters, and to Dundalk which would surely greet him like a hero.

On June 16, he sailed back across the Atlantic. He was not working his passage this time, though. Now he was a passenger on the steamship, *St Paul*, a gleaming new, twin-funnel steamer of the American Line. He arrived firstly, via Liverpool, at Newry, on Tuesday June 29, an event that was reported at length in the *Dundalk Democrat* under the headline: "A Dundalk Celebrity: Home-coming of Tom Sharkey, the Pugilist". It reported that the crowds gathered at about one o'clock to meet the boxer's ship. "The news of his arrival in Ireland, by the Newry route rapidly spread throughout that town, and hundreds of people congregated to await the arrival of the steamer. Loud cheers were given as the vessel came into the quays, and the now celebrated pugilist was seen on deck accompanied by his father who had gone from Dundalk to Liverpool to meet him. He was quickly recognized and cheer after cheer went up with a heartiness equalling that which was bestowed on James J Corbett on his arrival in Kingstown [now Dún Laoghaire] three years ago. There was a rush to shake hands with Sharkey and hundreds grasped him by the hand."[4]

His father took Tom, his younger brother, John – who had been living in America with Tom - and some friends (followed by fans) to Warrenpoint, allowing the fervour in Dundalk, about 14 or so miles down the coast, to rise to fever pitch. Eventually, word spread that Sharkey would be arriving on the 7:15pm from Newry. He understood something of his level of celebrity – having stood at the centre of 10,000-strong boxing crowds and having been seen off at Newry by a large crowd of well-wishers – but could anything have prepared the ex-patriot Irishman for the welcome Dundalk was planning for him? "A Prime Minister might envy the reception Sharkey got in his native town," the *Dundalk Democrat* wrote. As the time of the train's arrival approached, "a continuous stream of men and boys was flowing towards the station, while along the road were numerous representatives of the other sex".

Crowds lined the roads around the station while friends, the most keen fans and members of Sharkey's family bought tickets so they could be on the platform as the train pulled in. As it did, there was a rush to the boxer's carriage and Sharkey "stood a fair chance of being torn in small pieces by his demonstrative admirers. Not in all his contests with Fitzsimmons and Maher and Choynski and the rest, did he receive much rougher usage".

Reporters clamoured to get a word from the boxer, until local dignitary and family friend, James Gosling, and Sharkey's brothers pulled him free to meet the rest of the cheering crowd at the station door.

"The excitement was tremendous. Men and boys lined the way and sat on the wall and fences and cheered themselves hoarse. They tried to carry the pugilist, but his weight is not a trifle and he induced them to let him ride on the car."

He mounted a car with his brothers, mother and sisters, which slowly moved off as the town's Emmet Band struck up "See the Conquering Hero".

Now, a community which had no idea what its hero looked like – one imagines even his own family would have been startled to see the manly appearance of the 23-year-old fighter they had last known as a child or youth – had its first chance to feast its eyes on "Sailor" Tom Sharkey, the man who had given champion "Gentleman" Jim Corbett the run-around. Where American newspapers had often sought to put down the man, who went into the ring against their heroes, as if he were just a bare-knuckle dockyard puncher, the Irish reporter choose to celebrate and romanticise as he looked up at the fighter perched on the motor car.

"Seen on his elevation, he gave the lie to one's preconceived ideas of what a prize-fighter might be," noted one onlooker. "There was no brutal looking bruiser, with bulldog head or the savage marks of fistic battles, or of dissipation that so many of the fraternity indulge in. A fine massive head, set squarely on a broad pair of shoulders, a neck showing immense strength, were what struck one most about him. His comparatively short stature must tell against him in the ring. His countenance shows no marks either of bad usage or a bad life. Indeed Sharkey is, in many respects, a model fellow, never touching liquor and retaining, through all the vicissitudes of his life, a strong love for the old sod and the old people."[5]

Sharkey, clothed in a tall hat and frock coat, muttered "modest" words of thanks as he went on his way. Members of the crowd muttered at the fine clothes, the air of "prosperity and prominence" as the group moved towards the small thatched cottage in Hill Street, where he had been born and where his parents were still living. "It was typical of the good fellow that this should be the Mecca of his transatlantic journey," wrote the *Dundalk Democrat*. "A big car load of trunks went on to Bullock's Hotel but their owner spent the first hour or two amidst the scenes of his boyhood, talking to his old neighbours, fighting his battles o'er again, and enjoying the sweets of home-coming just like any big boy fresh home from school."

To get to his home, Sharkey had to travel over the short Hill Street bridge, coming down over the rise to his house. It must have been a most remarkable scene. In the beautiful summer's night, tar barrels blazed on the bridge to mark his return. It was not unusual for the poor families who lived in this area of the town to see their sons, daughters, brothers and sisters head off to the United States, but here was one who had made enough money to come back, if only for a few weeks: they were determined to create something special; the "joy overflowed the place and brightened its most squalid recesses".

Sharkey went to visit one of his sisters, now a Mrs Lappin, at the Quays – where he had run around as a snotty, dirty-faced kid and had his head turned by ships leaving on dangerous voyages to far shores - and along every street he was cheered and applauded.

The *Dundalk Democrat* reporter sat down with the "local lion" at the rooms of the Young Ireland Society, in whose gymnasium Sharkey planned to train during his visit. "There is nothing of the bully about Tom Sharkey, nor has he any of the side which is so characteristic of some returned Americans," the writer remarked. "He is a nice quiet fellow, who talked pleasantly of old days in Dundalk, and of his experiences in the Navy and subsequently in the prize-ring. He speaks remarkably well, with a good deal of the Yankee accent."

The reporter described Tom's exotic lifestyle: his home in San Francisco in "one of the loveliest climates on the globe", his travels to different parts of the United States to give sparring exhibitions; and the fact that the "Californians are never tired of seeing him, and never grudge any price to gain admission to the theatres where he exhibits".

"There is money in the business in the States, and Tom Sharkey has got a good deal of it in his comparatively short career. He is a tremendous favourite with the Irish in America and more especially with all those who are or have been connected with the Navy."

As Corbett was refusing to fight and as Sharkey had been awarded victory over Fitzsimmons (albeit before "Ruby" Bob was champ), Sharkey reckoned he now only had to beat Maher in a rematch to be world champion.

Sharkey's return allows a glimpse at the pride felt not only by his hometown, but by his family. His father, a "fine, hale, good-humoured gentleman" who had worked on the railways of Louth all his life, glowed over the son who was conquering America, saying, "A father never had a better son."

Mr Sharkey said Tom not only wrote to him "every fortnight" but had also sent him a black Malacca gold mounted walking stick which had been presented to him when he left the navy. Made from "very fine cane", the stick had a gold head and was worth about £20. It was inscribed: "To Tom from his shipmates on the *USS Philadelphia*, the 10th of November 1896."

Tom's father revealed that the boxer had resolved, before the Maher fiasco, to visit home. "No matter how the fight goes, father," Tom had written, "I will come home and see the old land again, and bring my brother back with me."

His son was looking forward to having a "good time of it at Blackrock, ducking himself in the sea". He added, with the fact in mind that as many did not approve of prize-fighting in Ireland as in the United States, that, "I am sure that he will always act honourably and never discredit his birthplace or his country."

Tom Sharkey had not been home for five or six years, having left Dundalk at the age of around 18. The fact that rumours and stories persisted through the American press that he had left at a much younger age is dealt with in the *Dundalk Democrat* of July 3, 1897. Under a headline "Some 'News' from an American Paper", the writer states: "Those who don't love the trans-Atlantic style of journalism say the American papers are as unreliable and inaccurate as they are sensational. A copy of the *New York Daily News* to hand gives the following description of Sharkey's departure: and the account of himself which the imaginative reporter puts into the pugilist's mouth will open the eyes of that stout ex-sailor himself and of his people."

According to the *Daily News*, the passengers of the *St Paul* included a "happy pugilist", Tom Sharkey, who "calls himself the champion of Ireland". Arriving at the pier before nine o'clock – with Lynch and others to bid him farewell – Sharkey had apparently told a city reporter: "This will be my first visit home since I left it 14 years ago, or when I was only nine years old. The place I came from is Dundalk, County Louth. It isn't a country village. It's a town and my father was postmaster there. There was a family of 15 when I left home, but now I have two brothers and three sisters living, besides my parents."

"Do they know you're going over?" asked the *Daily News*.

"No, that will be a surprise. I've kept in communication with them, and they know how well I've advanced in pugilistic honours, but they won't know I am going to make a call on them till I get to London. Then, I'll telegraph. It's about a day's trip then from London to my old home. I expect to be away altogether about five or six weeks."

As well as the repeated Sharkey or journalistic embellishment about the age he had left Ireland, the statement that his visit would be a surprise also appears to be inaccurate. The interview with Sharkey's father, quoted above, in which he talks about Tom's letter saying he would return home after the Maher fight, was conducted by a Dublin-based reporter the week before Sharkey's return home.

Stories reported in Ireland were generally sympathetic to Sharkey, particularly compared to an often cartoon-like portrayal of him in America. Tom, no doubt, contributed to this disparity: he liked to tell a good tale and could get away with it in America; there was much less bravado at home. Consequently, the stories told at home in 1897 confirmed his having last been in his hometown in around 1891. The facts of his leaving would often change but at this time of scrutiny – his family were all there to greet him home – it was likely to ring true.

"I little thought, when I left Dundalk six years ago, of making pugilism a profession," he said. "After I left here, I went on a voyage to China and afterwards to Australia and while there, I took the notion to join the US Navy. It was from seeing a fight between two well known pugilists while I was in the Navy that I first got the idea of entering the ring. I thought I should be able to do better than either of them."

Sharkey's account was confirmed by his father at the time of the same visit home. "He has been away about five years," said Mr Sharkey. "He left here to join the American Navy. As a boy he was always fond of the sea... He was always a very quiet boy but if he did have occasion to lift his fist, the fellow opposite him always got the worst of it."

The *Irish News* reported: "Six years have lapsed since Sharkey, then a raw stripling of seventeen, quitted his native town, like many another lad to seek his fortune. He had, for a couple of years before this, been engaged as a general hand on coasting schooners, but fighting in any form was absolutely foreign to him. After a couple of voyages in foreign-going ships, he entered the United States Navy. It was then, in the rough pranks which he played with his mess-mates, that it commenced to dawn on him that he

A CELEBRITY HOMECOMING

could use his fists. Encouraged by the patronage of the officers, he went in more strongly for the game, and in 1895 resigned the sea with a roll of fourteen fights, representing £27 to go in for the sport in real earnest."

The excitement at Sharkey's return home rose when it was reported that Maher was coming home to Ireland too, having just got married.

Sharkey had issued challenges to Fitzsimmons, Maher and Corbett before leaving for Ireland. In July 1897, Fitzsimmons had been world champion for four months and had only been fighting exhibitions since winning the title. He was not in a hurry to meet a true challenger.

Sharkey, on the other hand, was. He had deposited $2,500 with Al Smith to bind a match with Maher for $10,000 a side and said if Maher could not get the money he would fight for half that amount. Before Sharkey had left New York, there had been discussion in the American newspapers as to where the fight would be: Sharkey had suggested any of the clubs in England or Dublin, or in Carson City.

The jury, of course, was out on how Maher and Sharkey compared after June's abandoned fight. That meant Sharkey was desperate for a rematch. He felt that, as Corbett had backed out on his agreement to fight Sharkey and as Sharkey had beaten Fitzsimmons, he now only had to beat the other man in the frame – Peter Maher – to be able to claim he was champion of the world.

In addition, Sharkey was desperate for a rematch, eager to show that he was the greatest Irish-born fighter on the scene. Perhaps he had "forgotten" where he had come from a little bit, allowing himself to be promoted as a San Franciscan, and perhaps home fans would favour Maher, but as the *The Irish News and Belfast Morning News* noted, "The almost triumphant reception accorded Sharkey on his return to his native town…was proof positive that no matter how affairs may go in the coming struggle, he has attentive admiration of a very considerable section of Irishmen fixed on him".

When Sharkey visited Belfast, he was again the centre of attention but it was noted: "Sharkey's success has in no way turned his head, for there is nothing in his manner to suggest the bluster and brag which one generally sets down as characteristic of prize-fighters". He was modest, without any side, and spoke with candour about himself.

The air of prosperity noted on his arrival home manifested itself in his physical appearance and apparent sartorial elegance. On going out, he dressed in a suit of fine black cloth which showed off his broad shoulders. He was always clean shaven, nodding at admirers from under a spotless silk hat.

The kindly *Irish News* notes no "ostentatious exhibition of jewellery", but the trademark single diamond stud which "gleams brightly in the bosom of his white shirt and a gold curb chain extending across his vest" must have turned heads among the poor families of Hill Street and on the streets of Belfast.

In conversation, he was "urbane" with a "sincerity of style". A news reporter concluded: "It is hard to believe that this brawny young Leinsterman means to have a bold try for the World Championship before his twenty-fourth birthday."

Sharkey was certainly talking boldly about the mooted rematch with Maher: "Unsatisfactory though the (June) contest was, it gave me cause to feel confident that I shall defeat him when we next meet, and what is more, I am sure I shall win easily. He is the easiest man I ever put on a glove with."

Maher was making similar noises about Sharkey, although unlike Sharkey he was quite happy to make unsubstantiated threats and claims about the fairness of the contest. After arriving in Queenstown from New York, the Galway-born, 28-year-old fighter said he was "most anxious for another fight".[6] Having been away for two-and-a-half years, he brought his home fans up-to-date with his "many battles", of which he had "won nearly all; those that I have not won were drawn". He said: "The last man I fought was Tom Sharkey, and that contest, as you are doubtless aware, ended in a draw in consequences of the interference of the police. I had Sharkey completely at my mercy when the police interfered. Sharkey's manager and a backer laid three to one before

A CELEBRITY HOMECOMING

the fight commenced that it would be stopped and, right enough, it was stopped. The fight was for $12,000 and out of that sum I had to agree to pay Sharkey, if he lost, $3,800. I was forced into it, and if I did not agree there would be no fight. Sharkey is the easiest man in the world to beat and if the fight had not been interfered with, I would have whipped him in the next round." (Fights being broken up by the authorities, though, were far from unusual; indeed Maher would be involved in a similar incident in February 1899 in a fight with Tom "Stockings" Conroy.)

Maher also happily laid into Fitzsimmons, claiming he was the "most lucky fighter in existence".

Maher said he would wait only six weeks for the fight with Sharkey or he would return to America. Sharkey said that if the fight was to take place in London, Sharkey would train at Bangor, on the Belfast Lough, no doubt to raise important support from Irish boxing fans. "I always get strong with bracing sea breezes, and Bangor would suit me to a T," said the former sailor, who also had a sister living in the town.

Perhaps, Sharkey would have preferred to fight for the world title on this side of the Atlantic, telling the *Irish News*: "I do maintain...that the American Press, with few exceptions, have been against me during my career. Why, I don't know. I certainly never give them an opportunity by demeaning myself to hurl foul and disgraceful epithets either at any man I had engaged to fight, or respecting any pugilist living. Even my personal self-respect has been too carefully safeguarded to allow even a loophole for such unfair treatment."

However, the *Police Gazette* in New York was reporting that Buck Connolly, representing Maher, was in meetings with Lynch over the fight, and that while Connolly would not allow Maher to fight Sharkey in his back yard, San Francisco, the fight would either be in Carson City or Johannesburg. It would take place around November 1st at the highest bidding club. Negotiations to draw up articles for the fight were watched over by Gazette editor, Sam Austin, although, as the Horton Law prohibited the signing of articles in New York, the two managers had to go to New

Jersey to cement their agreement. It would be a "scientific battle with gloves, according to the Marquis of Queensbury [sic] rules, for $5,000-a-side and the best purse". The gloves would be the "smallest size and weight permitted by law in the State in which the contest may be held". The fighters would agree not to fight anybody else in a competitive contest without the other's consent.

Lynch cabled Ireland and ordered Sharkey to return by the middle of August.

Back on the streets of Ireland, Sharkey had to do more than strut his stuff in his smart suit: the people wanted to see him fight and exhibitions were quickly arranged in which local fighters had a chance to make their name against the tough "Irish-American". Veteran master of ceremonies and promoter, Tom Boyce, said Sharkey vowed to give his "townsmen a chance of seeing his prowess in the exhibition of the noble art".

On Friday, July 16, while the sun blazed outside, he fought the Ulster champion, Joe Craig, in front of an "enormous gathering" in Dundalk town hall. It was, onlookers mused, another example of how the town's heart had warmed to its "candidate for champion", with the crowd picking higher prices than were "usually made for admittance to the most high class entertainment in the town hall". And while the crowd in the five shilling seats was not "immense", the two shilling six pence and one shilling areas were packed out.

The punters had plenty of variety for their money, though. As well as boxing, there were musical items and gymnastic turns, such as rope skipping and club-swinging. Famed local musician, Mr TV Parks, entertained at the pianoforte.

Tom Sharkey first took the stage to illustrate the art of bag punching. The town hall crowd watched Sharkey approach an eight-foot high platform which was stood on four posts at the centre of the stage. A leather ball - larger than that used in Gaelic football – hung down on a length of stout cord from the centre of the platform. Each time Sharkey thumped the ball it smashed the wooden roof just over his head.

He opened with "grinding" work, punching the ball with both

hands in rapid succession, and then went onto the "fancy work", such as "catching the ball on the fist and on the points of the elbow alternatively", rapidly moving around it.

Occasionally, he stepped forward to illustrate that a knock-out blow is not in the arms alone, but in the force of a "lunge of 160lbs of bone and muscle".

The bone and muscle was easy for all to see too. Sharkey's green costume exposed the "gnarled and knotted wealth of sinew and muscle that nature endowed him with".

"The muscular development of his arms and shoulders is enormous. His deep chest lacking but half an inch of 50in circumference, his bull-like strength of neck; his agility of movement, and the precision with which he caught the whirling ball every time were all points that excited the enthusiastic admiration of the audience." Sharkey punched four one-minute rounds against the punch ball, missing only once.

Then, Mr Parks and a Mr C McAlester offered a change of pace, dueting on "The Moon Has Raised Her Lamp Above" from the light opera, "Lily of Killarney". The tender, sentimental tune quietened the audience for the moment – they even asked for an encore – but then it was the turn of three locals, Tom McKittorick, Sammy McConnell and M Casey, to enter the ring and fight it out for medals to be awarded by Sharkey. They were to show that there might have been something in the Dundalk water which inspired a certain style of boxing. Sharkey-watchers, for instance, would not have been unfamiliar with the words of the *Dundalk Democrat* when it described the fight between McConnell – small but strong - and McKittorick as displaying a "good deal more rough and tumble than science". The referee, Tom Lynch, the 10-stone champion of Ireland, eventually awarded the fight to McConnell when McKittorick was injured.[7]

Casey then gave a very pretty exhibition of Indian club swinging to an accompaniment played by Mr Parks and Dan Molony gave a couple of comic songs, including "A Pity To Waste It".

Casey then fought Lynch to warm him up for his bout with McConnell in the second half of the evening's entertainment.

This opened with "The Snowy Breasted Pearl" from Mr Parks and continued with Casey defeating McConnell to be declared the Champion of Louth. Later, the new champ fought E Doran for the Challenge Cup, but the bout was so even it was declared a draw.

However, there was little even about the night's big attraction: the sparring match between Joe Craig and Tom Sharkey. Sharkey appeared in green pantaloons, Craig in red. Sharkey's fitness showed for, although he was stronger and, this time, bigger than his opponent, he was also far lighter and more nimble on his feet. He moved around the Northern Champion, dodging and feinting, and rapped Craig with his glove pretty much when and how he liked. In the fourth and final round, the local newspaper reported, although "Craig stood to his guns like a game one, it was plain that the Dundalkman, if the fight were in earnest, could have knocked him into the middle week [sic] any time".

The audience, one guesses, had seen something of what they wanted – Sharkey fight - but they would have liked to have seen Sharkey knock out his opponent. That was certainly the case when the exhibitions moved to Belfast, for another four rounds with Craig and another bout of bag punching on Friday, August 6, 1897, at an event organized for Ginnett Circus. Again, many marvelled at his strength and physique and the *Irish News and Belfast Morning News* reported the following day that Craig again could not get a "single look-in" and Sharkey's exhibition of ball punching "raised the audience to a high pitch of enthusiasm" with a "large number rushing into the ring at the close to grasp the Irish-American by the hand". However, the turnout was not as great as at Dundalk. The reporter noted: "Sharkey deserved a larger attendance than foregathered in the circus last night, as his reputation is such as should have insured for him a packed building considering that the manly art has always been well patronised in the city. But the Belfast public evidently do not place much store on exhibitions. They must have the real article - a finish fight - or nothing."

Not all of Sharkey's fights were covered by the press. Official records show he also fought Joe Craig in Belfast on July 23 in a professional fight which saw Craig knocked out in the first; list a second round knockout of Pat McCourt in Warrenpoint on July 30; and a first round knockout of Tom Parks in Dundalk on August 7.

The exhibitions and the razzmatazz around them were well reported and there was just time for some more before Sharkey left for the United States.

The *Newry Reporter* watched him entertain a well-attended event at the town hall Warrenpoint, where he again sparred with Joe Craig. Mr Parks again played piano but all were apparently upstaged by a previously unknown gentleman of Newry named Roger Kelly, who pulled off "most of his clothing" and "made an announcement that he would box any man in the room – Sharkey his preference. He was laughed out of his pugilistic intentions by the audience and retired somewhat crestfallen".

The exhibition on Tuesday, August 10, at the town hall in Dundalk was tame by comparison, although it did give Tom the chance to say goodbye to his home town and to share the bill with a relative, for what was almost certainly the first time.

The farewell event was held to raise money for local charities and the hall was again full. During the bag punching, the ball came away under the ferocity of Tom's display. He then gave an exhibition of skipping which it was explained looked like "exercise the ordinary young girl takes with her skipping rope" but was "part of the pugilist's training". A reporter told readers: "It gives him that agility which enables him to escape a blow that might otherwise be a 'knockout' and to deliver his own thrusts with lightning rapidity." Sharkey was now claiming that skipping was at the heart of his training and that he had once "skipped for nine hours continuously".

The exhibition with Craig again showed off Sharkey's prowess, prompting a local boxing enthusiast to comment: "His agility was very remarkable, and those who say that Sharkey has no science are very much out of their reckoning. Nobody has denied that Sharkey has enormous strength and great endurance. He has 'science' as well."

Doran and Casey fought again, this time for fun, and then the other Sharkey took to the ring. John, younger than Tom and a little stouter, did not have his elder brother's experience, but he had travelled back from his base in America with Tom and wanted to box. He had the Sharkeys' broad shoulders but also lacked height and reach. He fought gamely with a bigger man named Guest and after three rounds, a judge could not choose between them. A deciding round was fought and young Sharkey lost.

The exhibitions and the musical accompaniment were running their course now. As someone wrote having heard another love duet from the stage: "This item is getting a trifle hackneyed, but it is too good not to be always enjoyable." Tom was itching to get back into the ring proper. The crowd was now aware that Tom was preparing to return to America and, when he told them he was going to fight Peter Maher for the world championship and "he hoped to win it", they cheered enthusiastically. The home crowd, which had feared it had been forgotten, had seen Sharkey, who had left an anonymous teenager and come back a world celebrity, and it liked what it saw. The *Dundalk Democrat* wrote in tribute: "During his stay…Sharkey won the good opinion of everyone who met him. Scores of people who expressed horror at the name of prize-fighter were delighted with the quiet manly young fellow, who may be an exception to the general run of professional pugilists, but who is certainly a self-respecting and respectable man, and impressed all who observed him with that belief. In his approaching contest with Maher, he will have the sympathy – the secret sympathy at any rate – of everyone in his native town. It is more than probable that if he wins it, he will retire from the prize-ring, and devote himself to a quieter and less rigorous style of existence for the remainder of his days."

Retirement for Sharkey as victor was actually unlikely: Tom knew that if he beat Maher, he would have to take on Fitzsimmons to be the undisputed champion. Then and only then, surely, would he hang up his gloves. Of course, it certainly seems true that this first trip home had softened Tom and maybe he had intimated that he was looking for a way to give up the ring some time in the not too distant future. Certainly, there were moving scenes when he left by way of the *Earl of Erne* for Liverpool the day after the final exhibition and following a farewell banquet at the Bullock's Hotel.

His brother, John, was at his side ready for the return to the United States, and their father was travelling as far as Liverpool. As they moved towards Steampacket Quay they had an unofficial escort which "swelled to very large proportions before the ship left the wharf". Onlookers reported: "The big fellow was very visibly affected on parting with his mother and sisters, and manifested an emotion that one might not expect from a man of his rugged and hardy character."

Tom climbed on board the boat then reappeared on the bridge with his brother and father and with the omnipresent Mr TV Parks, who was also travelling as far as Liverpool. As Tom looked down, a tremendous cheering rose up from the crowd on the quay. Sharkey spoke, saying his farewell and expressing his gratitude for the warm welcome he had enjoyed. He spoke about the regret he felt on again leaving his native land, his home and his friends. Then, feeling the swell of pride from the crowd, he told them he was determined to beat Maher "at all hazards". The cheering rose up again and continued as the steamer slowly slipped past the crowded wharf. They waved and they shouted and, as they watched Sharkey's figure shrink into the distance, they wondered if he would return to their town as the Champion of the World.

CHAPTER SIX
Hard as Nails

A curious little piece of news was reported in the *Dundalk Democrat* a few weeks after Sharkey's return to the United States. Peter Maher claimed that he had come to Dundalk during the sailor's visit but had been unable to find him.

The newspaper pointed out that if he had indeed visited the town, he had managed to keep his presence very quiet. "He does not say whether he came to fight with the Dundalk man, or to talk politics or the weather, or for what object he wanted to meet him," it said. "But if he had called at Bullock's Hotel he would have heard of Sharkey any time, or if he had stopped in the square and questioned the big policeman from Anne Street barrack (who knows all about pugilism) he would have learned all he wanted to know about the Dundalk man. Is his statement a pure piece of silly brag, or what?"

Maher's attitude caused the newspaper to ask: "Will the fight take place at all?"

The question was being asked in the Sharkey camp too, even before he got back to New York at the end of August 1897, although it was not concerning the boxer yet. On the way, he had fought Punch Vaughn at Liverpool on the 16th and knocked him out in the third. Two days later, on Wednesday, August 18, he had sailed for the United States on the steamship Umbria, a Cunard liner which had once made a record-breaking six-day, four-hour passage across the Atlantic. Sharkey was welcomed back with an invitation to umpire a baseball game between St Louis College and the West New Yorks at Weehawken and to referee a contest between two bantamweights at New London, Connecticut.

On first setting foot back in the United States, Tom told the *New York Sun*: "I have returned for the express purpose of fixing up the necessary details for my forthcoming match with Peter Maher. It appears to me that the match is as good as made although not one of the clubs hereabouts has made any decided bid for it. As soon as Maher gets here and managers are convinced that we mean business, offers sure enough will crop up rapidly."

However, it was not going as smoothly as Tom hoped. There were wrangles over money. A $20,000 purse from San Francisco's Knickerbocker Athletic Club, was turned down. Billy Brady tried to negotiate a $15,000 purse with a potential lucrative 49 per cent of the Veriscope receipts.[1] Danny Lynch accepted and wanted to sign, but Maher's man, Connolly, demurred. The New York correspondent of the Sporting Life reckoned there was a lot of kidding going on, designed to "draw further bids from Brady or whoever may want the fight". As time went on, Lynch began to hang back too. It was, the observer noted, a "peculiar" affair.

In the wings now, was another name – Joe Goddard. Goddard was a New South Wales-born, old bulldog of a fighter. Already well into his mid-30s, what he lacked in science, he made up for in strength and stamina. He had held the Australian and the South African heavyweight titles. Maher, it was said, wanted to fight him.

But in October, the *Brooklyn Daily Eagle* reported that the Knickerbocker had received news that Goddard had signed articles to fight Sharkey through the club on November 18. The fight would be fought over twenty rounds at the Mechanic's Pavilion, the scene of Sharkey's incredible encounters with Choynski, Corbett and Fitzsimmons the previous year.

Sharkey entered the ring ten pounds lighter that Goddard's 190 pounds but his recent form and comparative youth had him at 10/7 favourite. However, the bout had none of the pulling power which a rematch with Maher would have had. Fans were not particularly interested in seeing Sharkey take on the "decrepit" Goddard so the turnout was low, consisting, according to one San Franciscan, of only a few Sharkey fans from the navy and the early fights. "When time was called, two small wedges of humanity culled from Sharkey's partisans at Vallejo and Mare Island huddled together on either side of the gallery adjacent to the ringside and faintly cheered the sailor," he said. Elsewhere the ushers and policemen almost outnumbered the few isolated occupants of the reserved seats and boxes.

Goddard looked out over the house and sniffed. He reckoned it was not worth risking a beating for such meagre receipts. Word spread that he would not fight and, though small, the raucous crowd hissed and shouted: "Coward! Coward!"

No fighter of that era, let alone a man who had knocked out Joe Choynski twice and Peter Maher too, was going to take that kind of taunt from a bunch of sailors.

"I'll fight," Goddard shouted back angrily. "Even though I never get a cent."

Sharkey made his entrance first. Goddard was right behind him. He looked drawn and bony; Sharkey looked at his peak. Predictably, then Sharkey took an early lead, catching Goddard square on the jaw in the first round and sending him crashing to the floor. Before 30 seconds of the second round had passed, Sharkey did the same and Goddard went down again.

But Tom failed to capitalise on his early success and stood off for the next two rounds, as Goddard made a series of wild rushes. The technique of both fighters got uglier in the fifth, as the mismatch descended into "a little slugging and plenty of hugging, butting and elbowing". It was a precursor to the sixth, when a final rally at close quarters saw Sharkey in battling hard against the other fighter, who was more than three inches taller than him. Now, according to the *Brooklyn Daily Eagle*, Sharkey caught

Goddard with a right full in the face and the older man started to fall – and so did Sharkey. Goddard hit the floor with a thump and the Irishman stumbled on top of him.

The former sailor was up quickly, waiting for Goddard to regain his feet, buzzing around ready to finish him off. But Goddard was not getting up. It took him several seconds to steady himself by gripping onto the ropes and by that time the referee was giving the decision to Sharkey.

It was hardly satisfactory. A mismatch which ended untidily. One reporter, who favoured Goddard throughout calling him "Joe" and the other "Sharkey", reckoned the Irishman had been as "unfair and rough as could be tolerated without actually committing a foul". A New York newspaper added though: "The decision was just, but Sharkey's victory is far from creditable, it being the popular impression that Goddard was hurt more by his collision with the floor than from Sharkey's blows, which were at all times wild and miserably timed."

This was criticism from a familiar quarter, however. In California and back home, the view looked quite different. The *Dundalk Democrat* wrote: "We are glad for the honour of our townsman to see by a Californian paper just to hand that the Dundalk man fought a fair fight, and comes out of it credibly."

A San Francisco reporter added: "Tom Sharkey is the coming champion pugilist of the world. Last night in San Francisco he clearly demonstrated his superiority over Joe Goddard and advanced one step nearer the highest rung of the ladder."

The newspaper said nothing about Sharkey falling on his opponent. In fact, it stated, that "he won in the sixth round, when Goddard was counted out after a wallop on the jaw that would please any man on earth".

Sharkey had slipped in the fourth, after battering Goddard with a right and a left, it noted, and after that, had sought to finish the fight quickly, going at the other "like a hurricane". Goddard was "practically helpless" and twice he went to the floor in the short period of the sixth round.

Sharkey had made it clear on his visit to Ireland that some of the newspapers were out to get him. But none could deny that he was fighting the best and making a good account of himself. Even the writer who tried to besmirch his victory over Goddard had conceded the referee's decision was just. Nothing would dampen his enthusiasm or confidence. Another champion embarrassed, he raised his right hand and commanded silence of the audience. Again, he issued, a familiar challenge. He was ready to meet anyone in the world, he said, but this time he added: regardless of their colour.

This was quite a challenge.

Sharkey, like many immigrants, had found America to be a land of opportunity – albeit, as a pioneer of the modern age of a rough and bruising sport. But black people were still second class citizens. Writer Wayne Rozen notes that, between 1901 and 1910, 754 blacks were lynched in the United States. Racial hatred and prejudice in wider society was reflected in and around the boxing ring. The first black man would not fight for the heavyweight title until 1908 and the seven-year title reign of the winner of that bout would reveal as much about America's attitude to race as to sport (see Chapter Twelve). When Sharkey, whose friends and sparring partners included black heavyweight Bob Armstrong, made his statement in 1897, it was not going to get better for a long time.

There were, though, black fighters making names for themselves, fighting their opponents and society's prejudices. George Dixon had become featherweight champion in 1890 and was widely-regarded as one of the greatest little fighters of the time. Baltimore-born Joe Gans was working his way through lightweight contenders across the country and would win the world championship in 1902. In Tom O'Rourke's ranks was a powerful welterweight, Joe Walcott, the "Barbados Demon". O'Rourke wanted to pit Walcott against Sharkey. He offered to bet $7,500 against $15,000 that the smaller man could stay twenty rounds with Sharkey.

The Walcott bout, though, was another which withered on the vine. Sharkey's next fight would be a repeat of a match made two years earlier. And his second fight with Choynski would be as shocking as the first. The fight took place at San Francisco's

Woodward's Pavilion on March 11 and Sharkey began a narrow favourite but started the fight at even money. It was rumoured Choynski had "gone stale" but there was nothing in the Californian's appearance to suggest it were true. A couple of inches taller than Sharkey, he was trimmer and lighter, despite being five years older. The two men knew each other well: as well as the bruising eight-round bout from which Sharkey claimed victory, they had sparred together the previous spring when he was training for Maher. They had boxed daily and, drawing different conclusions from trading gloves, each believed he was harder than the other.

A crowd of between 5,000 and 7,000 turned up for this one which was good for the fighters as they were fighting for 60 per cent of the receipts.

The fight ended in the eighth when Choynski went through the ropes and crashed into the front row. At this point, the ever-present officers of the law intervened and the referee abandoned the fight.

Once again, Sharkey had been unable to conclusively prove himself better than a rival. And, once again, opinion was divided on Sharkey's performance with his critics sharpening their knives again.

So, while a New York writer cabled Ireland with the news that Sharkey gave Choynski "some severe punishment", was "in splendid condition" and "as hard as nails", and had "sent his opponent right through the ropes", the reporting back in the United States was less supportive.

According to the *Brooklyn Daily Eagle*, just on arriving in the arena Sharkey was "greeted with hisses and hoots by the big crowd in the galleries, with whom he has been most unpopular since his fight with Fitzsimmons." It went on to describe a fight in which Sharkey had "rushed Choynski through the ropes" and which had been stopped by the referee. Sharkey, it said, had then rushed the referee and been threatened with arrest.

The *New York Times* laid into Sharkey, claiming the "sailor's disgraceful tactics may end his career in San Francisco". It added: "His unpopularity has increased ever since his fiasco with Fitzsimmons in this city two years ago."

According to the critics, Sharkey had punched in the clinches, after agreeing not to, and had wrestled Choynski to the floor in the fifth when the police first threatened to intervene. His punches had put Choynski on his knees prior to sending him out of the ring. Choynski, though, was "game" throughout and, according to the *Eagle*, the referee Green ignored claims that Sharkey was fouling. It said the "crowd was so thoroughly disgusted at this performance". The *New York Times* concluded Sharkey "hurled" Choynski through the ropes onto the front row of the audience so that the referee, on the instruction of the police, stopped the fight. It said loftily: "Last night's exhibition by the sailor probably ends his pugilistic career so far as getting another match in San Francisco is concerned."

That prediction was incorrect, as were estimations of Sharkey's falling popularity in San Francisco. Events of his later life suggest that the city, and Vallejo too, never fell out with Sharkey and he never lost his fondness for it.

In fact, negotiations had already been under way well before the Choynski fight for what would be the biggest fight of Sharkey's career so far.

Regardless of the doom-sayers, it would take place in San Francisco and, although many of the circumstances of the event would be bizarre, it would be the start of the biggest eighteen months of Sharkey's career, at last culminating with a full shot at the heavyweight title of the world.

The contenders during the 1890s kept gathering. Corbett had held the title from September 1892 and March 1897 but had mainly fought exhibitions, creating a logjam behind which a queue of men eager to have a crack at his crown had formed. Fitzsimmons – who would not fight at all during 1898 - was not keen on letting his title go either, and while fighters would happily put on more than one exhibition a day sometimes, title fights remained few and far between. Title-holders could make a lot of money touring as champ.

This was a bad time to be a heavyweight: there were two top fighters at the head of the pack and a blistering bunch at their heels.

Sharkey, Choynski and Peter Maher (who started 1898 with three victories against tough opposition) were all contenders; as was the middleweight champion Charles "Kid" McCoy, who wanted to fight for the title in the heavier class too.

There was now a new contender who was very familiar with the former champion, "Gentleman" Jim, having fought seven exhibitions with him in the spring of 1897. He had taken Gus Ruhlin and Joe Choynski to twenty round draws later that year. He knocked Joe Goddard out in four rounds in February 1898 and eleven days after the Sharkey-Choynski battle, he knocked out "Mexican" Pete Everett in three. His name was James Jackson Jeffries, and he was known to all as Jim. Now, the Ohioan, who boasted the title "Pacific Coast champion", was gunning for Tom Sharkey.

It would be a match, a relationship, which would produce forty-five rounds of the most bone-crunching, skull-rattling, courageous boxing ever witnessed, and seal a friendship which would last until both men had breathed their last, weeks apart, many years later.

Shortly before Christmas 1897, the *San Francisco Daily Report* dismissed rumours of a Sharkey fight with another contender, Peter Jackson. Jackson – although champion of England and Australia - was too fat, at 216lbs, to be able to train, it was said. He was an "old has-been", a heavy drinker. Remembering Goddard's uninspiring performance, the public would have none of it. What the people wanted, said the newspaper, were the people of today. The "next big pugilistic event" would be Sharkey versus Jeffries, it predicted, a match which would "draw a gathering of spectators from the ends of the earth". Jeffries was clean-living too, said the newspaper, compared to Jackson. "Jeffries' 220 or 230 lbs represent good beef and sinew and not Scotch whiskey; while Peter Jackson was drunk on the street today in open daylight. Who would go to see a match in which he would cut a figure?" The newspaper's sporting editor met with Sharkey, who wanted to be seen eager to fight the new man. "If Jeffries refuses to make this match, he will hurt his own career. The public that have never failed to show their appreciation of him will not fail to believe that Jeffries is afraid of Sharkey. If Jeffries be the great pugilist advancing to the championship, let him come to the front and show that he is not afraid. The East knows Jeffries not. The East does know Sharkey and the unanimous opinion of the sporting writers in the Sharkey-Maher contest was that Sharkey had far the advantage over Maher and was the real champion, despite the interruption of the fight."

So, stated the newspaper, "if Jeffries expects to win the championship of the world, he cannot do so unless he first meets Sharkey."

And, to keep Sharkey's dream of a world title alive, he must meet Jeffries.

Jeffries stepped up to the plate. While early betting in San Francisco was generally in favour of the "local" sailor, Jeffries – who was training across the bay in the city of Alameda - wagered more than $500 of his own money that he would whip Sharkey before the twenty rounds were up.

By the day of the fight, May 6, 1898, with thousands of dollars being wagered in the last 24 hours, the odds had turned marginally in favour of Jeffries and there was huge excitement outside the Mechanic's Pavilion. Even newspapers which enjoyed sticking the knife into Sharkey described the up-coming bout as being one between "two of the most formidable looking fighters of the Queensberry age" who would "enter the 21-foot ring to decide the question of supremacy". It was "the most important ring event that has been arranged since the Corbett-Fitzsimmons affair at Carson". At least one newspaper claimed that the "one who is hailed winner will be regarded as the coming champion of the world".

Word in the city was that this was going to be an exciting and close contest, and there was a clamour for tickets which rivalled the Fitzsimmons-Sharkey match of December 1896 and which saw upwards of $14,000 taken on the gate. Every nook and cranny of the pavilion was taken and it was this which would ensure the strangest start to any fight.

The ring was surrounded by banks of elevated seats. As fans – chatting, bragging and joking – took their seats, there was a crashing in the west side of the pavilion and the bank of seats there suddenly collapsed, bringing the people down in a confused heap. For a while there were real fears that people had been killed but as dishevelled figures were helped out of the pile it became apparent those early fears were unfounded. There had been no serious injuries.

Now, the uproar was even greater. They had come to see a fight and this whole stand had collapsed. There was shouting and complaining and laughing and pointing, and it took the police half-an-hour to calm things down.

Just as they did, a second section of gallery seats, this time on the northeast side of the building, crumbled. Then another bank, in the northwest corner collapsed and the mood really took a cold turn as a state of panic developed. In the third collapse about 500 people were thrown to the floor from heights of between 3ft and 12ft, and were tangled together on the ground. People were stumbling about as more seats came down with a "terrific roar" and the pavilion was a mess, with about five or six thousand strong crowd now bustling about on the main floor. There were injuries now too and about half-a-dozen people were taken to hospital.

Has there ever been a stranger start to a boxing match featuring two heavyweight contenders? The preliminary bouts had not even started yet. Had the seats started crumbling during the big fight, with the stands full and the fans bunched, crowded and screaming on their feet, then that night would surely be remembered as one of the great tragedies in sport.

There was no safety-first mentality here, it seems. The bets had been laid. The fighters were in the house. What were a couple of collapsed stands? A few dozen bruised and frightened spectators? A boxing bout that began to look like a scuffle was shut down and everyone locked up, but this – nothing! The police calmed everyone down, assured the crowd that no-one had been hurt, that there was no danger and it was on with the show.

Sharkey – accompanied by Tim McGrath and "Spider" Kelly - and Jeffries entered the ring at 10 o'clock and time was called four minutes later.

Both men had talked confidently about their chances, both

were very fit and eager to win. But they started by sparring cautiously, probing, moving quickly around the ring. They landed, but nothing that was hurting the other. In the fourth, they exchanged punches more freely. Jeffries backed Sharkey into a corner and produced a left to the head which was countered by Sharkey with a right to the body. Swinging back, Jeffries thundered a left into Sharkey, and blocked a left, going into a clinch and forcing Sharkey against the ropes. Jeffries hooked Sharkey on the jaw with the left. Sharkey rubbed his jaw, and some fans even saw a smile on his face. Then, the other leapt at him, forcing him into another clinch.

Neither gained the advantage during the first half of the twenty scheduled rounds. Then, in the eleventh, Jeffries knocked down Tom with a right on the ear, and followed that up with a number of strikes which obviously hurt. Suddenly, Sharkey, whose footwork had been quick and nimble throughout, seemed tired. He fought on and used the twelfth to stay out of trouble and get his wind back. But Jeffries came after him again soon after and Sharkey had to take a lot of punishment. He looked distressed before the three crashing punches struck his jaw in the eighteenth. He was now bleeding badly from the mouth. But this was Tom Sharkey: he would not go down.

Both men appeared tired as they came out for the last round, but they then set upon each other ferociously. Jeffries landed several times on Tom's body and face but he could not knock Sharkey out. Sharkey struck Jeffries on the jaw with a left and a right. Their gloves were crashing together and into each other's bodies as the gong sounded to mark the end of the contest. The crowd went wild.

The referee, Alec Greggains, who Sharkey had defeated as a rising star two years earlier, gave the match to Jeffries. But this was no shame on Sharkey. Jeffries had been unable to knock him out even though Sharkey was a massive six inches shorter than Jeffries' 6ft 2 ½ inches and was giving away about three stone.

The narrow defeat, albeit to a man who would become considered by many – including Jack Johnson, Jim Corbett, boxing writer Nat Fleischer, modern boxing historian Tracy Callis and Sharkey himself – as the best heavyweight of all time, and to a man with a considerable physical advantage over him, struck Sharkey deeply. By beating Sharkey in what some had called wrongly a heavyweight title fight, Jeffries had cemented his right to fight for the real world title against Bob Fitzsimmons. He just had to wait until Fitzsimmons was ready.

Sharkey remained among the contenders, but his reputation had grown given his strong performance and display of courage. His confidence and technique had grown too, and he would rampage through some greats in the coming months as he continued on a collision course which would eventually take him back into the ring with Jeffries for what has been described as 25 rounds of hell.

In stature though, Tom remained much shorter than the other leading fighters. And now he prepared to fight with another man close on six inches taller than himself, Gus Ruhlin, an Ohio-born boxer nicknamed simply the "Akron Giant".

First, Tom took on his sparring partner Henry "Slaughterhouse" Baker, of Milwaukee, in a one-round exhibition in a play called *The Ensign*, in San Francisco on May 9.[2] Then, on June 9, he fought two four-round exhibitions, against Jim Scanlon and John J Cavanagh, both at Allegheny, Pennsylvania. (Another exhibition would follow the Ruhlin fight when Sharkey would take on Louis Jester at Middletown, New York, on July 1, and spar for two half-minute rounds.)

All was probably soft preparation for Ruhlin, who although a little older had less ring experience than Tom. While training at New Dorp, Sharkey said he just wanted to battle through everyone else to get back at Jeffries. "I'll admit that I have nothing to gain by defeating Ruhlin but I was forced to fight him as he was the first one to accept my challenge," he said. "Should Jeffries refuse to meet me, then I will go after Fitzsimmons and I have no doubt that he will take me on. I am in this business for reputation and at the same time, money. I have plenty of the latter and propose to post $5,000 after the fight with Ruhlin to show that I mean business. I will issue a challenge to any of the heavyweights for a meeting. I mean business and I am sure that if Fitzsimmons wants to fight he will give me the first chance."

He was asked: "How about Corbett?"

"Oh, I can lick that fellow four times every week day and seven times on Sunday," he said, knowing the message would get right back to 'Gentleman' Jim's camp. "I have no use for him, whatever. I want to meet men who can fight."

Ruhlin's manager, Billy Madden, understandably had more faith in his fighter. "I have not the slightest doubt but that he will win. I have put him through a course of training such as he never received before and when he steps into the ring tonight many will be surprised at the fine physical condition. I have heard a great deal about Sharkey being the favourite but I cannot quite understand why such is the case. Ruhlin certainly put up a great fight against 'Kid' McCoy, who is acknowledged to be one of the cleverest men in the ring today. Had that fight gone a few more rounds Ruhlin would certainly have won. He will enter the ring tonight full of confidence and the contest will be one of the best that has taken place in New York in some time."

Alex Brown, the official referee of the Greater New York Athletic Club, was chosen to officiate after Madden and John Quinn, talking for Sharkey, blackballed well-known middleman, George Siler, of Chicago. Brown, they agreed, was a man whose honesty could never be questioned.

In the end, there was not much for the referee to do. The destination of the $7,500 purse was decided quickly, cleanly and without fuss in the first round. The terrific right which Sharkey delivered that night put Ruhlin's lights out after just two minutes and seventeen seconds of fighting.

It was just what Sharkey needed. The New York press had been hostile to the Irishman, commenting on his San Francisco fights from afar in coverage coloured by the Fitzsimmons/Earp affair. There was not much the New York sports knew first hand about Sharkey. He had been greeted warmly for his efforts to help Sullivan in 1896, but the police intervention in June 1897 during the Maher fight had left sports unsure of Sharkey's quality and worth.

So, he had a lot to prove on June 29 at Coney Island. He did his bit. The *Brooklyn Daily Eagle* noted grudgingly: "The affair introduced both fighters to the New York public, but there is little to be gleaned from their initial appearance here save that Sharkey's reputation as a terrific hitter is sustained while Ruhlin goes on the record as one of the most headless fighters of the day."

Even before the fight started, the contrast between the men was stark. Ruhlin climbed into the ring and stripped street clothes off to reveal his fighting suit. He was clean looking, lithe, appearing more an athlete than a heavyweight boxer. Sharkey arrived in the ring with his bathrobe carelessly thrown open at the front, exposing his tattooed chest. Sharkey, though only 177 pounds, looked as hard as hell. Ruhlin was so much taller than Sharkey that, at 190 pounds, he looked "almost thin". One onlooker said: "The whole muscular development of (Sharkey) is away above the ordinary, but his trunk is something extraordinary. Through the breast he is thick as his chest is wide, one of these reservoirs of hitting power that betokens a terrific swinger as well as a hard puncher and from which the muscular arms work with great force in every kind of blow."

Longer than the fight itself, was the argument over the rules which proceeded it – while the men were in the ring. The fight was being officiated under the rules of the club: these differed from the Marquis of Queensberry in that they allowed no hitting in the clinches or in the break-away. That didn't suit Tom Sharkey as he naturally wanted a chance to get in all the infighting possible but he had had to concede this point to Choynski and was now being made to do it again. It favoured the taller man to have clean breaks. Ruhlin triumphed and clean breaks were announced.

When the ring announcer introduced Ruhlin as the "Akron, Ohio Giant", someone quipped from the gallery: "Oatmeal". Sharkey was presented as the "Pride of the American Navy" and stuck out his chest for all to see the four-masted brig tattooed in red and blue. "Remember the Maine," shouted someone else.

Ruhlin, it turned out, put up as good a defence as a bag of oatmeal. He should have used his advantage in reach to stay clear of Sharkey's "battering ram" fists; instead, after only a brief moment of caution, he mixed it at close range. Early on, Ruhlin put out a left for Sharkey's face, but it was half-hearted and Sharkey put more effort into his left counter than his defence. The former sailor swung a left and right in quick succession: a distinct move in which he held his muscle-packed body and huge arms rigid while moving his great trunk on a pivot.

Ruhlin caught Sharkey once, with a straight left on the nose. It angered the Irishman and O'Rourke cautioned, "Be steady, Tom", from the ringside. Sharkey probably did not hear. His reaction was instinctive, bringing his perfectly-trained and honed body to bear on his opponent in a power injected with equal doses of courage and rage. As Ruhlin again led with his left, Sharkey swung his left across. Ruhlin's head went down to duck the blow and his jaw received a smashing half-armed swing from Tom's right. Ruhlin spun like a top and crashed down in a heap, his right arm doubled up under him, his body gasping for air.

A cry of surprise went up from the 3,000-strong crowd. Sharkey stepped back toward his corner while the referee bent over Ruhlin and clicked off the seconds with his right hand. Ruhlin did not move.

A huge cheer went up and O'Rourke slapped Sharkey on the back. The Irishman ran over to Ruhlin's corner and attempted to talk to him but the defeated man just gazed at him. He looked like he did not know where he was.[3]

As Ruhlin was led away, Sharkey was appealing for hush. "He's going to challenge the world," exclaimed one fan excitedly.

Sharkey was issuing another challenge from the ringside. "Gentlemen, I thank you one and all for my cordial reception in New York. I will fight Fitzsimmons, Corbett, 'Kid' McCoy or anybody in the world for $10,000."

None of those three men were in the crowd, but they got the message alright. Corbett and McCoy, in particular, knew Sharkey had to be reckoned with. The huge confusion surrounding who was next in line to succession for the heavyweight crown was summed up perfectly in the ring on July 8, 1898, just before an incredibly brutal bout between Goddard and Maher, in which both men took a dreadful pounding. (Goddard eventually threw in the towel in the eighth but Maher was so badly hurt he collapsed in his corner.) Just before the big bout, Sharkey, Corbett and McCoy took to the ring to make the usual challenges. Billy Delaney was there too, on behalf of Jeffries, while Martin Julian spoke for Fitzsimmons. Julian was hissed for challenging "anyone Mr Fitzsimmons has not already defeated" and continued, "Mr Fitzsimmons will meet McCoy at the middleweight limit or Jeffries in the heavyweight championship or will box Corbett." Sharkey was being slighted and told Julian that Fitzsimmons had never defeated him. Julian relented: they all had a say. "Each wanted to meet everyone else and they are as far off as ever," observed one writer.

Corbett and McCoy were the first to sign to meet but the contest would be cancelled on the death of Corbett's parents (Corbett's father shot his wife and then turned the gun on himself). However, on making the agreement, Corbett had said he would fight Sharkey next, proposing a ten round contest in New York City. "If I fail to beat Sharkey, I am willing that he take the entire purse, as I propose to put myself in perfect condition," Corbett said.

So confident was Corbett of his return to form that he proposed McCoy and Sharkey as aperitifs for feasts with Jeffries and Fitzsimmons.

Sharkey – working with "Spider" Kelly and Tim McGrath to train a young Chicago fighter named Eddie Santry – had riled Corbett with perhaps one of the most outrageous challenges issued at that time; and boasting was at least as hotly contested as the heavyweight title itself.

In the *New York World*, just over a fortnight after his blitzkrieg over Ruhlin, Sharkey delivered a message to both Corbett and McCoy. "I want to meet each of them in a ten-round bout, and to allow thirty minutes rest between times," he said. "These fellows have been doing a good deal of talking about what they want to do to each other, and have disregarded me entirely. Now, I don't care anything about advertising. I am for fighting. They can fix the money end of these bouts and any arrangement will be agreeable to me. We could fight for a percentage of the door receipts at the

Lenox AC, or for a purse, the winner to take 60 per cent or all. I am not particular. All I wish is a chance at them and fair play."

The money was coming in – the newspaper described Sharkey as "parading Broadway now-a-days, looking prosperous as a millionaire" – but it was recognition and the title that he wanted. But while Jeffries was taking on Sharkey's sparring partners, Steve O'Donnell and Bob Armstrong, in a double affair, Corbett and McCoy would have provided very different opposition.

It would have been a crazy proposition and, Sharkey probably realized it would not come off. There was no mention of Jeffries in it; a sign no doubt of the respect Sharkey held for him already. Jeffries was already known to feel similarly too and was said, by the *New York Journal* to be "simply spoiling for a fight, [with] no one he would sooner meet than the sailor".

Sharkey, it was said, wanted to go around picking off the others, and the dollars, before stepping into the ring with Jim Jeffries again.

If you challenge the world for $10,000, a friend is supposed to have told him, "you will get called."

"Why, who will call me?" asked Sharkey.

"Jeffries," came the reply.

"Oh, well," Tom Sharkey is supposed to have said. "I intend to face a good many men before I meet Jeffries again."

Appetite for a Sharkey-Jeffries fight in New York was growing. Jeffries wanted a clear decision over Sharkey and to show the East Coast crowd that he had been worthy of the decision in San Francisco.

When the Corbett-McCoy match was cancelled, the way was clear for Sharkey. "Gentleman" Jim's comeback would begin over 25 rounds against the former sailor at Manhattan's Lenox club, at Lexington Avenue and 107th Street, on Tuesday, November 22. It would be the biggest contest the club would host so far. Excited fans would pay anything from $3 to $20 to see it and there would be $20,000 (three-quarters to go to the winner) on the table for the fighters.

Sharkey stayed at the Martin Hotel, Broadway and 41st, in the final run-up. He felt in the best condition, ready to enter the ring at 174 pounds, only half-a-stone lighter than Corbett.

"Honest" John Kelly had been agreed on as referee. The crowd was expected to be large with folks coming in from across the States. Seventy prominent followers of the turf and ring arrived from San Francisco. There was special trains from Cincinnati, Boston and Philadelphia.

On the night before the fight, New York was buzzing. Crowds of boxers and their fans wandered along upper Broadway and through the Tenderloin area of Manhattan with its red-light district and its bars, best known to criminals and the city's vice squad. The bars and hotels between 23rd and 42nd streets were packed with sports from out of town. In the corridors and cafés, they talked about possible outcomes of the fights, weighed up the talents and skills of the two men, threw money down. One observer stated that the former champ had the larger following, all eager to match money wagered by Sharkey fans: "Wads of greenbacks were handed in semi-reckless fashion by the bettors and one would think that the wealth of the Klondike had been brought to New York."

Gamblers made Corbett the 10/8 favourite and he told a reporter who greeted him two days before the fight: "I feel better than I ever felt before in my life, thank you." If Sharkey won, Corbett said, he would admit the Dundalk fighter was the best man in the world.

New York fight fans noted the difference in the two gladiators, not just in style – the old mauler and the scientific boxer – but in look. Corbett contrasted with tree-trunk Sharkey. He did not have the bulging sinews; but his skin was clear and tight over "panther-like muscles". To match his technique, Corbett was expected to make a fuss with the referee about the barring of punching in clinches, where Sharkey's shorter, more powerful arms made his fists as deadly as wrecking balls. The Corbett camp was said to be very pleased that the fifth condition of the articles of agreement had precluding hitting with one arm free, meaning the fighters would have to break clean from the clinches without hitting. Some of them looked for Sharkey to forget himself and lose on a foul by not observing the essential points, but Sharkey's people said that Tom would not lose his head at any stage of the game.

It was said Corbett had never worked so hard to get into shape for a fight, training at Asbury Park, West Baden Springs and at the Lenox club itself, running ten miles a day, bag-punching, wrestling, eating food prepared by his wife, sparring and going to bed early – except when he fancied a night in the theatre.

Corbett's trainer, Charley White, boasted: "Jim is a better man tonight than he was when he entered the ring at Carson City [against Fitzsimmons]... He has lost none of his speed otherwise and his footwork is very nearly perfect. I think the fight should not go more than fifteen rounds and Jim will be the winner. If he loses, he will have no excuse, for no man was ever in finer condition for a fight than he is at present. His chance of defeat, however, is very remote to my mind and I have never entertained a thought of such a result."

All was set; but a year-and-a-half since his last competitive fight, Corbett might have chosen easier opposition.

On the night, Sharkey had "all the better of the match", according to the *Brooklyn Daily Eagle*, although the end was another muddle, with Corbett this time at the centre of the fiasco. Once again, as with every bout of the period, all the tensions were there: the law appeared to be itching to break the whole thing up; reputations and egos, even of challengers and contenders not in the ring, were stretched taut on the line; huge sums of money, including much from some of the most powerful people in the city, were being laid down.

And this area of Manhattan had seen nothing like what was happening that night. Between 5,000 and 9,000 spectators were jammed into the old Ice Palace. Touts were selling $10 seats for three times the face value. The clamour for tickets came despite widespread fears that Chief of Police Devery, who sat at ringside, would stop the fight. (Whatever else would go wrong that night though, Horton's Law would not be transgressed.)

The betting intensified, too, as the minutes ticked down to the bell. The scene ringside looked like the Stock Exchange. Noisy gamblers shouted and bargained with the bookmakers and it was estimated that the total sum at stake when the bout began had reached the neighbourhood of $200,000.

At 10:25pm Sharkey took his place in the southwest corner of the ring but, for once, the arrival of one of the main men was not at the centre of people's attention.

The "out of ring" diversion was bizarre. It had been agreed – because of ill-feeling between "Kid" McCoy and O'Rourke – that McCoy and Maher should be barred from the clubhouse. This posed a problem for McCoy, a man whose reputation as a shifty trickster seems well-deserved, as he had been paid to write a story of the fight for a New York newspaper. The ever-resourceful McCoy put on a false beard and wandered into a box somewhere opposite Sharkey. The club's detectives saw through the disguise and started to kick him out, with the boxer noisily appealing for help from the spectators as he was pulled by the collar.

McCoy ejected, Corbett appeared, playing dramatically to the crowds. His team boasted this was a world championship fight but the crowd hissed its displeasure at that claim. The "mangled Queensbury rules" were confirmed that "no hitting in the breakaway, no hitting in the clinches and both men to step back when ordered". Sharkey, noted the *Brooklyn Daily Eagle*, "was the only one to comply".

The bell rang at 11pm and Corbett's confidence at first seemed well-placed, when he caught Sharkey with a left to the mouth. "That's it," shouted someone. "Jim is going to jab him to pieces with his left."

But Sharkey rarely seemed to notice single blows. In the second, he backed Corbett into a corner and landed a hard right, and then another, which sent the former champion sprawling to the floor. Corbett clasped Sharkey as he fell and came up still smiling, but he was dazed by the blow and went into a clinch that kept him safe until the round closed. The *New York Herald* noted Sharkey's "new science" was "splendidly in evidence" and Corbett's backers were seeing "thousands of dollars getting away from them".

In the third and fourth, Corbett placed one suspiciously low right on Sharkey's stomach and took every opportunity to lean into his opponent. Both seemed unhurt until the seventh when the fight was almost ended by crushing blows from both men.

Corbett opened with a right on the body and a left on the jaw and, as Sharkey rushed, Corbett had a clear right which smashed into Sharkey's face. The blow, it was said, would have dislocated any ordinary man's neck and was heard all over the building. But it did not stop Sharkey. He attacked with both fists at close range right into Corbett's gut, putting a wobble in Corbett's legs. Jim leaned heavily on Sharkey. Both men were tired but Sharkey's engine was still running. He led for the jaw with his left just as the round closed.

Now, further bets went down with 2/1 offered on Sharkey. Someone bet $1,000. The sailor was hurting Corbett and, though Corbett's showiness still persuaded those in the gallery, the writers and bookies ringside knew he was struggling. On the bell, he rushed Sharkey and was met with a lightning left into the stomach which all but carried him off his feet. The former champion boxed back but Sharkey landed another right and Corbett ended the round, his breathing hard and troubled.

One of the hacks wrote that the ninth and last round was "indescribable". Sharkey rushed, the men clinched, broke away and rushed together again. Now, they were in close, fighting like tigers, short, fast jolts to the body; as they battled, Corbett's manager, George Considine, then his second, Con McVey, made unscheduled appearances. With Corbett's ribs under siege, Considine crawled halfway into the ring, directly in front of Kelly, then shuffled back. Then, McVey jumped up and crawled in-between the ropes. He was claiming a foul and waving his arms around, but Chief of Police Devery reached up and caught him by the collar of his sweater, hauling him out of the ring.

The police officer's attempts, though, were not enough: Kelly had no choice but to stop the fight and award it to Sharkey. He stared at McVey with his back to the fighters before turning, separating them from a clinch and sending both men to their corners. Corbett made as if to strike McVey but he did not. "Put up job!"

yelled a chorus at the ring-side. "He did it to save Corbett!"

As the crowd should have been celebrating, Tom Sharkey was denied the pleasure of a clean victory. All around him was pandemonium. The crowd had not paid between $55,000 and $60,000 on the gate just to witness, as they reckoned it, Corbett "give up".

Then, the clamour got worse when, after about ten minutes, Kelly persuaded the announcer, Charley Harvey, to declare all wagers null. He was drowned by whistles before he got to the end of his sentence. Kelly claimed he did not think it proper that thousands of dollars should change hands on such a decision. The fans knew the decision stank: only two weeks earlier and at the same club, Dave Sullivan had lost to George Dixon in exactly the same way but the bets stood and the wild betting sports were well aware of that. "To deprive Sharkey's backers of their winnings, while Sharkey still gets the purse, because Corbett's seconds deliberately committed a foul, is palpably unfair," pointed out one expert. Sharkey, too, had money on himself which he would not be allowed to collect – although there was more than $16,500 prize money to soften the blow.

Word went round ringside that Kelly had been told to say this by men from Tim Sullivan's office as he had put a great deal of money on Corbett. Then the rumours and accusations intensified: now fans were saying that McVey himself had stepped into the ring to stop Corbett from losing and to save all the powerful men who backed the former champion.

A shadow fell over the fight; but this time, the Sharkey camp was not under it.

In fact, Sharkey had the sympathy of all, even the sports fans who trudged off into the rain, swearing and griping about their empty pockets.

He had totally outboxed the former champion and richly deserved a clean victory. Corbett's once-feared left jabs had barely left a scratch on the former sailor. By the end of the eighth, Corbett was bleeding from the mouth and lips, and was holding his right side as if in pain. His legs were weak.

"The condition of the men at this time may be described by the odds," reported the *Brooklyn Daily Eagle*. "They were 2 to 1 on the sailor, with no Corbett money in sight and, in the opinion of the judges present, the fight was Sharkey's to a certainty. Sharkey's apparent absolute indifference to the hardest of the ex-champion's blows and his fearless and unceasing rushes could not but have carried [the] fight. Had not Corbett's seconds realized this, they would never have taken the step that cannot but push Corbett further down the toboggan slide of pugilism."

The referee had favoured Corbett, too, said observers. Not once had "Honest" John made him step back after a clinch and Corbett "had all the best of the distorted rules". Sharkey's former nemesis, the boxing writer for the *Eagle*, said Corbett had "played continuously for a foul", while Sharkey aimed only for the face, despite the other's height advantage. Sharkey did not want to risk being accused of hitting below the belt; he stood up, delivered one crashing left in the eighth which totally took the wind out of Corbett.

The newspapers concluded someone on Corbett's side had created the "most monumental fake ever perpetrated on the sporting public". But what could be the reasons? "Had a decision gone against Corbett on a knockout or on points, the ex-champion would have been relegated to a rear seat forever," said the *Brooklyn Daily Eagle*. "That Corbett's backers could not afford to lose on anything but a foul was apparent. It was the almost unanimous opinion of the crowds that saw the fight that had the affair progressed it could only have ended in defeat for Corbett. In eight rounds of utmost exertion, Sullivan's conqueror could not shake Sharkey nor stop his rushes for an instant." A foul by a corner-man was the only way, too, that Corbett could get out of the battering he was taking and still be able to claim a rematch at a later date.

White was cleared by fans early on, but doubt remained over McVey's and Considine's roles. Whether he favoured Corbett or not, or whether he was persuaded to call the bets off, Kelly had had no choice but to give Tom the fight. But why had McVey, an experienced second who had been behind Corbett in all his big fights, taken such ridiculous action?

Rumours had started even before the fight that Corbett's team were looking to pull something. It was said that six hours before the fight, Harry Beecher, the sports editor of the *New York Journal*, had called his staff together to tell them he had been tipped that "there is a put-up job to give the fight to Sharkey on a foul in the ninth round." The referee Kelly had obviously heard the same rumour.

The slow drip of information left a bad taste in the mouth of those involved and watching the game. The *Brooklyn Daily Eagle* sniffed a big story.

A first point concerned the police chief, Devery, and his decision to sit in Corbett's corner.

Devery and the referee, Kelly, were close friends of the politician Senator Timothy "Dry Dollar" Sullivan, whose men had wagered thousands on Corbett and whose money was being thrown about the ringside by, among others, his brother Danny Sullivan. (Timothy Daniel Sullivan, also known as "Big Tim", was a key figure in the politics of Tammany Hall, a street level political power broker with fingers on every pulse in New York's Five Points district. An assemblyman, senator and congressman at various times in his career, he knew the businessmen and mobsters of every nationality. Sharkey would know him well too, as we will see later.)

It was not until the harm had been done, onlookers said, that Devery pulled McVey back and the "chief's action at that time was of a kind that only emphasized the fact that Corbett's second had broken the rules".

The "all bets are off" decision made it a case of "heads I win, tails you lose" for Corbett's powerful backers. They had considered the ex-champion a sure winner and had bet thousands: their money could be absolutely covered by a trick of making a foul should Corbett look on the verge of collapse as he did in the ninth.

The full extent of the betting on the fight became apparent as news came in from around the States. It was reckoned more than a million dollars was wagered upon the battle, with a quarter of that being laid down in San Francisco alone. New York sports were betting in excess of $300,000. Opinions were clear that Kelly exceeded his powers when he called bets off; that had he believed the fight not to be on the level he should have declared it a "no contest".

The *Morning Telegraph,* named as the authority for the payment of bets by many stake holders, brokers, bookmakers and pool room operators in many big cities, declared that all wagers must be paid on the Sharkey win. Kelly, it was said, had not one precedent for the ruling he made.

Boxing officials also moved to block the loophole which allowed a second to "foul" for a boxer in trouble. The *Police Gazette* rules were to change so that should a second climb into the ring he would be arrested as would "any outsider who tried such a trick, the fight to go on uninterrupted".

The Lenox club began an investigation a week later. Senator Timothy Sullivan, who represented the club, announced proceedings, saying the Lenox club had been wrongly accused of being party to the fiasco. He said the club had been immediately determined to hold an investigation, but had waited a few days while public feeling and press interest cooled down. He declared the club to be absolutely honest. It had no animosity or favouritism to show, and was prompted only by a desire to set itself straight in the public eye.

The hearing proper was held at the Police Gazette Building. Tom O'Rourke, who was manager of the Lenox, appeared not for it, but on Sharkey's behalf. Sullivan spoke for the Lenox. The principals were to be asked to answer to "charges which the city shall prefer." The newspaper reporters who flocked to the event asked what this meant: Sullivan, O'Rourke and White muttered that it basically meant Corbett was being accused of faking the McVey episode to save himself from a knockout.

Sullivan and the other Lenox directors just wanted someone from the Corbett camp to take the blame, and remove any stain from the club's reputation. The lowly paid second, McVey, was the man for that dirty job – even though he did not come to the hearing.

Senator Sullivan sat at the head of the table. Around the room were Corbett, Considine, Tom Sharkey, O'Rourke, White, "Honest" John Kelly, Teddy Foley, Assemblyman Timothy P Sullivan, and George Gray, the former manager of "Kid" McCoy.

Gray testified first, claiming he was told by a friend about seven days before the contest that the fight would end in the ninth round, and that Sharkey would be the winner. Sullivan asked Gray to produce his informer and promised to give $500 to any charitable institution if Gray could get his friend to repeat the assertion. No-one was forthcoming, of course.

Kelly was the only one to tell Sullivan that he believed "somebody got to McVey".

The Corbett team set the scene for Corbett's story: that he has fighting perfectly well, not losing to Sharkey as all independent observers had stated, and it was silly old McVey who had panicked and stopped the fight.

Considine admitted he had every dollar he was worth on Corbett but he said he knew nothing of any deal or put-up job to stop the contest.

White said he could not account for McVey's actions. "In my opinion," he said, sticking to the team's line. "Corbett was far from whipped when McVey interfered. I didn't see any foul committed on Sharkey's part, and in the seventh round, when McVey yelled foul I asked him to stop."

Corbett smirked when Sharkey was called and told the hearing he felt he was winning from the start and would have knocked out his opponent in another round.

Then the former champion himself became the last person called on. "I won't believe McVey was bought," he said. "He has been with me for years. I have supported him and he has eaten my bread and butter. After we returned to my dressing room on Tuesday night, McVey said to my brother Tom, 'I could not see the big fellow licked and I got into the ring. That is all there was to it'."

Corbett went on: "I was not licked by any means and am willing to fight again. I want to state right here that I had the better of it from the second round, in which Sharkey knocked me down with a hard blow on the jaw."

Corbett's pomposity pricked Sharkey and an "interesting exchange of compliments" then followed, as described by the *New York Times*.

"Why, you didn't have a dead man's chance to lick me?"

Sharkey shouted.

The boxers squared up.

"I never faked in my life," Corbett spat.

"Neither did I. But you did fake in San Francisco when you had our fight stopped."

"You are too ignorant to know when a compliment is paid you," answered Corbett, indicating just how much the young Sharkey had hurt the then champion on that night in June 1896.

Corbett slammed his fist down with a bang on the table.

"I am 'Gentleman' Jim and always will be. You had your say and I want mine without being interrupted."

At last, order was restored and Corbett said McVey was impelled only by honest motives in doing what he did.

As the *New York Times* suggested, this was music to the Lenox judges' ears. They quickly "considered the investigation at an end".

"I came prepared to hear you say that McVey entered the ring to claim a foul," Sullivan told Corbett. "This you have not done, but have accepted McVey's actions in good faith. In trying to sift the many charges of crooked work which have been made, the club directors have done their best to clear up the matter. The bets, the club has nothing to do with."

Corbett showed his usual "oratorical ability", it said, but his speech was "rather nullified by the bouquets he threw at himself for making it". Considine's interference had been acknowledged but he was left off the hook. "No one was under oath and so far as a balancing of accounts with the public goes, the investigation was worth nothing."

Top referee, George Siler, claimed to be telling the inside story of the fight in March 1900 when he wrote that, despite claims about what great shape he was in for the Sharkey fight, Corbett had, in fact, been "negligent in his preparatory work…until a few days before the day of the fight, when he was informed that the contest would have to be on the level".

Corbett later wrote that this was "one of the most bitterly discussed fights of the last thirty years, and certainly was the bitterest for me, for the sports writers called it 'a fake'." He claimed a string of excuses, saying his brother, Joe, had warned him about Sharkey's endurance and so he had chosen to take it easy and said he had been hindered by a lame ankle caused when he fell from Sharkey's punch in the second.

Despite Corbett's bravado, the fight and the smell that hung over it signalled an end in sight. He was being talked about as being "out of the game" and when he challenged Sharkey to a charity bout it was "generally regarded as a weak attempt to stave off the oblivion that is creeping over him at a rapid rate".

Corbett would have another crack at the title but in August 1900 he took on Charles 'Kid' McCoy at Madison Square Garden and there were more cries of fix. Gamblers even stopped putting money down, so strong were the rumours that Corbett and McCoy had agreed to spilt their share of the gate ($33,810) fifty-fifty. Real fans could not believe Corbett would risk his reputation again. In the fifth, McCoy went down. Corbett biographer, Patrick Myler, writes: "Many spectators were not convinced the knockout was genuine…The ringside reporters were divided." The mutterings of fraud continued for more than a week until the *New York World* revealed Corbett had run away to England with his manager, George Considine, and a beautiful vaudeville singer named Marguerite Corneille. Left behind in New York, his angry wife, Vera, made claims that both the Sharkey and McCoy fights had been fixed. When confronted with the claim about the Sharkey fight, Corbett growled: "I never faked a fight in my life. These stories about fakes are started by soreheads in New York."

Sharkey, meanwhile, following his win over Corbett in November 1898, remained in the ascendancy. He was quickly challenged by the iron-fisted, former bare-knuckle middleweight, Charley Mitchell, of England, a bout which would have made an intriguing contest but was never to go ahead. He was also in discussions with the champion, Bob Fitzsimmons, who was still jealously guarding his crown and used the scandal around Corbett to bluster: "There's only one honest fighter in the world… and his name is Robert Fitzsimmons".

Sharkey, though, was a fighter who did not remain out of the ring for long. On December 30, he again defeated Joe Goddard, this time over four rounds in Philadelphia. His target now was McCoy, with a twenty-round meeting on January 10, 1899 at the Lenox. The winner would pick up 75 per cent of the $20,000 purse plus a percentage of the door, but for Sharkey it would mean much more: finally, a shot at the title. Whether he would face Fitzsimmons for the crown, depended on events during the last dramatic few months of the nineteenth century.

Tom Sharkey in fighting pose.
(Photo courtesy of Chris La Force)

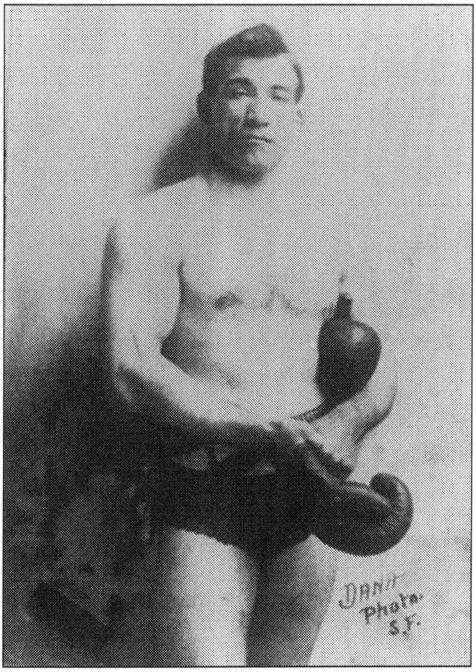

An early photograph of
Tom Sharkey in San Francisco.
(Photo courtesy of Chris LaForce)

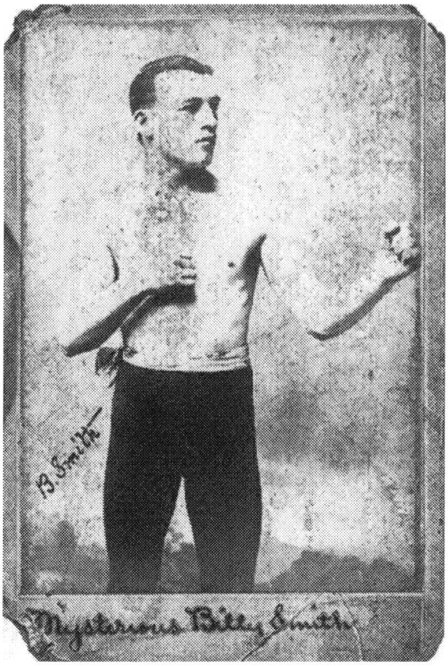

Mysterious Billy Smith.

Tom Sharkey as depicted on a
cigarette card at the turn of the
19th and 20th Centuries.

Preparing to take on all-comers. (Photo courtesy of Chris LaForce)

A rare photograph of Tom Sharkey sparring with Bob Armstrong. (Photo courtesy of Chris LaForce)

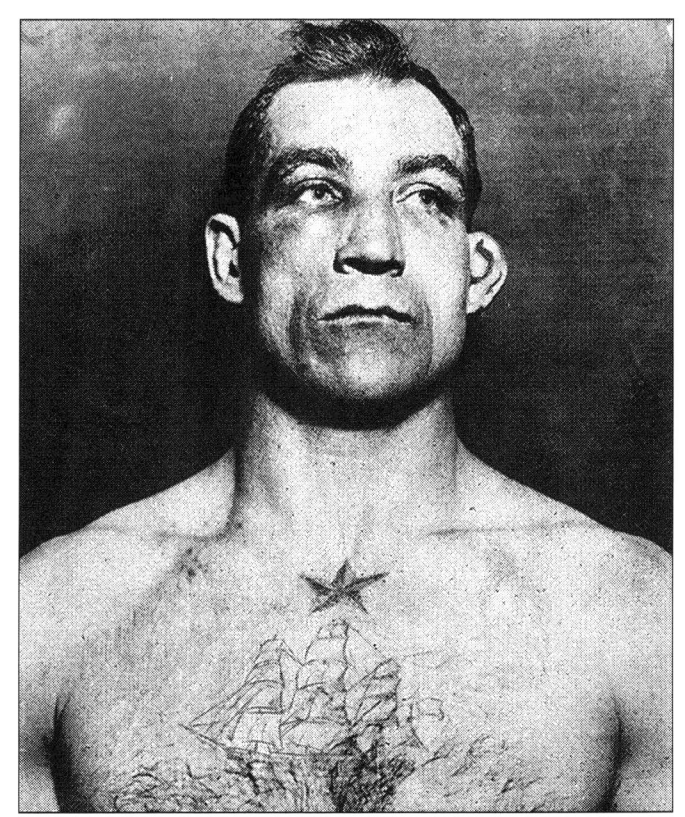

Tom Sharkey's famous ship tattoo - and the look of a fighter.

Celebrity prize-fighter and world title contender. (Photo courtesy of Chris LaForce)

Tim McGrath.

Punch Vaughn, an opponent from 1897 knocked out by Tom Sharkey in the third round.
(Photo courtesy of Tracy Callis)

Tom Sharkey, businessman and celebrity.
(Photo courtesy of Chris LaForce)

A postcard showing Tom Sharkey's bar in New York City in the early years of the 20th Century.

Tom Sharkey and Jim Jeffries sparring on their vaudeville tour for Marcus Loew. June 11, 1926 (Photo courtesy of Pete Ehrmann)

Tom Sharkey in later years, still striking a fighting pose.
(Photo courtesy of Pete Ehrmann)

A portrait taken on February 4, 1944, when Tom Sharkey was a civilian guard for the US Army.
(Photo courtesy of Pete Ehrmann)

Tom Sharkey congratulating his greatest fighting foe and long-time friend Jim Jeffries on his 70th birthday. The date was April 22, 1945.
(Photo courtesy of Pete Ehrmann)

Tom Sharkey meets Jack Sharkey.
(Photo courtesy of Pete Ehrmann)

Tom Sharkey was born in a cottage which stood just behind this row of houses, near the gated alleyway, in Hill Street, Dundalk. The cottage no longer exists.
(Photo: Authors' Collection)

The quay at Dundalk today. It was here that the teenage Tom Sharkey found work on board ship, eventually making his way to the United States. (Photo: Authors' collection)

Hill Street, Dundalk, is a pleasant area today, but back in the years of Tom Sharkey's childhood it was described as a "dilapidated, troublesome neighbourhood". (Photo: Authors' Collection)

The Tom Sharkey mural above the bar in Byrne's, Dundalk. (Photo: Authors' Collection)

Byrne's in Hill Street, Dundalk, one of the few places in the town where Tom's life is commemorated. (Photo: Authors' Collection)

Tom Sharkey's grave in Golden Gate National Cemetery, San Bruno. A proud sailor to the last, he was buried with military honours. The incorrect birth date on the headstone reflects the error identified by the authors in Sharkey's military record. (Photo by Scott Groll)

CHAPTER SEVEN
Fair and Square

There were no advanced ticket sales for the Sharkey-McCoy fight so there was a rush to be first to arrive at the club. In the standing area around the ring, men "of all conditions" were leaning on each other's shoulders to get a good view.

When the place had filled up, the brightly-lit globes which hung above the spectators were turned off and, according the *New York Times*, the battleground "presented a weird appearance" with "tier upon tier of white faces…rising one line above the other in the semi-gloom but not a face except those of the men in the ring and those of the men grouped around the roped arena could be clearly distinguished."

All eyes stared down past the eight padded posts and the three circuits of thick rope and to the padded canvas floor of the ring where the action would soon unfold. The gladiators would be lit by four arc lights, which were suspended over each corner of the ring and supplied by a circle of gas jets hanging under a white sheet which was stretched immediately above the ring.

The crowd was about to witness what the *New York World* would describe as nine-and-a-half rounds of the "most beautiful fighting ever seen anywhere" and the *Brooklyn Daily Eagle* called the "fight of the decade".

After the preliminary bouts, Sharkey was the first to climb into the ring, choosing the same corner where he had sat in his fights with Corbett and Maher. He was wearing a thick grey and brown bathrobe and, as he sat in his corner, he smiled to friends on either side. Reporters ringside said he looked "the picture of fitness and confidence" and "whistled a little Irish tune to himself when the waiting became tedious".

McCoy strolled into the ring less than a minute later, throwing his weight against the posts and ropes, and utterly ignoring the presence of his rival. He wore a long, white bathrobe - like a "driving coat" – and sprawled down on two campstools in his corner. His brother, Homer Selby, tied McCoy's colours, a small silk American flag, to the middle rope.

McCoy stated that he weighed 156 pounds and Tom O'Rourke declared that Sharkey weighed 173. Sharkey was three inches shorter.

McCoy walked over to Sharkey's corner and examined the adhesive tape bandages on Sharkey's hands and let Sharkey see his own. Always the showman, McCoy then retired to his corner, where he sat in an armchair, his feet stretched out onto a second chair. "The crowds laughed at his unusual display of household furniture and the long array of bottles that were seen in the corner. The old timers turned up their noses, while many credited the Kid with common sense in providing for his own comfort."

Sharkey stripped and showed the crowd his costume of green trunks and an American flag for a sash.

McCoy wore a pair of white silk running trunks that were halfway to the knee and were held up by an old silk American flag. He was quite a character, 'Kid' McCoy.

McCoy – real name Norman Selby - was a boyish-looking 26-year-old who had fast become one of the most notorious figures ever to step in the ring; a talented fighter, yes, but a trickster too. According to Myler: "The numerous stories told about his trickery, mostly apocryphal, are a treasured part of boxing folklore." He was said to have once filled his mouth with loose teeth and spat them out during a bout, horrifying his opponent and delivering a knockout punch on his unguarded chin. He also scattered thumb-tacks on the canvas when he took on a fighter who fought in bare feet. One particularly dirty trick involved Peter Maher. McCoy sent him a fake telegram, shortly before they were due to fight, saying there been a sudden death in the Irishman's family. As another writer, Graeme Kent, has noted: "McCoy was a brilliant boxer and an extremely shrewd operator who had sailed close to the wind on a number of occasions."

His name lives on with us to today as a way of describing the genuine article. Myler reckons this relates to confusion with a lesser-known fighter named Peter McCoy, who was also known as "Kid". He says a newspaper once ran the headline, 'Choynski is Beaten by the Real McCoy' and the phrase stuck. Kent prefers a story more in keeping with 'Kid' McCoy's trickster image. He says that McCoy, trading on the drawing power of his name, sometimes booked himself to appear in different places at the same time and sent along ringers. "Promoters had grown wise to this ploy and had insisted on the Kid being less generous with his doppelgangers," notes Kent. "To reinforce this point they had taken to billing the boxer as 'the real McCoy', a phrase which later entered the lexicon."

According to boxing historian, Tracy Callis, of the *Cyber Boxing Zone*, McCoy would not be short of tricks before the Sharkey fight either. At the time, with no films of an opponent available for study, fighters often hired men who had sparred with or fought against their upcoming opponent. The story goes that McCoy and his entourage kidnapped big Bob Armstrong, a frequent sparring partner of Tom's, and frog-marched him to McCoy's camp to find out about Sharkey's strengths and weaknesses. However, Armstrong was angry and fed McCoy incorrect information.

But there was power and skill as well as trickery. He had won the middleweight title in 1897 by knocking out Dan Creedon, and bravely took on larger men like Sharkey, Ruhlin and Choynski, trying to make up for his lighter build by using speed and his famous 'corkscrew' punch, which he would drive into his opponent with a last-minute twist of the wrist aimed at ripping the skin.

McCoy's fight with "Sailor" Tom Sharkey had been billed as a battle of Science v Strength. McCoy had bet $100 on himself; Sharkey later either wagered the same or twice as much on himself, depending on the source. The majority of gamblers figured science would be victorious over strength and they made McCoy – who had fought about twice as many professional bouts as Sharkey - favourite. Perhaps they were forgetting the new science in Sharkey's boxing.

Certainly, guys in the know figured the betting did not tell the whole story. Few boxing experts could call this one and the main view was that McCoy had never met a man "capable of giving him good punishment" like Sharkey. All agreed that the winner would move into the first class of heavyweights and that if Sharkey won he should "naturally be looked upon as a formidable opponent of Bob Fitzsimmons".

Speaking from his training camp in Asbury Park a few days before the fight, McCoy admitted Sharkey was the "best heavyweight fighter next to Bob Fitzsimmons". Sharkey showed respect to his opponent also, saying McCoy was a "good, strong, clever, young fellow", with considerable science.

Meanwhile, in his office in New York, Owen J Kindelon, a correspondent of the *Dundalk Democrat*, was showing no such restraint. The people of the home town were still excited from the Sharkey visit; they were following his career closely now. The *Democrat* wanted something stirring for its readers and although logistics meant the article would not be published until well after that fight – and Tom could have lost by then – the writer went for it. "It seems a very short time since I sent a few views on the battle of Corbett v Sharkey; now Tom is ready for business again," he explained. "He is like the Irish 69th New York Regiment in the little war with Spain, he'd as soon fight as eat - but the 69th didn't get a chance to do either. Therein is Mr Sharkey more fortunate than the 69th in the army, for he can fight and his business manager, Mr O'Rourke, can do the preliminaries to perfection.

"Thomas has some advantage in this fight, over his trial of

prowess with Corbett. He is a Hercules, Selby (or McCoy) is a spider. McCoy (or Selby) is credited with having science, whereas Sharkey is accused of having only strength. But that was discussed to a threadbare finish when last he won, and I believe he will tonight be proclaimed champion of champions, like the gladiators in a Roman Amphitheatre, who, from a multitude, dwindled down to two, and, when they cast aside all impediments, and stood foot to foot and blade to blade, the Roman Empire held its breath, as a miser does his hoard."

Again, before the fight, Sharkey's opponent would insist that hitting in the clinches would be outlawed. A clinch, referee Tim Hurst would say, would not need to be a hold either, it could just consist of one man placing his hand on the other's shoulders to save himself from punishment. The *Brooklyn Daily Eagle* said: "Sporting men, generally speaking, consider this statement absurd, but they feel that Referee Hurst will use good judgement and will not allow McCoy to get out of tight places in so easy a manner." That debate continued right up to the bell when a *New York World* reporter asked the referee: "What constitutes a clinch?"

"When either man is holding the other so that he cannot strike," replied Hurst.

"But if one man grabs the other in such a way as not to prevent him from hitting, is that a clinch?"

"Certainly not," came the reply, "for if either man tries that he'd get his jaw broken."

In the ring, the fighters stripped to their trunks, as Hurst prepared to call time, Sharkey stopped smiling and became a picture of concentration.

The fight started at 10.40pm, with McCoy skipping out of his corner leanly. Although Sharkey was shorter, McCoy "looked like a mere stripling" in comparison. "Sharkey…looked gigantic enough to make two of him," reported *New York World*. "It seemed a conflict between Hercules and Apollo."

McCoy began confident, lighter on his feet; dancing around, feinting, smiling "maliciously", working Sharkey backward. Tom seemed very grave, anxious even.

Sharkey defended a right hook at his ribs. McCoy hooked his left lightly on Sharkey's cheek. Sharkey countered with his right, catching McCoy lightly on the back of the head as the Kid rushed toward him. Both fighters took breath, getting the measure of the other. Sharkey was not rushing in.

McCoy dashed in with a sudden left hook and then a right onto Tom's ribs. McCoy came again, driving his left in on Sharkey's belly and when Tom came back with his right he only found the Kid's shoulder.

At the end of round one, Sharkey looked "annoyed, puzzled and serious", while "McCoy skipped away like a young deer".

McCoy, it seemed, was finding the whole thing amusing, although the writers ringside were still waiting for the Sharkey rush.

Round two. Sharkey made an early left for his body but the Kid threw in his right shoulder and stopped him. Tom came again but the Kid responded with a fierce left to the Irishman's cheek, before clinching.

Then Sharkey dashed in and smashed the Kid on the ribs with his right, driving him against the ropes, but McCoy moved away and grinned.

In the next move, Sharkey clinched and "seemed to try to throw the Kid down". Some of the crowd hissed.

Sharkey was struggling to keep up with McCoy's speed. McCoy was displaying the 'scientific' performance expected: neatly blocking, ducking and side-stepping. Sharkey's strengths would have to be a steady, determined aggressiveness, ever going forward. Again, as before, Sharkey would have to be prepared to take a dozen of his foe's blows for the privilege of landing one.

Twice McCoy dashed in with his left and Sharkey was left flailing at him. Sharkey charged him like a bull and McCoy slipped out under his arm like a "bit of quicksilver".

Tom then backed McCoy into a neutral corner but, before he could hit, the Kid clinched and held him safe. Then, as Tom rushed him again in the opposite corner, the Kid stood and powered a short jab into Sharkey's ribs.

The next round continued where the previous had left off. Tom stood in the centre of the ring, with the Kid circling around him "like a hawk around a rooster". The Kid sprang, bringing a left upward into Tom's belly. The punch made Sharkey grunt and as he tried to recover the Kid caught him on the left cheek, reddening it.

Tom punched back and only caught his opponent's shoulder again. Sharkey dashed in with a straight left for the body, but only hit the Kid's breastbone lightly as he skipped away. Now the Kid went in for the kill with his corkscrew punch to Tom's left breast, following it rapidly with a straight right jolt on the chin which knocked Sharkey onto his backside.

Tom rolled over and got up to his feet. Too quickly: he had not recovered. McCoy unleashed a left onto his jaw and again sent him to the floor.

The crowd was alive now. Twice Sharkey had been down, although he would not stay down. The end of the round was greeted with deafening howls, cheers and whistles, and the noise levels raised again as the two fighters came out for the fourth.

McCoy was smiling but Sharkey appeared to have recovered completely and would not let his opponent keep the upper hand. McCoy caught him twice in the face with his left and the hard, straight on the mouth, but Sharkey danced away and stuck out his tongue in defiance.

McCoy sparred and jabbed, then half a minute later, unleashed a hard left which almost closed Sharkey's right eye.

McCoy came with another left on Sharkey's right eye, then a punch in the stomach.

Tom responded with a "terrible right counter that might have knocked his head off", but the Kid was clutching him, keeping his face safe from the blow.

The pair began to wrestle and give each other's necks a twist in the clinches. The *New York World* felt Sharkey was tiring, saying he was walking "with slow and heavy steps". McCoy was certainly outpacing him and if Sharkey got close, McCoy would clinch. But fewer of McCoy's strikes were getting through now and, in the sixth, Sharkey unleashed a blow into McCoy's belly which made him wince. Sharkey, puffing heavily, swung his left wildly, reddening McCoy's shoulders and breastbone. He pushed the Kid into a corner and drove a left hook up into his belly.

The blows were sapping McCoy's strength. He caught Sharkey twice in the seventh – a left on the mouth, a right on the jaw – but the blows only dazed the sailor for a moment.

As they clinched early in the eighth, Tom muttered to McCoy: "Are you tired?"

The Kid laughed and flicked him on the mouth with his left glove.

Sharkey responded to the flash of McCoy's teeth by swinging an uppercut that caught McCoy in the middle of the belly just above the belt. The Kid held Sharkey's hand and forced it down so that it fooled many into thinking it was a low blow.

McCoy pitched forward and fell on his face. He lay on the floor groaning with his face contorted as if he were in horrible agony.

The referee rushed over and stood between him and the sailor. But Hurst was not fooled: it was a bit of McCoy trickery. The *New York World* reporter, "who sat right before the fighters, was absolutely certain that there was nothing foul about the punch."

McCoy writhed around on the floor for several seconds, and then promptly jumped up and landed a right hook on Sharkey's jaw. He was, one observer said, "more active than before he went down, and began to dance all about Sharkey."

McCoy's grinning did not last. In the next round McCoy cannily ducked a swing but as he lifted his head caught a massive left fist straight in the face. Seconds later a left to the stomach and a hard right to his shoulder almost sent him through the ropes. Three more times Sharkey swung his left to McCoy's belly, but the Kid defended with his right forearm. The blows drove him back, but did not get fully home.

With nine rounds down, a murmur went round that despite his fancy footwork and science McCoy was on the back foot; he had underestimated his opponent. Sharkey was growing stronger, breaking through the other man's longer reach, backing McCoy around the ring. McCoy defended his belly with his forearm, just keeping the sailor out. Sharkey stuck out a mocking tongue: "Bah!"

Now they were near McCoy's corner; Sharkey had the Kid close upon the ropes and dancing about for a chance to escape. Then, as Sharkey appeared to be about to make another painful hook to the belly – making McCoy employ both hands to protect himself - Sharkey switched aim and swung a devastating blow upwards instead. Sharkey's left fist crushed into McCoy's chin and drove the man back against the post – had it been an undefended right from Sharkey it might have killed McCoy, said one observer. The back of McCoy's head smashed against the gas pipe that fed the lights around the ring. McCoy's body then flew forward "like a swimmer plunging off a springboard" and crashed face downwards.

His arms moved, trying to push himself back up on his feet, but the effort was too much. Referee Hurst counted, making the ten and counting McCoy out, but neither fighter seemed to hear. McCoy struggled up to its feet, made a feint at Sharkey, then turned to run away. Sharkey made a straight right hand drive at him and sent McCoy downward against the ropes. Hurst turned Sharkey away: "I counted McCoy out the other fall; you've won!"

Now everyone heard McCoy counted out. Yells went up all around the building as McCoy staggered away in the arms of his seconds. He looked like a "whipped and penitent school boy". There was sympathy among the 6,000-strong crowd as fans liked McCoy for always mixing it with bigger men than himself, but Sharkey was the undoubted winner. He had been down at one time but, as the *Brooklyn Daily Eagle* said, his "wonderful physique...saved the day". It said: "It was a case of the cleverest middleweight against a terrific hitting heavyweight and the result proves that McCoy's style of fighting and McCoy himself, have no place in the latter class." The *New York Times* wrote: "It was a battle in which cunning and science were combined on one side against brute strength and fearlessness on the other, and in this case science and cunning were vanquished."

The McCoy fight had shown an improvement in Sharkey's technique. Mr Kindelon, of the *Dundalk Democrat*, was overjoyed: "Sharkey's performance...was a revelation to those who saw him two years ago. His ring work and generalship were so superior to his exhibition when he first came out that the improvement was almost incredible…The engagement was altogether the finest piece of fighting ever seen here. It was nevertheless a contest of strength against science, a case of a fighter who could take a punch against a clever man."

He added: "You'll notice excuses by the score why McCoy didn't win. But the real reason is that which other defeated candidates can all give, if they will. They were 'up against' their master, who has given them all lessons, and whose physical perfection is more than they can overcome."

After once again communicating exactly what he meant with his fists, he then issued another defiant statement in his own words.

"I won this fight fair and square," he said defensively. "I simply knocked the man out and did it in good time. I thought I would win about the tenth round and told my seconds so. My eye was blackened a little but otherwise I am unhurt. The blow that knocked me down was a dandy, but I knew I would recuperate. The Kid can hit hard and is fast, but I have some speed myself, and as for hitting hard, I let the public [be the] judge of that. When I got up from the knockdown blow I was still strong and the one minute's rest put me alright again. McCoy is a good game fellow and I give him all the credit in the world, but he can't whip me, nor can anybody else in the world whip me. I think I am the best man in the world."

He added: "I have met them all and each time got the money. Nobody can say anything about this fight but the fact that I knocked my man out. I am ready to fight anybody for the championship of the world."

The *New York World* recorded on its front page that strength had defeated science and that "dancing around didn't win"!

"[Sharkey's] victory was due to his marvellous strength and his quickness and the coaching of Tom O'Rourke," wrote its boxing expert. "Each one of these equally helped to win the battle for Sharkey."

McCoy, he stated, had the advantage "not only in height but in tremendous reach, cleverness and agility" and had for the first half of the fight kept Sharkey "guessing and completely mixed up".

In the third round, he wrote, Sharkey had been dropped "as heavily as if he had fallen from the roof of the building".

"Moreover, it was not like Peter Maher's punch of a year ago that knocked him down and sent the sailor bounding up in the air again, but it shook him so that when he tried to rise up from a sitting position he fell over on his side," he said.

But McCoy had played around with Tom like a cat playing with a mouse before killing it.

The Irishman had kept coming, and coming, and with the power of those punches he had just needed one to land.

McCoy went on to effectively accuse the Irishman of a lucky punch.

"I am defeated, but I still think I can whip the man who got the decision. I had Sharkey practically knocked out in the third round, as any one who saw the fight will agree to, but I made the mistake of being too cautious and waiting for a better opportunity to finish the job.

"The blow he struck me, which sent me down, was one of his wild swings, all of which I had been able to avoid with ease, and it was entirely a chance that it landed. However, it did land, was effective and it's my fault."

McCoy complained about two punches in the eighth and ninth which his side had claimed were fouls - although the referee and the press had felt both were on the level.

"I don't like to make any claim of foul work against my opponent," said the trickster with reference to his own well-known dodgy dealings, "but I was struck twice very low."

He finished with a final flourish, again stating that he would beat Sharkey should they meet again.

"I realize that I was up against a hard game in going against a man considerably heavier than myself," he said, "but anyone who saw the third round of the fight will agree with me when I say I have got a very good chance to defeat Mr Sharkey if we meet again."[1]

But they would not meet again. His defeat of Kid McCoy had set Sharkey up for much bigger things.

Fitzsimmons admitted Sharkey was now a better man than when they had fought with Earp more than two years ago. He claimed to be looking forward to facing Sharkey: "I will lick him a finish you can bet on that. I have him now just where I want."

Tom, however, took time to enjoy the money from the McCoy fight. As well as his winnings, he collected $15,000 from the gate receipts and spent a few days hanging around the "big hotels" with his friends as they cashed bets all over the city. He was becoming a name in the city now and when he went to the cycling, a dozen policemen were needed to hold the crowd back from McCoy's conqueror.

On visiting Harvard University, a Dr Sargent who worked at a gymnasium attached to the campus, took a look at Sharkey and said he was, "considering his height, the finest physical specimen" he had ever seen. He said the sailor's chest and back were wonderful. Sharkey returned the compliment to the institution by wandering through the college grounds, and describing himself as "much impressed" with what he saw.

The crowds at an even more unlikely venue were much impressed too. In April 1899, a series of moving pictures from the McCoy fight were added to the Royal Aquarium, Westminster, London, and a large number of people queued at St Stephen's Hall to see the twice daily showings. One or two defective parts of the films had been cut out and the pictures were "an improvement on others previously exhibited". According to the *New York Times*: "This is said to be the first time a fight at night-time has been shown by means of the cinematograph. A vivid representation of the contest is given, the whole of the ten rounds being seen in every detail." It was to be Sharkey's first representation in a moving picture, but certainly not his last, with ring fights and Hollywood eventually to feature on his CV.

He deserved a rest. Since that Fitzsimmons fight he had fought Maher, the battles against the local contenders at home in Ireland, Corbett, Goddard twice, Choynski, twenty rounds with Jeffries, Ruhlin, McCoy as well as more than a dozen exhibition matches.

Fitzsimmons, in the same period, had fought up to thirty exhibitions but only one competitive fight, the one in which he had snatched the heavyweight crown from Corbett. Jeffries, billed as the "the only undefeated heavyweight in the world" in a dig at the champ Fitzsimmons' defeat to Tom, showed Sharkey good faith by declaring he was entitled to a rest and said he would seek to fight Fitzsimmons, McCoy or Corbett first. However, he said, he was not backing down on his deal with Sharkey: when the sailor was ready they would fight again.

They would fight that year but not until November. The delay was hugely significant because the first person to fight Jeffries would be the world champion, Bob Fitzsimmons. Jeffries and Fitz were matched to meet on June 9, 1899, and if Jeffries were to take the title, Sharkey would be next in line to snatch it straight away from him.

There were fights, of course. Sharkey liked to be in the ring to pick up the dollars. He fought Jim McCormick (some reports call him Jack) in Philadelphia only twenty days after beating McCoy, although it did not last long: Sharkey knocked him out after two minutes and fifteen seconds of the second of the six scheduled rounds. One reporter noted: "The bout lasted as long as it did probably, because the sailor wanted to give the great crowd present something for their money." McCormick, a local boxer, more of a wrestler than a fighter, went down twice, the second time after a right in the stomach and a left on the jaw.[2]

He fought out a six-round exhibition match in New York on February 1, with Tommy Ryan on the invitation of Monarch Athletic Club. The fight went fine but when the chancellor of Syracuse University heard that a member of the club wanted to invite the fighter to visit the athletic class and "exhibit himself to the students", he barred Sharkey from coming anywhere near the students: the chancellor was no fight fan. Ryan, a 28-year-old considered one of the best middleweights in the world, was on home turf and put up a good show against Sharkey in front of the 1,800-strong crowd, although neither man tried hard to damage the other.

Though there were continuing rumours about fights with Mitchell, Fitzsimmons and Corbett, Sharkey would only fight a series of exhibitions between April and October 1899.[3] The man he traded punches with was generally Bob Armstrong but he also fought Tim McGrath and Jeff Thorne, and spent time acting as second to George Dixon. All formed part of his training for the biggest fight of his career, although some more than others. Some of the Armstrong fights formed part of a theatrical show entitled *Sidewalks Of New York* which, the *Pittsburgh Dispatch* noted, also featured Tom playing a "character in the drama" and – in the third act – a daredevil performance from Paul J Tustin who would dive from the top of a 50-foot tower into a tank of water to rescue a 'drowning' woman.

The articles for Fitzsimmons' defence of his title against Jeffries were signed on February 10 when Martin Julian, for Fitzsimmons, and three members of Billy Brady's Jeffries team met at the Bartholdi Hotel and settled upon a fight between Fitzsimmons and Jeffries. Jeffries' decision over Sharkey in California, gave him first chance: the rest would be decided afterwards, depending on the outcome. Tom O'Rourke, who was at the Bartholdi, had decided to hold Sharkey back, to make money on the exhibition circuit, even though Sharkey wanted to fight. "I am willing to stand the brunt of the fire sent after me for not allowing Sharkey to fight Fitzsimmons. It was not Sharkey's fault that I did not consent to make a match with Fitz before October. It was due to the business methods which I have always pursued since I entered into pugilism. It is my idea to make as much money with Sharkey as a card between now and next fall as the public will allow. I did not take Sharkey in hand for nothing. He is under contract to me and cannot do as he pleases. In the last year, Sharkey has fought Jeffries, Choynski, Goddard, Ruhlin, Corbett and McCoy and I think he is entitled to a chance to reap all the benefits that both Corbett and Fitzsimmons have enjoyed. If Sharkey had his own way he would fight the Cornishman in four weeks, for he sincerely believes he can beat Julian's man easily." What O'Rourke wanted for Sharkey was a crack at the winner of the world title fight and by February, he was already negotiating for Sharkey to fight the winner that November. Nothing else was going to be good enough.

While Fitzsimmons had easily avoided challenges to fight, Sharkey flinched at criticism that he was avoiding competitive fights. He was particularly angry at comments attributed to Jeffries about their first fight, a bruising encounter which he still believed he could have won. In a letter to newspapers from Baltimore, where he was staying on March 23, 1899, he wrote: "In referring to our contest at 'Frisco all he need do is reprint the account given in the 'Frisco papers of the fight and his dull brain will see printed therein that I, Tom Sharkey, should have received the decision, and at the worst, a draw, and that if the fight had continued five rounds more, big Mr Jeffries would have been on the floor." Sharkey claimed to be a more popular draw with the public too, claiming to have made a record $48,000 (probably from the McCoy fight) as opposed to the $2,100 he claimed Jeffries made in New York in a fight with Bob Armstrong. "But we will let bygones be bygones. If Mr Jeffries is sincere and he would be lucky enough to beat Fitzsimmons, I will meet him thirty days after."

The Jeffries-Fitzsimmons bout was set for the Coney Island Sporting Club. If Fitz won, O'Rourke boasted that the Lenox Club would offer a purse of $50,000 for a meeting with Sharkey. It would be the biggest purse ever given for a battle in the prize-ring but the "battle would warrant it". Sharkey, said fight watchers, had "to be reckoned with", while McCoy "has not weight enough to stand in the class" and Corbett had "gone back for all time".

Fitzsimmons was looking forward to the Jeffries' fight as a "picnic", training at Bath Beach and enjoying his daily game of quoits. Boxing expert and referee, John P Eckhardt, backed Fitzsimmons. He said there were only three men in the same class now: "The strength (Fitz) possesses is approximately the strength of the strongest heavyweight known to pugilism with the possible exception of Jeffries and Sharkey."

On June 9, 1899, Fitzsimmons finally came out to defend his crown.

All the smart money was wrong. Jeffries was to record a clean and complete victory over Fitzsimmons, connecting a blistering right to his jaw in the eleventh. The crowds gasped. They had come convinced of a Fitzsimmons victory, and hoping for one too, but they were stopped in their tracks in the second, when Jeffries first laid the champion out. Fitzsimmons smiled confidently though and, getting to his feet, boxed on, cutting the Boilermaker's eye. Jeffries, fighting from a crouched position, wore the same expression throughout: one of grim determination. In the tenth, he knocked his opponent down for the second time. It was then that the 8,000 spectators sensed the end. In the next, Jeffries caught him with a left, which made him wobble and drop his guard. A long second passed, in which Jeffries saw Fitzsimmons open and unprotected. He despatched a second left and then a right which sent the champion crashing to the canvas. Fitzsimmons wept when he came round: he had lost his title.

Billy Brady, who had managed Corbett to the championship, was delighted to have a second winner in his stable. "Let them all come to (Jeffries) now – none of them can class with him."

Jeffries was, the newspapers reported, the first "real American champion" since the 1860s and John C Heenan, boasting as he did "three generations of American-born ancestors".

John L Sullivan said: "All Americans should rejoice at his victory. He is an American and we have needed an American champion. Besides, he is young and able to defend the title for many years to come."

Jeffries first defence would have to be against the other contender: Sharkey. Could the next champion be an Ireland-born warrior who fought with the colours of the Stars and Stripes wrapped around his middle and like Jeffries, harked back to the tough, pre-science days of Sullivan himself?

Within days of Jeffries' victory, he was formally matched with Sharkey, the fight to take place the following November 3. Jeffries, unlike some of Sharkey's other opponents, also quickly agreed not to amend the Queensbury rules. 'Infighting' would be allowed with each man having to protect himself in the clinches and breakaways.

By August, Sharkey was in training for the championship, while Jeffries was touring England, France, Scotland and Ireland. In Ireland, Jeffries was hissed as he left Cork for refusing to fight a local celebrity named O'Connor saying it would be "inadvisable" considering his approaching fight with Sharkey. He was welcomed in New York, though, on September 22, with excitement already growing about the Sharkey bout.

On his return, there was concern about an injury to Jeffries' left arm which was investigated by Dr Henry Frauenthal. At the training quarters at Lock Arbor, New Jersey, Dr Frauenthal subjected the injured arm to "fifteen minutes of hot air treatment and at its conclusion, Jeffries declared that his arm was a great deal better". On October 20, he was back to his routines of bag-punching and wrestling. Four days later, he sparred six rounds with Tommy Ryan and the arm was "as good as ever it was". The *Brooklyn Daily Eagle* stated: "Jeffries punched often and hard with it and did not spare it and he found it all right at the finish. Nevertheless, his medical adviser will stay with the champion during the remainder of his training."

Sharkey, who was aged just 25, had also started to feel the effects of six years in the ring. He had began to suffer from rheumatism and was taking time to relax at Sulphur Springs (now Clifton Springs) in Rochester, New York, where thousands travelled to take in the health benefits of the spring waters. He was also, one newspaper reported that summer, looking a little "stout", although he claimed to be as fit as a fiddle and ready for Jeffries. A physician, Dr C Sichel, checked in at New Dorp to see the sailor did not overwork himself.

On the eve of the fight, the boxing writer of the *Brooklyn Daily Eagle* described the sense of anticipation which breathed through Coney Island. "The lull before the storm is here. The lull of a day or more in which the aspirants for the world's championship are resting up and storing away the energy that they have learned to generate each day in training… Today, there is but one obstacle in the way of Jeffries' undisputed right to hold and keep the title of champion. Today, there is only one rung in the ladder that the sailor Sharkey, has not climbed upon and beyond. Sharkey put away Ruhlin and then Corbett and McCoy; Jeffries jumped to the top by beating the great Cornishman. Both have passed through preliminaries and the semi-finals of the ring just as if they had been drawn by lot to mow down the lesser lights preparatory to meeting each other in one grand final.

"It is now the final that will take place tomorrow night, down by the seashore and when Referee Siler shall have formally made his announcement of the winner, that man will be the champion, the absolutely undisputed champion of the world."

Jeffries was 10 to 7 favourite. He had $8,000 on himself; Sharkey had thrown down $5,000. "In all of the prize-ring archives there has been no such battle as will be recorded there tomorrow night, that is if the men live up to their known capacities." Around $100,000 was being bet on the fight three thousand miles away in San Francisco. A reporter in Los Angeles tracked down Jeffries' mother, the wife of a farmer and evangelist. "Of course, I want Jim to win," she said. "Jim has always been a good son and brother – a great deal better, in fact, than many young men who make a profession of religion and who stand high in the church. What mother would not want her boy to succeed?"

The hype was incredible, although interestingly, the two boxers had done little to add to it. "Not an unpleasant feature of the whole affair," said one writer, "has been the absence of any semblance of mud slinging by either man. Each thinks he will win to a certainty as witness their wagers, and the men of this class are not prone to compliment their adversaries, especially on the eve of battle, when keened down by their training and bolstered up by their admirers. But in this case neither has stooped to the blackguarding so frequently heard and neither has said much of anything – certainly not much of the foolish stuff that is put into their mouths."[4]

Late on the morning of the day of the fight, Jeffries and his handlers arrived at Martin Dowling's hotel on Coney Island. Experienced middleweight, Tommy Ryan, who had fought Sharkey earlier that year, was part of the team.

Sharkey arrived to some fanfare, with fans already there to watch his arrival via the 39th Street ferry. Together with Tim McGrath, Frank McCormick and Eddie Sweeney, he headed to the Sagamore Hotel, Surf Avenue, and "ate a hearty dinner of a big steak and vegetables and drank two cups of tea". He then slept through the afternoon.

Outside the rain battered against his window. It was a breezy November afternoon on the island and cold too. Inside the club, though, the temperature would be raised – not just by one of the most astonishing boxing matches ever fought but by the "great warmth…of the lights for the Biograph". In all, to support the cameras, there were 400 lights around the ring. Each had the power of 200 candles; a combined total of 800,000 candle power in all. A large sign out in the front featured a warning from the fire department: No Smoking. The significance of the operation to film the fight would become immediately apparent that night when all entered the club.

Referee George Siler was tracked down at the Sagamore Hotel by a reporter, who was still interested in the fighters' agreement to allow hitting in the clinches. "I have not seen the men for a talk over the rules," he said. "They know they are to fight Queensberry and that is all."

"Will they break clean?" asked the reporter

"No. They might fight themselves free."

Can they clinch and hold, as allowed under the Queensberry Code in England, he was asked.

"Oh, yes," said the referee smiling. "They may hold and fight with one hand."

"This certainly was promising for a lot of terrific fighting," noted the reporter after his chat with Siler.

And how right he was!

CHAPTER EIGHT
Ninety-nine Minutes of Hell

One of the largest crowds ever to gather at an indoor sporting arena watched Jim Jeffries learn a valuable lesson the night of November 3, 1899: it was easier to win the world title than to hold it.

More than 10,000 fans, who had stumped up something close to $100,000 at the door, watched this astonishing fight. "How many foot tons of energy were represented in the struggle at Coney Island...no man will ever know, but it is a certainty that in no twenty-five round fight ever seen before was there such terrific punching, from start to finish, combined with an ability to take it as fast as it came and go back for more," wrote the *Brooklyn Daily Eagle*. "[This] battle was probably the fiercest that the American fight-going public ever witnessed for it was between men both of whom are of gigantic physique, both game to the core and masters at the game of boxing," stated the *New York Times*.

If the battle was fierce, the conditions were even more savage, thanks to the age of the motion picture which had arrived, but with the most primitive technology. Crowds entering immediately saw the strange scaffolding of the Biograph Film Company which was suspended from the ceiling with its electricians and technicians and the intense white brightness of the 200 arc lights.[1] Extensive tests had already been made for the filming with bouts between Dixon and Bolan and "Mysterious" Billy Smith and Jim Jeffords filmed in the days before the fight. "The films have been developed and positives made and run in the Biograph," explained the *Brooklyn Daily Eagle*. "They were both entirely successful. The figures of the men will appear slightly larger than life size and every detail will be shown as definitely as it is possible for the finest lenses made to record it."

The cameras themselves were placed on a platform at one side of the ring, about fifteen yards away outside the ropes. There were four; each was loaded with 1,280 feet of film, long enough to record a round and intermission. The preliminary appearance of the men on the platform and the intermissions, as well as each round, was recorded, making 110 minutes of film in all. But it was the arc lights which created the problems, producing a blinding light and pushing the temperature in the ring to "easily a hundred…and possibly more". A sweating reporter noted: "It was almost unbearable for those who occupied the seats at the immediate ringside. But Sharkey and Jeffries stood it for an hour and forty minutes of the hardest kind of slugging which fact requires no further illustration of what a perfectly trained man can endure." It was later claimed Jeffries lost twenty pounds under the heat; Sharkey, a smaller man, lost nine.[2]

One of the reasons that the fight became so brutal was the styles of the men. Both were extremely tough fighters. Jeffries did as he did with Fitzsimmons, using his weight as a millstone around the neck of his opponent; Sharkey used his elbow in clinches a number of times. These were two men that fought hard to win and gave no quarter. Each was a virtually immoveable object of packed muscle and iron bones; battlers built on aggression and stamina, who would grit their teeth and go on forever. "Sharkey is probably the most wonderfully aggressive man in the ring today. Whether he is fresh or groggy, he follows his opponent around the ring ceaselessly, taking his punishment with a lion's heart and landing his blows with a speed and brute force that make him at all times a dangerous man...Jeffries is no less a fighter, he has a head that is cooler than the sailor's and as he is in the business of winning fights, he claims everything in the hope that he may get something."

The champion was afforded the right to occupy the northwest corner of the ring, the same place he had sat the night he had defeated Fitzsimmons. His seconds included Billy Brady, Billy Delaney, Tommy Ryan and Jack Jeffries. Sharkey was attended by Tom O'Rourke, George Dixon, Morris Kelly and Tim McGrath.

The fight was to start at 10.15pm. Tom Sharkey wore his green trunks with the Stars and Stripes as a belt. Jeffries looked determined as he advanced to the centre of the ring to shake hands with the Irishman. He towered above him.

Jeffries was about 214 pounds; Sharkey was 187. The champion was taller, with a longer reach. But Sharkey showed "not a particle of fear of the giant", forcing the battle from the first. Sharkey rushed regularly but was "over anxious to end it quickly and very wild". The fighters clinched often and, according to the *Brooklyn Daily Eagle*, "the crowd with its usual ignorance of the Queensbury rules hissed the sailor for fighting himself free from the clinches". At times, "the men came together...like two freight trains colliding and there were few sports who concluded that the human beings could stand such blows and keep their feet".

There was big money on this fight. Jeffries was 10 to 7 favourite. Martin Dowling bet $10,000 to $7,000 on Jeffries; Billy Roche, the manager of George McFadden, had $700 on Sharkey; the black politician, Charley Anderson, placed $3,000 on Jeffries against a four-man syndicate of Sharkey men who laid down $2,180; Tom O'Rourke, it was reckoned, had about $15,000 in all, riding on his Irishman.

The *New York Times* noted: "The fight was a greater betting affair than any heavyweight contest that was ever fought in this country, for almost every man in the clubhouse had a choice and almost everyone was willing to back his opinion with his money."

And, by the end of the night, no matter who they had backed, whether they were richer or poorer, they were satisfied in one thing: they had seen a fight.

ROUND ONE: *Sharkey rushes but honours even*

Sharkey rushes in swinging with his left, landing on Jeffries' jaw. They break and spar cautiously. Sharkey rushes with a left swing but Jeffries sends him back with a left jab to the face. In a third rush, Sharkey forces Jeffries to the ropes without at first doing any damage. Then sends a right to Jeffries' cheek and Jeffries clinches. Sharkey breaks, comes back on attack and gets a stiff left hook on the face. They clinch and are separated by the bell.

ROUND TWO: *Sharkey twice sprawls on canvas*

They meet in the centre of the ring. Sharkey gets in close and gets his left to Jeffries' face. Jeffries backs Sharkey into the northwest corner. Sharkey mixes it up and gets a right hander on the side of his head; off balance, he goes sprawling. Jeffries backs away.

Jeffries lands an incredible left on the chin which sends Sharkey down in a neutral corner. He's up quickly. Sharkey fights like a demon but they stay in clinches.

ROUND THREE: *Sharkey lands left and right to face*

In a rush, Sharkey is caught with a right to the body. Sharkey lands a left on Jeffries' ear. Jeffries drives him back with a left and right to the body. Sharkey slips. He gets up and rushes, landing right and left on the face in the breakaway. Jeffries rushes Sharkey to the latter's corner and Sharkey slips again. They clinch and are hooked together when the bell rings. Siler cautions Sharkey for holding during the intermission.

ROUND FOUR: *Both men still fresh and fighting hard*

Jeffries comes out in a crouch with Sharkey standing tall. Sharkey blocks his face well. Jeffries laughs and Sharkey returns the smile. Both fighters are a bit wild but Jeffries lands some heavy blows in the sailor's chest. Jeffries is cautioned for using a right to the body while holding. The referee separates them from a hard clinch. Jeffries jabs his left straight to Sharkey's eye.

ROUND FIVE: *Ferocious fighting, to body and face*

Brooklyn Daily Eagle describes ferocity of fighting as "appalling". Sharkey, says the *New York Times*, was rushing like a demon. Round opens with Sharkey the quicker on his feet, sending a left to the face and two fast rights to the head at close quarters. Sharkey rushes again and is repelled by a hard right on the body. Jeffries lands again in the same spot and Sharkey clinches. They break, Sharkey rushes in with a terrific left on the body but he misses on his next try and gets a left in the face. Both men exchange very hard lefts in the face and cross counter each other hard over the heart. Sharkey shoots his left to the face and Jeffries sends back his right to the body. The bell finds them in close quarters, fighting hard. Sharkey strikes a right to the head as the gong sounds and the punch is not allowed.

ROUND SIX: *Sharkey cuts Jeffries and takes initiative*

Sharkey has advantage in speed and aggression. He hooks his left to the neck and drives a right with fearful force to the body, forcing Jeffries to another clinch. Both men hold with their lefts and deliver two hard right body blows. Sharkey uses his left on Jeffries' chest and, says the *New York Times*, the "big fellow's brain is jarred from the blow". Both fight fiercely, Sharkey having the best of the infighting. Jeffries sends his left to the body and Sharkey counters with a left on the mouth. Jeffries' mouth and ear are bleeding. The *Times* concludes: "This was Sharkey's round". The *Eagle* says that from the moment Jeffries mouth begins to bleed "Sharkey's aggressiveness gave him a decided advantage".

ROUND SEVEN: *Sharkey shakes the champion with a left to the head*

Sharkey rushes but O'Rourke tells him to keep his head up. He is first to land with his right on the neck. Jeffries sends his right and left to the body and Sharkey catches him with a left hook on the neck. Sharkey plants a hard right on the body, then a left to the head which shakes Jeffries. Sharkey swings his left to Jeffries' head. Jeffries clinches hard and lays over on his man with such force that the referee has to keep Sharkey from falling. This was another round for Sharkey, says the *New York Times*.

ROUND EIGHT: *"Fearful" punches; Jeffries tries to throw Sharkey over*
The crowd's cries swell for Sharkey as his "aggressive tactics won him many friends".
Jeffries, defensive, near his corner, is attacked. Sharkey's left goes around his neck but he follows it with a right hard to Jeffries' ribs. Jeffries returns a right on the ribs. They regroup. Sharkey lands two hard straight lefts on the head. Jeffries clinches again and seems unwilling to break. Jeffries, says the *New York Times*, throws his entire weight on Sharkey. Then they mix "with fearful force", both landing heavily on neck and body. Jeffries seems tired but still meets Sharkey's next rush with right and left jolts to the body. In a clinch, Jeffries rushes Sharkey to the ropes and almost throws him over. The bell finds them locked on the ropes; Sharkey's cauliflower ear is "broken open" and bleeding profusely.

ROUND NINE: *Both fighting hard; Jeffries footwork keeps him safe*
Sharkey rushes again; Jeffries is on the defensive. Jeffries trips with his left on the ropes but steadies himself. He meets Sharkey's rush with a left hook on the ear. Sharkey rushes again and Jeffries drives a terrific right under the heart. They clinch hard and the referee forces them apart. Jeffries drives his right to the body and Sharkey clinches. They break; Sharkey hooks two beautiful lefts to the jaw. Jeffries rushes Sharkey to the ropes. Sharkey is now very steady and fighting but Jeffries' footwork and ducking is serving him well. Both land lefts as the bell rings and Sharkey laughs.

ROUND TEN: *Jeffries attacks Sharkey; blood streams down the Irishman's face*
Jeffries looks to some to be a beaten man. He is worried and distressed until he cuts Sharkey's left eye (by smearing his glove over it in a clinch) and gets fresh heart. The heat from the lights is fierce now with both fighters and the spectators near the ring in running sweats. Jeffries strikes a left on the face; Sharkey hugs

Jeffries around the neck. Jeffries shoves Sharkey to the ropes. Jeffries swings his right to Sharkey's bleeding left eye. They mix very roughly until the bell sends them to their corners.

Round Eleven: *The hard exchanges continue; Sharkey slips*
Sharkey leads the attack but is met with a left on the ear. Jeffries rushes, sending his left to the body and his right to the injured eye. Sharkey comes back with a left to the face. He is repelled with a hard right under the heart. They exchange rights on the body. Sharkey slips on a wet spot and goes to one knee as Jeffries jolts his left to the chest.

Round Twelve: *Trading blows to fell an ox; Sharkey increases lead*
They come to a clinch with Jeffries jolting his right to the body. Both miss lefts for the head. Jeffries swings his left on the ribs and meets Sharkey's rush with a right under the heart. Sharkey lands his left and right on Jeffries' head. Jeffries replies with left and rights to Sharkey's body. They clinch and break. Sharkey lands a left full on Jeffries' neck. "Every blow in this round seemed heavy enough to fell an ox but both men went to their corners smiling," says the *New York Times*. The *Eagle* sums up: "Sharkey increased his lead and tore the champion's right ear."

Round Thirteen: *Sharkey on offensive from first to last*
Sharkey is again the quicker on his feet. They clinch without landing and break away only to spar. Jeffries slides in with a right on the body and Sharkey comes back with a terrific swing on the neck which makes the big fellow stagger. Jeffries ducks Tom's left swing for the neck and Sharkey turns completely around to land a back-hand blow on Jeffries' ear. It is a pivot blow but, while Jeffries' seconds yell foul, the Irishman escapes caution. They reach the bell with Sharkey the aggressor and Jeffries blocking.

Round Fourteen: *Sharkey hurts Jeffries with a left to the mouth*
Sharkey opens again with a rush; his left for the head just misses Jeffries as he quickly side-steps. Sharkey is cautioned for holding

in a clinch. Jeffries gets his left to the body twice. Sharkey forces Jeffries to the ropes and crashes a "well-directed" left jab which lands full on Jeffries' mouth. The Californian grunts audibly. "Sharkey out fought his man in this round": the *New York Times*.

ROUND FIFTEEN: *Sharkey's "fearful" blows split open the champion's nose*
Jeffries comes out very cautiously, crouching along the ropes. Sharkey swings his left up to the chin and then sends another home with great force on the body. Jeffries tries a left for the face but Sharkey gets inside the blow and swings his left twice with "fearful effect" on Jeffries' head and face. Jeffries comes back with a good left on the face which almost put Sharkey to the floor. Sharkey replies with left and right to the face, splitting Jeffries' nose; the blood comes in streams. "The sight of the blood on Jeffries' face seemed to make a demon of Sharkey who fought fiercely," says the *New York Times*. Jeffries plants left and right jolts to the sailor's body and they are fighting fiercely when the bell rings.

ROUND SIXTEEN: *Sharkey's straight left sends Jeffries on to the ropes*
They rush to a clinch twice before doing anything. Jeffries gets in a right drive under Sharkey's heart and Sharkey swings two lefts to the head. They clinch. As they break Sharkey gets a straight left to the damaged nose, which sends Jeffries back to the ropes. Sharkey follows up but the big fellow clinches. When they break, Sharkey whips his left twice over to the face drawing blood from Jeffries nose and mouth. Jeffries counters with a right swing to Sharkey's damaged left eye. The *Eagle* reports: "The sailor was just as willing as ever, and some awful blows were exchanged. The fifteenth and sixteenth were the sailor's."

ROUND SEVENTEEN: *Sharkey hammers the champion's bruised face*
Referee Siler took some "stimulants" such was the heat. Jeffries ducks at a feint several times and the crowd jeers him. His face becomes a "nasty sight" as Sharkey hammers it relentlessly. In a neutral corner the Irishman sends three lefts in quick succession to the

boilermaker's head and gets nothing in return. Jeffries eventually counters with a right on the body. They exchange lefts on the head and they fight at close quarters till the bell rings. Brady complains that Sharkey sends a late blow but Siler refuses to interfere.

ROUND EIGHTEEN: *Sharkey's left to Jeffries' jaw makes the champ shudder*
Sharkey opens with a left swing for the head but Jeffries hooks him; they clinch. After the breakaway, Jeffries lands a right swing on Sharkey's ear but the sailor comes back at him with three left hard jabs to the face. In a clinch, Sharkey hangs on to Jeffries' neck with his left arm, dragging Jeffries across the ring. They break clean and Sharkey swings his left with fearful force to the jaw: Jeffries shakes "from the top of the head to the soles of his feet". Jeffries gets careful, goes on the defensive until the end of the round. It is "decidedly Sharkey's on points, barring the hugging", says the *New York Times*.

ROUND NINETEEN: *Sharkey lands but Jeffries ends on top*
Sharkey rushes but Jeffries lands first with a right, hard to the heart. Sharkey hooks his left over to Jeffries' ear. They clinch and Sharkey brings his left hard across the stomach. Sharkey leads left to head. Jeffries ducks and put his left hard in on the body. Sharkey rushes again, sending his left to the head and, in a half-clinch, sends his free right hand onto the body three times. Jeffries clinches and after they break, Sharkey swings his left to the cheek and crosses his right over on the opposite side. Both blows jar Jeffries but he comes back, jabs his left to the body and then into Sharkey's face. The sailor staggers.

ROUND TWENTY: *Sharkey again strikes Jeffries' damaged nose*
Sharkey forces Jeffries to a neutral corner but fails to land a left hand swing. They break from a clinch in the middle of the ring and Jeffries sends his left straight to the mouth. They exchange left swings on the ear and get into another clinch, until separated by the referee. Sharkey sends two straight lefts to Jeffries' nose

bringing the blood in a stream. The pace increases but no further damage is done.

Round Twenty-One: *The fighters of this mammoth battle laugh with each other*

In the centre, they clinch and Jeffries shoots his right to the body. Sharkey responds with two rights on the body. Jeffries lands another right on the body and jabs his left in Sharkey's face. Both hook rights on the body while they laugh at each other, semi-good naturedly. They clinch and after they break, Sharkey swings his left to the neck. Jeffries sends a straight left to the mouth just before the bell. The *Eagle* reports: "In the twentieth and twenty-first Sharkey did the better work and the worse he made Jeffries look, the more the champion improved." Jim Corbett described a left which landed on Jeffries' jaw and once more "dazed the champion…Sharkey's round". Still no-one was calling the result.

Round Twenty-Two: *Two vicious uppercuts from the champ turn the battle*

They move cautiously. Jeffries is first to land with a right to the body. After a clinch Jeffries sends his left to Sharkey's injured eye. Three times they clinch and break and each time Sharkey lands a back-hand right on Jeffries' face. Jeffries steps in with two fearful right uppercuts under the chin which "would have killed an ordinary man". They turn the tide against Sharkey who turns to his manager O'Rourke and laughs – but he's hurt. Tommy Ryan and other men in Jeffries' corner shout: "Go on! Go on !" But Jeffries fails to follow up his advantage. Sharkey wobbles as the bell rings and looks all in.

Round Twenty-Three: *Sharkey's tiredness shows as Jeffries senses victory*

They come together fearlessly again with a rush and Jeffries shoots his right to the chin. They clinch and when they break Jeffries smiles and feints with his left; they clinch again. Both miss lefts for the body. Jeffries jabs a straight left to Sharkey's injured eye. Jeffries jabs his left to the sailor's stomach and forces him across the ring where they came to a clinch. Jeffries jabs his left to the sailor's face and makes him stagger. Sharkey clinches.

Round Twenty-Four: *Sharkey clinches and battles on but another round is lost*
Jeffries is now the quicker out of his corner. They clinch and after they break, Sharkey sends his right over to the neck. Sharkey tries his left but falls short and receives a hard smash on the ear. As Sharkey comes in close, Jeffries shoots his right to his opponent's chin. Sharkey clinches again. They break. Jeffries reaches the sailor with a right swing on the ear. Sharkey rushes, swinging left and right wildly for the head but fails to land, and Jeffries catches him with a right on the jaw. They clinch at the bell with Jeffries now decidedly the better man.

Round Twenty-Five: *Jeffries loses glove but remarkable battle continues to an end*
The fighters laugh and shake hands good naturedly. Jeffries leads for the head but Sharkey ducks. Both swing rights. Sharkey's is blocked; Jeffries lands. They clinch. Sharkey swings his right very roughly for the head but falls short, and Jeffries hooks his left hard to the jaw. Sharkey staggers. In a clinch, Sharkey slips to the floor, pulling Jeffries' glove with him as he falls. The referee picks up the glove and tries to adjust it. Meanwhile Sharkey tries to get at the Californian. Jeffries breaks away from the referee as Sharkey leads for him with his right and Jeffries sends his right over Sharkey's shoulder. The referee gets between them and as he does the bell rings ending the fight.

After 25 three-minute rounds of violence, aggression and courage, it was for the referee, George Siler, to choose the winner. He chose Jeffries. And although Jeffries is considered one of the all-time greats, the debate has raged for more than a century as to whether Siler made the right decision. Didn't Sharkey at least deserve a draw?

The verdict on the night met a storm of protests from the Sharkey team with even the neutrals believing Sharkey deserved a draw. He had forced the fight virtually until the twentieth round and had taken a pounding towards the end. He had ignored his physical disadvantages throughout, shaking off Jeffries' punches for some time. He had shaken Jeffries to the core in the sixth and was considered ahead by round ten. He had, Sharkey said later, thrown the hardest punches of his life. Even at the end of twenty-first round the *Eagle* reporter reckoned those around the ring were predicting a draw.

At the end, the *Brooklyn Daily Eagle* picked out Jeffries' weight advantage as counting for "much".

"Jeffries leaned heavily and bore Sharkey into and once almost over the ropes," it stated. "The extra twenty-five pounds of weight was an enormous advantage. It was worth a thousand dollars a pound to Jeffries and, in many minds, that was what won him the decision, for Sharkey's aggressiveness and cleverness at equal weights would, to many minds, have turned the tide of battle into another direction."

Sharkey probably would have got more out of the fight if he had stayed clear of Jeffries' fists in the final rounds. Unfortunately, that was not Tom's way: he had to be the aggressor to the last. This time he ran into jabs and uppercuts which even he could not withstand. With tiredness sapping the energy from his legs, Sharkey's lack of height and reach showed too, making it easier for the powerful Jeffries to pick him off.

Jeffries had taken terrible damage to the face but Sharkey had fought on in the most incredible pain: Sharkey had received a number of agonising injuries in the fight, although it is a matter of debate when these occurred. Soon after the fight, newspapers revealed that from the third round he had been fighting with two broken ribs. In his autobiography, Jeffries provides a dramatic account: "I felt the fist crush into his ribs, heard a crack. I knew something was broken and learned afterwards that the blow caved in three of his ribs. In spite of that, and with one of his ribs sticking through the skin toward the end of the battle, the human cyclone refused to stop, but kept coming as before."

Forty years later, writing for a magazine, Sharkey would tell not one but two slightly different versions of the injury – after all, it was too good a tale not to wring every last dollar out of. "In the seventeenth round, a right-hand punch from Jeffries broke three of my ribs but I went right on," he said in one article. In another, written in the same year, he stated: "I fought Jim Jeffries twenty-five rounds at Coney Island with four broken ribs and a dislocated left arm and haven't used it as an excuse for losing yet."

The injury to his arm was also reported in the *Brooklyn Daily Eagle* on November 5, when it described Sharkey having his "arm in a sling" the day after the fight.

Many of the familiar political faces were absent from the Coney Island crowd, being instead busy on the campaign trail. It was the only thing which would keep these men "who would not miss a scrap for the sake of a prayer meeting" away from such a championship fight. However, there were still plenty of local dignitaries on display, from Senator Timothy D Sullivan and assemblymen, to assistant district attorneys and state prison officials (commissioners of corrections), to fighting greats like Sullivan and Corbett. After the fight ended and the cars came to pick them up, it said it was "doubtful if so many (cars) have gathered together at one time as were congregated on Surf Avenue, Coney Island".

The rain came down in torrents outside the club and the cabmen lined up for fares, each charging "exorbitant" prices. All evening a steady stream of carriages brought sports for the fight. Afterwards, prices were higher still and, as cabbies raced to fill their vehicles, there were a number of fights. One cab driver and a coachman began to push each other with their whips. The road rage escalated as they drew alongside each other and began a lively fist fight, which ended when the Hansom driver lost his balance and fell over backwards with a crash. Before they could restart a policeman arrested them.

It was not until early morning that the last carriage left the island.

Those who had not headed to the island were kept informed at the newspaper offices. At the *Eagle's* main office in Washington

Street, the crowds stood in the rain around the bulletins as they had "during the war with Spain". The street was blocked for an hour before the fight and for its duration as bulletins and round-by-round reports were put up on a board. It was mainly Sharkey fans who cheered every time a point was noted in his favour. The police struggled to cope as the crowds extended from Johnson Street, halfway to Myrtle Avenue. The scene was similar at branch offices on Fifth Avenue, East New York, Broadway and Bedford Avenue.

The *New York Times* painted a similar picture. "In no recent event have the habitudes of the uptown hotels shown so much interest as in the Jeffries-Sharkey fight," it said. Tickers were placed in every café attached to a hotel and were surrounded by dense crowds. At each place, someone volunteered to read the tape and all listened intently. At the Gilsey, Grand, Albemarle and Morton House, it was almost impossible to get into the cafés while the fight was in progress.

Jeffries' supporters made their headquarters at Corbett's saloon where the waiters could hardly move for fight fans. At John L Sullivan's place, people were so tightly packed they could get neither in nor out. At the democratic club, Mayor Van Wyck and Richard Croker received the fight news over a ticker. In Printing House Square, a Jeffries crowd stood without umbrellas or overcoats and awaited the bulletins. By the time they heard in round eight that Sharkey was "getting the best of it" they prepared for Jeffries' defeat. "It looks as if Sharkey will do this fella," said one. It was not until the twenty-first round the mood changed with a bulletin saying, "Sharkey is tiring fast while Jeffries freshens a little". A howl of delight began and grew with each succeeding round. At the bulletin announcing "Jeffries wins on points" the crowd gave a short satisfied cheer and melted away.

As the fans turned their collars up against the rain, a legend was already growing around the fight. The next day, the *Brooklyn Daily Eagle* sports team, which described the fight in five columns across its pages, enthused about the "unprecedented" display, a "fight unparalleled in the history of pugilism". "No prize-fight like that at Coney Island last night will be seen again for many days, unless

NINETY-NINE MINUTES OF HELL

the principals in it are Jeffries and Sharkey," it said. To the ordinary spectator, it said, this was the "perfect fight". It was a night of hard-hitting in which Jeffries started the crowd favourite. "But the plucky showing of Sharkey won over many who didn't care for his fighting so much at the start, and by the time the fight was called, the admirers of the Irishman were as numerous as those of the Californian." It described one magistrate in the crowd – a Sharkey fan. "By disposition, he is dignified. Before the second round was over last night, he was sending out a voluminous series of yells toward the ring which eclipsed the weird voice from the megaphone." As he smoked on his cigar, the announcer with the megaphone turned on the magistrate, telling him to stop smoking as it interfered with the picture taking.

"You will please not smoke," said the megaphone voice.

"Whack him in the ribs, Sharkey!" shouted the magistrate puffing away.

"No smoking!" yelled the man with the megaphone.

Eventually a police sergeant stamped over to put out the cigar. But the magistrate seemed not to notice. When the fight was finished he made a dive for the ring side, yelling: "Robbed! Robbed!"

"Never has there been such a struggle," reported *The Milwaukee Journal*, "and it was a struggle far more than a glove fight. Before it was half over, both men were covered with blood and their massive bodies were battered and swollen."

Sharkey was the aggressor for most of the fight, but after Jeffries "stood for 21 rounds taking the punishment of the best man in the world who could be found to go against him, he turned in and with a speed and strength that were a great surprise proceeded to administer such punishment no other man in the ring except Sharkey could have received and retained consciousness."

The *New York Times* stated: "That (the fight) went to the limit of 25 rounds was evidence of the wonderful condition and vitality of both men, for during the hour and forty minutes blows hard enough to have felled an ox were given frequently. Both men were badly punished - Sharkey showing a cut ear and a badly cut eye, while Jeffries was pounded on the neck with Sharkey's vicious left hand until the flesh there was as raw as a piece of beef.

"When the cheers that greeted the announcement that Jeffries had earned the decision of Referee Siler subsided, three enthusiastic cheers were added for the sturdy ex-sailor, who had taken manfully such a terrible beating from an opponent who had height, reach and weight on his side."

O'Rourke would later exclaim that, "If I ever had a man win a fight, Sharkey won tonight" but the *New York Times* noted that George Siler's decision was "satisfactory to the great majority of spectators".

It added: "The battle was a notable one for the reason that for the first time since John L Sullivan reigned supreme, the title was to be contested by two old-time fighters whose stock in trade was brawn and muscle.

"Not that last night's battle was devoid of the element that boxing instructors define as the science of self-defence but it was essentially a slugging match in which each of the principals made strenuous efforts to put his opponent out of the fight."

The status of the fight has grown in years since.

Jeffries told *The Ring*'s editor, Nat Fleischer, in 1950: "They came no greater than Tom Sharkey. I split his eye open, and his ear was swollen as big as my fist. When I landed a blow on it, it was like hitting a big wet sponge. Yet he wouldn't think of quitting. I also broke two of his ribs and still he kept coming at me. He was as game a fighter as I've ever seen."

Sharkey himself revisited the "hardest fought heavyweight championship fight" for articles written for *Liberty* magazine in 1939.

"The heat from the lights was terrific," he recalled. "Before I could take off my robe, the sweat was burning my eyes, running off my body, soaking my ring trunks. The kinetoscope company had furnished oxygen tanks for both corners. I didn't use mine and I don't believe Jeffries did his. Referee Siler bawled out some instructions and let the gong go."

He describes the left that put him down in the second. "Jeffries said (he) swung the hardest punch he ever let go of, in the ring or any place else. It lifted me off my feet, I hit the canvas on the back of my head with my feet in the air but I got right up.

"Round after round, we fought. Toe to toe, we stood and swapped punches. The roar of the crowd rumbled through the rafters."

He said the height difference meant he had "to leap off my feet to hit Jeffries" and claimed that the "beginning of the twenty-fifth round found me in pretty good shape, considering my broken ribs". He said that during the glove incident – egged on by his corner - his "fighting instinct was up and I wanted to make a whirling finish of the closing round. The referee was still engaged in fastening the glove when the gong clanged loudly. It was the signal that the championship fight was over. It was a weird ending."

Four decades later, Sharkey holds only that Siler's "decision was criticised by many. Some held that I had won; others that I was entitled to a draw".

He quotes Corbett's claim in the *New York Morning World* that it was the fastest fought heavyweight fight ever seen.

And he quotes Jeffries too: "November 3, 1899, is the date of the toughest championship fight in the heavyweight records. I am saying that and I know. I was in it. I'll make a boast if you want to call it that. I'll boast that I was the only champion that ever had to defend his title against Tom Sharkey when Tom was right – and Tom was right that night."

While the legend of the fight has never died, neither has the debate around Siler's decision.

Siler – a close friend of Tom O'Rourke, Sharkey's manager - released a statement after the fight. "It is true that there are some men who had wagers down upon Jeffries yet who admit that the sailor should have had a draw, but it is also true that there are others who had money on Sharkey, yet who say they lost fairly," he said.

"Throughout the fight, Jeffries did the clean punishing, his blows landed fair and square, while Sharkey's swings to the head were delivered with the forearm, the glove often failing to counter at all.

"Jeffries certainly had the better of the first six rounds and from then on till the tenth it was fairly even. Sharkey had a trifle the better of the next seven rounds, but Jeffries continued to improve and the last five rounds were all his. Sharkey was foul at times. He hit low at different times and hit in the clinches while holding. He twisted Jeffries' neck several times and cut Jeffries' nose with a butt, not with a punch. His head was constantly thrown into Jeffries' body and he roughed it almost throughout.

"All of this I took into consideration in making the decision for clean and fair tactics are what count. Sharkey was knocked down clean and was groggy at several stages.

"I gave what I think was an honest decision and was upheld by the crowd and I feel satisfied with my work."

The Jeffries' camp would be pleased with that assessment too. They reckoned that had more rounds been fought, their man would have knocked out the Irishman. Some argued that the glove incident could have seen Sharkey lose on a foul, but many see it as an interesting curiosity. Myler writing in *The Ring* more than 90 years later remarked that when Jeffries hit back at Sharkey with his bare fist "it was the only time a fight was contested with gloves and bare knuckles at the same time".

However, the day after the fight, a *Brooklyn Daily Eagle* reporter found that "Sharkey carried his arm in a sling and his temper not at all whenever the decision was broached". Jeffries' and Siler's ears "must have tinged at the small talk that was indulged in, in some quarters", it said. "Indeed it is an indisputable fact that today the general public accepts Jeffries' occupation of the championship title with a grain of salt and two grains of suspicions for while the keenest sports at the ringside admit that the decision was a fair ruling, there seems to be a keen desire, which is evidently parent to the thought, that the boilermaker was really second best in Friday night's argument. Jeffries won beyond a doubt, but Sharkey was on his feet and fighting at the call of the end of the battle."

It was the fact that the champion had not knocked out his opponent which was getting to "Mr Vox Populi", said the newspaper. "All of which brings up the old discussion about settling championship titles in a limited bout. No man of the trade of fisticuffs is actually finally beaten until he is counted out – and Tom Sharkey, the greatest glutton for fight that ever stepped into the ring, least of all."

Jeffries and Sharkey, it went on, "met under a set of rules. These rules prescribe that if both men in a fight are on their feet at the conclusion of the stipulated number of rounds the referee shall award a decision upon points. In their meeting, Jeffries outpointed the sailor and at the finish held the upper hand. And Referee Siler did the only thing, the fair thing, under the circumstances. Maybe Sharkey, would have won in a finish fight, and there are a horde of folk who think so. But under the conditions that prevailed at Coney Island, Jeffries was the sure enough winner. If Sharkey really could have won out in an unlimited battle, the sailor man is the victim of fate – in the form of twenty-five rounds."

Siler responded to the debate in a long letter to the *Chicago Tribune* a fortnight after the fight. "Things were toning down a bit," he joked over the hysteria. "A week ago, I was a highway robber; a few days later, a petty larceny thief; a day or two after that, a suspicious character, and today, I am considered honest enough to ride in a trolley car among honest people. Who knows but that in another week, I'll be honest enough to salute a policeman?

"I have not argued with anyone at length regarding the fight, neither have I gone into details, and probably would not, but for the fact that a number of soreheads – friends of Sharkey's and those who lost their money on him – still declare that he was entitled to a draw. Another reason for writing what will follow is that I have received scores of letters from friends in Chicago and throughout the western country, asking for an explanation."

Claims from O'Rourke that Sharkey won the fight were "natural", he said.

But he concentrated on the 'lost glove' moment and asked if O'Rourke – in egging on Sharkey to hit at Jeffries – was deliberately risking a foul so Tom would avoid a points' defeat and could argue for a rematch.

He also questioned the representations of the match in the news bulletins – raising an argument to protect himself which can be neither proved nor disproved. However, he does nail a problem for all researchers relying on subjective reports of any event, fights included. "Judging by some of the letters received, the ticker reports gave Sharkey all the better of the fight. I wonder if the general public knows who or what the operator is who sends out the reports. Do they know whether he is a youth of 20, who possibly never saw a fight before, and is therefore incompetent to send a correct and unbiased report, or a man of 30, whether competent or not, who has a bet on one of the principals?

"Operators, like spectators, have their likes and dislikes and are apt to be prejudiced. I do not wish to infer that the ticker operator of the big fight was prejudiced or that he was incompetent, but I do know of instances wherein the operators were novices at the fighting game. Still, their reports were devoured as being the proper goods."

He highlighted reports of the McCoy-Ruhlin fight at Syracuse, in which Ruhlin, according to the ticker, "slammed the life out of McCoy, when in fact McCoy did not get his hair ruffled, while Ruhlin was pummelled to pieces".

Siler was certainly not pulling any punches in defence of his controversial verdict.

However, his claim that some reports stated that "Sharkey hit Jeffries from three to four blows to one received" seems unconvincing: most ringside commentators were aware that Sharkey's 'style' was to brave out two punches for every one he could deliver.

Furthermore, he went on to claim that "Jeffries left the ring with a slight cut on the left side of his nose…and a slight cut on his forehead between the eyes…These were the only visible marks on his face." That claim – effectively that Jeffries was unhurt or showed few signs of injury from Sharkey's punches – certainly contradicts contemporary reports and Jeffries' own descriptions of the fight. On meeting the men the next day, one reporter described the cuts and bruises on both faces, saying: "Neither was a candidate for a beauty show. Indeed it may be said that neither had a face fit for publication."

However, the damage to Sharkey was severe – as we have seen, Sharkey's own descriptions show how he had suffered. "Surely Jeffries must have gained some points," said Siler. "Sharkey put up a wonderfully game fight. He was the aggressor and forced the battle. This however he was compelled to do being five inches the shorter man and therefore obliged to get in close."

Well, if O'Rourke, understandably, considering the reputation and money he had hanging on the battle, wanted a win, most argued for a draw. Siler responded: "A great many persons argue that Sharkey was entitled to a draw because he put up such a game fight against so big a man as Jeffries and that the contest went the limit. That may be a good way to figure a draw but not to my way of thinking."

The new marvel of moving pictures meant Bob Fitzsimmons would see the fight a few months later at the Brooklyn Music Hall and be able to give his opinion. As he watched the screen, reporters watched him, noting he never took his eyes from the scene and that he made the occasional remark. "That's a good one," he shouted several times as Sharkey got his left to the jaw and, at the close of the twenty-third round when Jeffries landed his right in a break-way, Fitz said: "I think that dazed Sharkey a little but he came back all right."

At the end, he was asked his opinion. "It is a good fight: a first class fight," he said. "Both men tired, Sharkey being apparently very tired in the last three rounds, but then twenty-five rounds is a long journey indeed, and I don't blame them for being weary, especially under the fierce heat."

What about the verdict? "I would not like to say, under the circumstances," he replied. "In the pictures, it is sometimes difficult to tell whether or not Jeffries is landing punches or is simply pushing Sharkey away, and then again I could not tell what he was doing with his right in the mix-ups for Sharkey's back is turned toward the camera much of the time. It was certainly a good, hard battle."

The boxing bible, *The Ring*, continued to illustrate the split in opinion about the fight. Three decades after the fight, Charles F. Mathison wrote in the magazine: "...Nine out of 10 persons in the arena were convinced that Sharkey had won the bout and the title. The soft-hearted Siler decided it would be cruel to declare the titleholder beaten when he was on his feet at the conclusion of the 25th round. Jeff had been outpointed in 18 of the 25 rounds, but that meant nothing to the referee, who apparently was there to see that Jeff kept his championship unless he was carried out of the ring on a stretcher." However, in July 1944, it ran another piece about the fight, called *99 Minutes of Hell*, that stated: "Sharkey lost the honours, but not until he had forced his opponent to fight a marvellous battle and was in no way disgraced by the outcome. But lose the fight he did... In the writer's opinion, no other decision could have been rendered, despite the big points' advantage Sharkey had gained in the early rounds. The condition of the men at the finish testified to the correctness of the verdict." The writer of the second article was also Charles F. Mathison.

In January 1960, *The Ring* tried to settle the debate. Its front cover asked 'Was Sharkey Robbed of the Heavyweight Title?' Inside, *The Ring* 'Detective', Dan Daniel, said the system in which the referee was the "sole arbiter" had good points but "placed too much responsibility on one man and too much faith in the bona fides of a single scorer of points". Siler had been "recognised as the best of his time" but a "good many veterans who saw the battle at New York's surfside still are arguing over (his) decision". Daniel stated: "If *The Ring* Detective finds that Siler made one of the colossal errors of fight history, and bilked Sharkey out of the world's championship, many of the Old Guard will rise to the writer's support."

The 'Detective' wrote: "For seventeen rounds, Sharkey kept Jeffries pretty much on the receiving end. In the eighteenth, Jim started to rally. However Tom's supporters felt that the worst Siler should have given the sailor was a draw.

"Most of those who contributed to the then remarkable take of $68,000 were vehement in their support of the idea that Sharkey had won."

Daniel then explored the reasons why Siler's judgement might have been affected. There were, he said, "extenuating circumstances". "The referee was not so old, only 53. Yet the terrific heat in the ring wore him down and when he got to his dressing room, he collapsed.

"The late Joe Vila, veteran columnist of the *Evening Sun*, New

York, who saw the fight, told me that the temperature in the ring was 112 degrees. The lights bounced their hot rays off tin reflectors and made the heat unbearable even as far back as the tenth row. The poor ringsiders got roasted at the high impost of $35 each."

Vila told Daniel: "Sharkey beat Jeffries and should have won the title. The customers were in a mood for lynching Siler and Tom O'Rourke, who ran the scrap, had to call out the police reserves to protect the referee from harm."

Daniel repeated Sharkey's later assertion that he suffered "four fractured ribs" while claiming that "Jeffries got a broken nose in this, perhaps, most vicious of all heavyweight championship fights", and he wanted to get to the bottom of the damage suffered by both fighters.

In 1926, *The Ring* heard that Sharkey had been taken to Dr John F Erdmann's offices on East 54th Street, New York, after the fight. It had heard that the doctor had "marvelled at the physical make-up and constitution of the sailor" but "never before had he seen a human being survive so terrific a battering". The rumour the magazine had heard was that Erdmann had identified "broken ribs, a broken nose, a battered face. His body above the belt was a bruised mass of flesh. Sharkey got perhaps the worst beating ever handed out in the modern ring."

It appealed for the doctor's thoughts on the matter but it was not until 1960 that Dan Daniel tracked him down. The doctor had gone on to become one of the top surgeons in the United States and was 80 when he talked to The Ring. He had not seen the fight but said Sharkey was "badly battered and bruised... It was apparent that he had been in a very punishing fight. I understand that Jeffries also was badly done up. But I did not examine him, and in any event, a comparison of injuries hardly would have offered any concrete evidence as to the winner. I do recollect that Sharkey felt he had won the fight. But, as I said, he was badly beaten up."

With Sharkey, Jeffries and Siler dead by this time, where else could *The Ring* turn? What about the film from the four cameras. Technologically, the Biograph Film Company had been a hit that night, having honed its skills at the Corbett-Fitzsimmons fight at

Carson City in 1897. The Jeffries-Sharkey contest had "made fight fans flicker daffy". Daniel stated: "When the pictures were shown in New York, those who felt that Siler had bilked Tom insisted that the movies backed them up 100 per cent."

He went on: "Billy Brady, Jeff's manager, must have had his doubts as to whether the flickers would back up the referee. He refused to see the first showing, but did view the pictures later in Chicago and came out with a statement that the screen proved conclusively that Jeffries had won.

"The truth of it was that the movies failed to show Jeffries in an impressive role. He had injured an already bad left hand in training and this had forced a week's postponement of the fight.

"Jeff did not score much with the left at Coney and the movies played this up, creating fresh furore at the expense of Siler. George continued to insist that the Sharkey claims dumbfounded him and the imputations concerning his honesty were scandalous."

Jeffries later claimed that at the time of the fight he was tired after a punishing vaudeville tour of Europe and the States. Whatever his energy levels, there seems little doubt that he was carrying an injury. He told *The Ring* – in a conversation at which Sharkey was also present and which was repeated by the magazine's 'Detective' - that before the fight he had been advised by a doctor to have the left arm placed in a cast and not to do any fighting for six months. But he had insisted on going through with the Sharkey contract.

While training for Sharkey, said Daniel, Jeffries had hurt the arm again when he was hit by a medicine ball thrown playfully by the wrestler, Ernest Roeber, a member of his entourage. The medicine ball dislocated the left elbow and in putting it back in place, Roeber was "more or less effective but thoroughly inexpert".

"I figured I had just one good punch in that left when I faced Sharkey that chilly night at Coney Island," Jeffries recalled. "I felt that I would have to let Tom have that punch early on in the fight. I spotted an opening in the second round and let go. Tom hit the deck. But he bounced right up again. I had hurt my left more than I had damaged Sharkey and for the rest of the fight I had to punch with my right only. No wonder I looked bad in the motion pictures."

(Interestingly, some contemporary newspaper reports appear at odds with this version of events. *The Brooklyn Daily Eagle* fight report states: "Jeffries was coached to keep his right under cover, save in the clinches, just as he did against Fitzsimmons and to win with the left. This Jeffries did fairly well, save at odd times, until the beginning of the twenty-third round and then he went out to win in a hurry.")

Continuing in conversation with *The Ring* and Sharkey, Jeffries stated: "You know I figured Tom to be a cinch."

Sharkey responded: "I sure felt like one when you busted my ribs, but I felt better after I got over that clout on your nose in the ninth, remember?"

"Should say I do" replied Jeffries. "Saw cobwebs for a minute."

Turning to the reporter again, Jeffries said: "When I climbed into the ring that night, Sharkey's billowy chest didn't scare me one bit. I had trained for weeks and trained hard. When the bell rang, I went in to finish it quickly but before the end of the second round I knew that Tom could not only protect himself but could sock. I watched Tom closely and at the end of each round he would go to his corner looking all het up and plumb tired. That would make me feel that I had him going and I would start the next with a rush. But Tom came up, feeling the same as I did and we'd bang away for another round. Those lights they rigged up to take moving pictures with were terrible. You'd feel all in anyway. Tom would bounce one off your head and those lights added to it to make you feel miserable. I'm sure the fans got a run for their money that night. If they didn't, I don't know what they would want! Siler gave me the decision after 25 rounds. That fight stands out as the most terrible one in my career."

Then Sharkey described how his career up until the final weeks of the nineteenth century had felt like a prelude to a victory that night at Coney Island and a full grip on the world heavyweight title.

"I figured I could knock Jeff off easy," he said. "My idle, John L Sullivan, had told me that I would be champion of the world some day and I believed everything John L Sullivan said. I was cocksure and confident of winning the championship that night. I hit Jeff with everything I had every time I hit and I hit as often as

I could flay my arms around. I had trained too and I was in great condition, the best of my career.

"Honestly I just itched before the first bell to clout him one and see how he would take it. I didn't think he would take it because I wanted to put everything I had in a punch and I did. But he took it and gave me plenty.

"Before the first bell I kept saying to myself: 'Tom, you'll be the champ after this fight - let him have it!" I kept repeating that to myself even during the rounds and in the waits but Jeff must have been saying something to himself.

"You know I knocked out those coast fellows, Jack Langley, Rough Thompson, Billy Tate, 'Sailor' Brown and Nick Burley. That gave me a lot of confidence and when I got Jeff, I really felt I could knock him over."

Both fighters agreed Siler's honesty was never in question. "The most terrible thing that happened in that fight was the charge against Siler, a great referee and an honest man," said Jeffries. "They accused him of robbing Sharkey. I don't know what made so many of the spectators turn against me."

The Ring felt it could make a judgement. It was not only veteran reporter Dan Daniel at the typewriter, remember; he was consulting his friend and editor, the great Nat Fleischer, the man who had founded *The Ring* in 1922. He was considered the world's most influential authority on the sport, would write forty million words on boxing during his career and who had refereed and judged thousands of fights himself.

The Ring 'Detective' selected to put the ghost to rest: "The questions now have to be answered once and for all time. Did Siler rob Sharkey of the heavyweight championship of the world?

"Was the referee guilty of straying from the straight and narrow?

"Was Siler guilty of poor judgement and could he have been upset by the beating he took from the lights?

"There is no basis for the charge that Siler had been fixed.

"There may be some grounds for the belief that Siler pulled a rock.

"*The Ring* Detective rules that, in any event Sharkey was entitled to a draw."[3]

Deserving a draw, but being judged the loser, Tom Sharkey's heart was broken on that rainy night at Coney Island.

As Siler grasped Jeffries' hand to give the decision, O'Rourke looked like he had "lost his last friend". He looked forlornly across the ring and exclaimed: "But how about the twenty-two?"

Sharkey, though, said nothing. He sat with his head held in his hands. He shook hands with the joyful Jeffries then smiled sadly and slumped onto his stool. Jeffries then came over to him, extended his hand again and said something into his ear. They were, said one reporter, "undoubtedly words of admiration".

The result of the fight was cabled to his parents and his father took a boat across the Atlantic to be with his son.

For some time, Sharkey's line on the fight would be that it was up to the general public to decide if he was robbed. It would take a long time for the hurt to subside. The *Brooklyn Daily Eagle*, now supportive of the warrior sailor, explained why. He was, it said, the "most aggressive man according to all who saw the battle that ever put on the gloves".

It said: "With two ribs broken, with the blood pouring into his left eye, destroying the little sight left there after the swelling had begun, with his body black and blue and covered with blood bruises and with his face beaten beyond recognition, Sharkey did not know that he was beaten.

"That was because it is the nature of this man to keep fighting while there is a breath of wind or a spark of sensibility. Sharkey will be knocked out only when he is as unconscious as a stone. A ton of coal might fall on this natural fighter and not quell his desire to give blow for blow. There was no stage of the game when Sharkey was not willing to take two blows even from the great giant who was towering over him, to give one in return.

"Sharkey is truly a 'bad sailor' with all that means. He is the most gritty and pugnacious son of Erin that ever donned gloves, and Sharkey, had he been grovelling upon the floor, would have still claimed that he was robbed of a decision."

CHAPTER NINE
Blood, Sweat and Tears

Sharkey and Jeffries recovered the day after their fight in the same Turkish baths. They were massaged, "cleaned and pressed", plasters were placed carefully over their stinging cuts and a soothing syrup was smothered over the bruises.

But the talk was all about a possible third fight. Sharkey, someone joked, wanted another fight "for he had one eye and one ear left". Jeffries said Sharkey could have it, even though the champion's nose was said to look "like a clothes line from under which the prop has fallen".

Sharkey posted $5,000 with George Considine to secure the fight. O'Rourke said: "Sharkey is clearly entitled to the first chance to meet Jeffries, as no man ever gave the champion such a close fight or such a hard rub. I fully believe Sharkey to be the best man and that the next time he will have no difficulty in winning the championship."

A few days after the brawl, he added: "Sharkey, while still confined to his room, is doing splendidly. His ribs have knitted well and he will be about again very shortly. His wonderful recuperative powers are coming to his aid and he is now able to move about a bit."

Sharkey, it was claimed, would punch Jeffries in the street if he didn't fight. Jeffries was not backing down either – although quotes from managers and camps often differed from the boxers themselves and, while some reports said he was leaving for a fight in Philadelphia, Jeffries himself said: "I do not think I will arrange another contest for six or seven months at least. I need a rest and propose to take it. When I do get ready to fight, Sharkey will have the preference if he then wants it."

Jeffries – who made about $30,000 on purse and gate receipts from the Sharkey fight and had also wagered $8,000 on himself – did not appear in a ring again for six months and then against a setup, Jack Finnegan, on April 6 in Detroit. Finnegan went out in one. A month later, Jeff met Jim Corbett in a famous 23-round fight in Coney Island, in which Corbett's legs gave out.

Sharkey made about a third of what Jeffries did on the Coney Island fight but $10,000 or $12,000 could still buy you a pretty good life at a time when the average hard-working American family was struggling to make anything between $500 and $1,200 a year. And there was more money to come for the boxers. The film of the Jeffries-Sharkey fight was already causing a stir. Estimates on the return from the moving pictures must have provided some balm for the boxers' aching bones and groaning muscles with some saying they were looking at between $50,000 and $150,000 each.[1]

Tom was already showing signs of his wealth and of an interest in spending it on women and racehorses – he already owned at least one of the latter, named Hesper, and would go on to own a stable of 16. Two weeks after the Jeffries fight, he was seen at a major horse show in New York where, although society was "brilliantly represented", the main non-horse event to hush the perfectly-dressed folk of Madison Square Garden was the "arrival and the settling down upon the scene of Tom Sharkey, the pugilist". According to the *Brooklyn Daily Eagle*, he "came, he saw and he conquered", strolling down the promenade "accompanied by two feminine friends, one a young person of many attractions". The young woman was "tall, fascinating of face and figure, and the eyes of every man she passed turned admiringly in her direction".

The newspaper was excited by her costume as any society magazine would be today, crowing over the "startling white dress and a hat with heaped-up feathers". Tom was "arrayed with equal care and particularity" in a tuxedo, a "wealth of shirt front" and a derby. The boxer was recognized by everyone and greeted them like a gentleman as he made his way to a private box. So, who was his charming companion? It is possible she was a Jennie Tuttle, the daughter of Fred Tuttle, a retired sea captain. Jennie, a 19-year-old, dubbed 'The Belle of Sheepshead Bay', was rumoured to be Tom's first love, with the *Milwaukee Journal* of August 8, 1900, even going on to claim that they had become engaged. However, Jennie was not to be the one. She would come later, would be no less attractive and would do even more to help change Tom, the boxer, into Tom, the man of society.

But Sharkey still believed his real prize – the heavyweight title – remained within reach. The Jeffries' defeat was painful but he quickly arranged fights to confirm the notion that he was still *the* contender to the big men.

Tom's ribs were ready by February 13, 1900, when he stopped Joe Goddard in four rounds in Philadelphia. Veteran John S Clark refereed the fight before 4,000 people at the city's Industrial Hall who saw the "Barrier Champion" outclassed. The fight – the third in which Tom had beaten Goddard - ended with little pride for Goddard who lunged at Tom after his own corner had thrown in the sponge. Goddard slipped to the floor dragging the Irishman with him. Tom was given a standing ovation.[2]

Six days later, he went to Detroit, Michigan, to fight the Californian heavyweight Jim Jeffords, who had only recently embarrassed himself in a sport in which simulation was rife. In November 1899, he had fought Tom's sparring partner, Bob Armstrong, in New York and, in the third round, had writhed on the floor in "well simulated agony trying hard to give referee Johnny Eckhardt the impression that he had been hit foul". Armstrong was held by the police as first the club surgeon and then an ambulance man were called to examine Jeffords. They could find no sign that he had been hit foul at all. One reporter noted: "It was a clear case of quit on the part of the Californian and he will find it hard work to get on another bout in this vicinity." So, now, Jeffords, who considered himself a heavyweight contender, was fighting in Michigan with ten rounds planned. Tom didn't need ten though. In the second, the men were breaking from a clinch when, on two minutes and six seconds, Sharkey whipped his right into the Californian's head and Jeffords went down. The Irishman packed a punch. It was some time until Jeffords recovered to talk. He then claimed a foul, saying Sharkey hit him in the breakaway when they had agreed to break clean. The referee dismissed this, though, and awarded the fight to Sharkey. He later expressed the opinion that Jeffords "laid down", an opinion shared by some of those ringside.

Despite the racial prejudice which was so strong in the sport, there was widespread love and respect for the little fighter, George Dixon. Sharkey fought with at least two black fighters in his corner: Bob Armstrong and Dixon, who were popular with crowds as well as peers. On February 22, 1900, Tom was eager to be at Broadway Athletic Club where a testimonial was being held for George, who for many years had successfully defended his world title but had recently lost it to Terry McGovern. It was a glittering get-together and raised $8,000 for the fighter. Sharkey, McGovern, Corbett, Ruhlin, McCoy, Choynski and Gans were among those who entered the ring for "friendly bouts". Sullivan, who had been invited to fight an exhibition with Tom, did not make it. He had been expected, according to the *Brooklyn Daily Eagle*, despite the fact that his "antipathy to colored fighters is traditional in pugilistic history because of persistent refusal to box or fight one" and he had "waived his prejudice and was one of the first to offer to box for Dixon's benefit".

Tom travelled to Hartford, Connecticut, and Baltimore, Maryland, for fights during March. On the 15th, he took on Texan Jim McCormick and knocked him out in just 38 seconds at the Coliseum. Sharkey, said onlookers, went at McCormick viciously, ignoring two hard punches to the face, and sent his opponent to the floor with a left to the body and a right hand uppercut. Then, on the 29th, he ended the career of heavyweight fighter Thomas Francis Conroy – who was known to all as "Stockings" – with a blistering second round knockout.

There was another easy victory in the summer when on June 8, he took on Yank Kenny, another opponent who stood head and shoulders above Sharkey. The fight, which was over in 135 seconds, provided a glimpse of the old Sharkey. Some thought Kenny would crush his opponent but Sharkey wanted it over quickly and moved his fists fast. He rushed like a bull and whipped two sharp left hooks to Kenny's jaw, sending the big man flailing back against the ropes. They clashed in close and two more rights to Kenny's jaw sent him down and out. He tried hard to get up but fell on his face, as the referee counted him out. Sharkey tried to lift his opponent to his feet but Kenny was too heavy and both fell. Kenny's seconds then helped in assisting him to his corner, where he soon revived.

Four days later, Tom was due to take on Philadelphian Jerry Miller in his home town. The turnout was small but, despite the money he was making already, Tom was happy to go on. However, Miller claimed there was not enough money in the house and the fight was cancelled.

The talk all year was of a rematch with an old foe: Bob Fitzsimmons. "Ruby" Bob had challenged Sharkey soon after the Jeffries fight and O'Rourke played a few games before agreeing Fitz deserved another chance at his man. Referee and sporting commentator George Siler said Fitzsimmons believed there was "one more good fight in him, and is doing his utmost to get on a match with some of the top-notchers and then quit the game for good". He added: "The public, I am positive, wants to see Sharkey and Fitz come together and as the former is both willing and anxious, why not match them? The fight would make the best drawing card New York fight promoters could put on the boards."

The fighters met in March and agreed to a 25-round fight later in the year. While huge money would again be involved, the men seemed so eager to fight that little negotiation was needed.

"Everything goes, Tom, but I prefer having the winner take all the purse," said Fitzsimmons.

"Pictures and everything?" O'Rourke cut in.

"Yes," said Fitz.

"That just suits me," said Sharkey.

The public wanted the fight because they remembered well what had happened – or what they believed had happened – back in 1896 when Earp awarded the fight to Tom.

It niggled Fitzsimmons too and he used it to snipe at Sharkey and O'Rourke.

"You get a copy of the rules, Tom, and study them, and I'll do the same," said Fitz. "I have fought so many different rules that I reckon I have forgotten them."

Sharkey took this in the same good faith and said: "All right."

But there was time to close a little of the old wound when Fitzsimmons stood up. Speaking first to O'Rourke, he said: "Now I want to shake hands with you, Tom. We have begun in a good, businesslike manner, and I want to finish the same way." He turned to Sharkey: "When we meet in the ring then it will be a fight. In the meantime I want no backbiting in the papers, and I have no ill feelings." The two fighters shook hands.

Such was the lunacy surrounding the sport though that all was bound not to run smoothly. O'Rourke, for instance, had a conflict of interest when being party to the choice of venue, decided normally by who offered the most cash. Being not only Tom's manager but also the manager of the Seaside Sporting Club, he quickly realised that if the fighters met elsewhere – probably the Westchester Athletic Club – on the winner-take-all plan, there would be nothing in it for him should Tom lose. Therefore, he quickly decided that the 60 per cent offered by the Coney Island club was better than the 67 per cent offered by the Westchester Club. Fitzsimmons saw through that game and told him all was off. Soon after, though, he was wandering along Broadway and met Sharkey at Thirty-Fourth Street.

"O'Rourke says he won't let you fight at Westchester under any conditions although that was the biggest purse," said Fitzsimmons.

"Well, he's not the boss," blurted out Sharkey.

Sharkey was angry with O'Rourke. He said he would sort it and shook hands with Fitz.

The Sharkey-Fitzsimmons rivalry then took a strange turn when Sharkey choose to back Fitz in a twist on his even bigger contest with Jeffries. When Fitzsimmons took on Jeffries' sparring partner, Ed Dunkhorst, Tom seconded Fitz. Fitzsimmons railroaded Dunkhorst, laying him out in the second. Tom may have been on Fitz's side that night but did he see the omens coming? Fitz, it was said, had "grown younger" and was bearing little resemblance to the man who had lost the world championship to Jeffries less than a year earlier.

Public interest in the Fitzsimmons-Sharkey bout was already massive. The August date set by the fighters was too far away for many, but the promoters did not want it too close to the Jeffries-Corbett fight planned for May. "Two big fights, such as that between (Jeffries and Corbett) and that between Fitzsimmons and Sharkey could not successfully, be pulled off within sleeping time of each other," wrote Siler at the time. "One would certainly suffer and the one to suffer in this case would be that between the two Jims."

What was also exercising Siler at the time was the possibility that the Horton Law might not remain on the statute books much longer. The law had governed boxing in New York since 1896 and allowed fights with no limit to the number of rounds, decisions by referees and the posting of forfeits and side-bets. There were calls for reform to tackle corruption and one senator wanted a stop to fights where there was more than a ten pound difference in fighters' weights. Sharkey had fought plenty of men much bigger than himself and his previous bout with Fitzsimmons had been one of the most controversial in ring history: it was, perhaps, fitting that the August bout would be one of the last fought under the Horton rules.

Tom began training in Sheepshead Bay, where he had bought a home, Claremont Villa, and had set up a training quarters with, according to visitors, a "big leather bag about fifteen times the size of a punching bag and stuffed with hair" hanging from the ceiling.

A New York writer for the *Dundalk Democrat* visited Tom. "I have heard Mr Sharkey say that as a boy leaving home he promised his dear mother he would lead a temperate life – and he has kept that promise," he gushed. "I've met him in company where the red wine flowed and he smiled and said: 'Apollinaris-water was strong enough for him.' And the young man who keeps a promise made to his dear mother in that way is worthy of honour and of success too and he is the most successful and one of the most sensible young Irishmen in America today. His country home, Claremont Villa at Sheepshead Bay, Coney Island is finer than Lord Claremont ever dreamed of."[3]

Preparing for Fitz, he set up fights with two other close rivals, telling sports on a visit to Fort Dearborn Athletic Club, Chicago, that he "whipped all the heavyweights" and "was going to start at the bottom again and repeat the trick".

He started in that city, on May 8, with Joe Choynski. It was Tom's first competitive fight in the Windy City. They met at Tattersall's with Choynski keen to beat the sailor cleanly after the draws of 1896 and 1898, and they both went at each other like "hurricanes". The Irishman had the game well in hand throughout and planted a killer left on Choynski's jaw just as the bell went to end the second round. The San Franciscan tried to get up but it was all over and Sharkey danced a jig to celebrate.

He then spotted referee George Siler sitting with the ringside reporters. Siler's decision in the Jeffries' fight was still uppermost in Tom's mind.

Sharkey leaned over the ropes and looked the referee in the eye and, according to Siler, said: "I suppose you would have called that a foul had you been the ring."

"Of course, I would," Siler joked.

Bob Armstrong led Tom away.

Then, on June 26, Tom took on Gus Ruhlin, the Ohio fighter who, almost two years to the day earlier, he had flattened in under half-a-minute. It was to be a fight which would have a lasting effect on Sharkey in more ways than one.

Sharkey's reputation with sports fans, despite or perhaps because of the defeat to Jeffries, and because he had taken all the great heavyweights, had never been better. He had most of the betting. To fans, Ruhlin was a second-rater, a fighter who had never made a particularly good showing against any man of reputation. Word in the saloons was that he would not last ten rounds but those closer to the action thought differently. Corbett was training Ruhlin and thought he had a chance. Even O'Rourke admitted: "This fellow Ruhlin is not by any means an easy mark. From the reports that I have heard about him, it is my opinion that he will put up an interesting battle."

Much was against Tom, as it had been so many times. Ruhlin had all the natural advantages on the Irishman. He towered six inches above Sharkey, while the Irishman weighed around 180 to Ruhlin's 195. Ruhlin's long range would ensure that Sharkey had to take considerable punishment to get near him with his own punches.

But there was something else that many of the 8,000 spectators at Coney Island claimed they witnessed in Sharkey that night: a staleness; feeling that he had trained too much, fought too hard.

From the off that made him desperately vulnerable to the big man. Ruhlin had learned some footwork and cleverness, and together with his height and reach, he made a more than formidable opponent. It seems crazy now that a Ruhlin defeat could seem quite so unimaginable.

Tom took a beating in the first round and he never recovered, but he was Sharkey, the fighting sailor, and he would never give up.

In the sixth, he took a wound which completely blinded his right eye for the rest of the fight. Throughout the second half of the fight, Sharkey fought on like a machine, not knowing exactly where he was.

By the 15th, blood was streaming down Sharkey's face. It seemed impossible he could fight on.

Blow after blow continued against him. Sent back by Ruhlin, he staggered under a right to the jaw. Ruhlin pressed on with both fists and Sharkey staggered down to the floor. The referee counted. A gasp had gone up from the crowd. Sharkey had never suffered a knockout before.

Tom drew himself to his feet but could not defend himself as Ruhlin came in again, raining down blows. He was down for a second time, but was again not out.

He clambered up. Ruhlin was in pain now too, almost unable to use his hands. The sailor staggered towards him and he sent soft, short lefts and rights to the head that "looked as if they would not hurt a child" but it was enough for Tom. He went down for a third time.

The fighters were in agony. Exhausted. Blinded by pain and tiredness. Like a bloody toy that would not stop but was getting the very last sources of power from its batteries,

Tom rose again. Ruhlin walked to him. Tom tried to clinch but Gus Ruhlin, using the very last reserves of his strength, stepped back and sent a straight left to Tom's face and a right hand uppercut to the jaw.

Tom toppled forward. This was it. He was all out. Referee Johnny White held Tom under one arm and waved Ruhlin to his corner. The sailor's seconds carried him to his corner.

Tom slowly came around, the shocked crowds of O'Rourke's Seaside Athletic Club hazily coming into focus.

He had taken a terrible battering, staggering to within five seconds of the end of the round, taking a punch in almost every moment of the three minutes, having respite only when he was on the floor.

Ruhlin came over and shook Sharkey's hand.

The *New York Times* reported: "The decisive battle and unexpected result were truly a surprise for the sporting public."

It added of Sharkey: "No soldier ever gave more desperate battle, no man sinking to unconsciousness ever clung more determinedly to his vitality. Even at the end, when blinded by the blows of his powerful opponent and dulled mentally by the battering of his foe, he clung instinctively to the massive frame of the man who was his master."

Its reporter concluded that the Irishman "did not give up his place in the line of first-class heavyweights without a desperate struggle".

Sharkey was still set on Fitzsimmons. Ruhlin had made himself a contender too. Folks in some areas still questioned Jeffries' hold on the title. One boxing writer claimed: "Since the Sharkey-Jeffries battle there are thousands of folk who cannot be convinced that Jeffries is entitled to the championship beyond all dispute and a series of battles between Jeffries, Sharkey and Fitzsimmons would fill the popular bill, as it was never filled before."

The reporter went on: "It is not to be disputed that such a series would be the greatest in the pugilistic lines that the world ever saw. It would give Fitzsimmons, Sharkey, Ruhlin, and McCoy the chance to meet Jeffries and the winner of the final bout would be entitled to the championship with a clearer and cleaner title than any one who ever held it before."[4]

Back home in Ireland, there was only a brief report of the "great fight" in which "Sharkey's colours were lowered by Gus Ruhlin". It stated: "The latter proved to be much smarter and a harder hitter. He avoided Sharkey's rushes and as the fight wore on inflicted terrible punishment. Sharkey became more and more distressed and in the fifteenth round was in a helpless state though he would not give in."[5]

Challenges flew all ways after Sharkey's defeat. But for many fans Fitzsimmons was still the man they wanted Sharkey to meet. While the men were on speaking terms now, Fitzsimmons still claimed to have been robbed in San Francisco. Fitz also agreed with fans – and now Tom – that the Irishman had been stale during the Ruhlin fight and was still a worthy opponent.

Fitzsimmons honoured Ruhlin first, taking him on at Madison Square Garden on August 10 (with Sharkey lending Bob his own sparring partner, Bob Armstrong, to help him prepare) and he defeated the Ohio conqueror of the Irishman in six rounds.

A fortnight later, Fitzsimmons and Sharkey fought at the Seaside Sporting Club. There was a great deal at stake: plans were being made for the winner to take on the champion, Jeffries, within a week, before the Horton Law was due to end.

In addition, both felt the need to drive away the dark clouds left hanging over the encounter by the San Francisco fight. As one commentator explained: "When it is said that no two gamer men than Fitzsimmons and Sharkey ever faced each other in the heavyweight class, one truth about tonight's battle has been told. When it is added that they are as hard hitters as can be found in the class and each anxious to efface unpleasant things said about their first battle in San Francisco three and a half years ago, it will be seen why the fight is such a popular one among the sporting men. As much interest has been taken in the affair as if the men were meeting to decide the championship. Had Sharkey not been beaten by Ruhlin a couple of months ago, the battle would probably prove the greatest drawing card of its kind ever put into the ring here."[6]

The night before the fight, Fitzsimmons dreamt he would beat Tom in two rounds. "I guess I must have dreamed the same thing a hundred times" he declared afterwards, "for I knocked him out with every kind of blow. At times, I would try to look on the other side of it and I would feel that he was going to put me out. But, no. The dream came out the same every time."

Reality appeared to be very different from Fitz's dream life. Sharkey had to get his shorter armed hooks inside Fitzsimmons' jabs. Four thousand men, their coats draped over their arms to help them cool down in the sticky, hot weather, waited to see who would come out on top.

And Tom did in the first, sending a terrific left jab to the mouth which sent Fitz's head back and following it with a right swing that would have removed his opponent's head from this shoulders had it landed there. Instead, it struck Fitz on the left shoulder and sent him down on his back.

Just as Fitz straightened up, the bell rang. Neither man heard it, nor did referee, Charley White, and they were beginning hostilities again when the seconds got into the ring. Sharkey felt he could have finished the fight there had the bell not sounded to give the Cornishman time to recover. "Maybe he would and maybe not," commentated the *Brooklyn Daily Eagle*. The *New York Times* thought Fitz was looking weak and unsteady.

However, Fitz, who by now had almost two decades of experience under his belt, could see the confidence in Tom's eyes. He knew Tom would start to rush him in the second and that is exactly what the Irishman did, eager as he was to drive home his first round advantage.

As Tom came in, Fitz sidestepped to the left and swung his right full into the sailor's face. It dazed Tom. The fighters were in close, their bodies almost touching. Sharkey battered at the Cornishman with blows that "would have felled a young forest", but Fitz returned the punches, a left hook connecting with Tom's chin and putting him down on one knee.

Sharkey took a long count and, when he got up, he did not rush. He let Fitz come to him and took a right and left to the face. Sharkey hugged. Fitz pushed him off and, dropping all pretence of a guard, he hooked his left on the jaw and swung a right onto the left temple. Sharkey's legs went but before he fell another left reached him, although he did not need it.

Sharkey soon came to his senses. Fitz came to his corner and they took a drink out of the same water bottle. They each had cuts over their mouths. In ten minutes, both men were out of the building.

Tom said later: "When Fitzsimmons put me down in Coney Island, I felt no pain whatever. I felt as you do in a nightmare, when you imagine you are falling off a high building and expecting a ton of bricks to come down on you at any minute. But I never hit the ground. Just as I thought I was about to be smashed to pieces, I came to my senses enough to hear the referee counting 'Five'. I knew what was going on after that, but try as I would I could not lift my head from the floor. In ten minutes after the fight, I was in my dressing room without a mark to show where I had been hit and felt no ill effects from the blow. Fitz didn't hit me so hard, but it felt as if someone had swung a crowbar on the point of my jaw. He has the hardest fist in the world."[7] The fighters were both staying at Cohen's Hotel. Tom shook hands with Bob's wife, Rose. "The best man won," he said. "Fitz is the real champion and he will surely beat Jeffries. I never knew anybody could hit such blows."

Fitz said that despite the shortness of the fight, Tom had hurt him. "Gee, but that young fellow can hit an awful wallop," he said. "My arm is very lame from that right swing that I caught on the shoulder [the blow that floored Fitz] and my back is lame too, from a right swing when he got mad and chased me." He had been "nailed…good and plenty" at the end of the first round, he said.

Sharkey's lack of reach, Fitz concluded, was a major factor in the Irishman's two defeats.

"After Ruhlin beat Sharkey, I told O'Rourke that Sharkey might have knocked Ruhlin out if he had stepped in a foot closer when delivering blows, for many of his swings were just a little short," he said. "Last night, I could hear O'Rourke calling to Sharkey, 'Step in, step in' and I had to laugh. The advice was all right, but he stepped in just as I landed him that right in the wind. My fist sunk in up to the wrist and Tom let out a groan… But he came back in game style, and it was just as I predicted - I had to stretch him out perfectly senseless before the decision was mine."

Fitz had crossed to where Jeffries was sitting after the fight and leaned over the ropes to hold out his hand. Jeffries, onlookers said, had reluctantly risen to his feet and caught the fingertips and shook them. There were no wordy challenges. Fitz was saying that he would claim the title if Jeffries did not take him on.[8]

So, where did that leave Tom? He was still making money from the fights – he and Fitz received half of the $25,000 purse that night – but for how much longer would he be an attraction?

The fight game was changing. The *New York Times* described the Fitz fight as a "remarkably brief struggle, the shortest in fact, that the most prominent heavy men of the ring have fought since boxing has been legalized in New York" but the Horton Law days were over.

On August 29, 1900, the boxers marked its passing at Madison Square Garden with exhibition bouts featuring Corbett, McCoy, Maher and Ruhlin. Tom entered the ring draped in an Irish flag and traded blows with a fighter named Jim Guilder. As he was leaving, the 5,000 crowd caught sight of Fitzsimmons arriving and there was a cheer. The two men shook hands and Fitz borrowed the sailor's gloves.

BLOOD, SWEAT AND TEARS

A colour illustration in the very popular weekly The *Utica Saturday Globe* on September 8, 1900, depicted Fitzsimmons, Corbett, Sharkey, McCoy, Ruhlin and Jeffries "Mourning at the Grave of the Departed" Horton Law. The fighters are wiping tearful eyes and laying their gloves like wreaths on the grave.

Tom was living off the image rather than living the boxer's life now. He was rich, very rich. He was lauded on the street. He was a celebrity and this brought him into contact with some of New York's most colourful characters. A central figure in city life was Timothy D "Big Tim" Sullivan, also sometimes called "Dry Dollar". Beginning as an enterprising youth with a single saloon, he developed into a businessman and politician of incredible power. His political style was "simplicity itself", according to Luc Sante, the author of *Low Life*, a fascinating history of New York between 1840 and 1919. "Boys, I'm a Democrat," he said. "I've been a Democrat all my life. I have voted the Democrat ticket straight all my life." Big Tim, Sante writes, was a "genius of the shakedown, which in its most basic form took on the contours of a slightly glorified racket. Local merchants, gamblers, whores, liquor vendors, saloonkeepers and the like would be required to buy tickets to Big Tim's clambakes, chowder suppers, and summer outings to College Point. For the latter, there would be a parade down to the dock with some retired boxer or other acting as Grand Marshall. The boat would be equipped with an open bar, stuss and poker tables, and private rooms for the more distinguished guests."

Sharkey became an honoured guest at Sullivan's colourful celebrations, including the parade held as "a wake for the now dead Horton Law".[9] Sullivan's annual outing on September 10, 1900, took the assorted revellers to Donnelly's Grove, College Point, and, according to the papers, was "probably the largest wake ever held" with at least 6,000 constituents and friends of Senator Sullivan in attendance to enjoy the eating, gambling and boxing bouts. A reporter noted: "Tom Sharkey probably gave his admirers the liveliest time as he ran amuck through the long line of gambling tables and in other ways let his friends know he was present." Sharkey, together with 'Kid' McCoy, escorted Sullivan on the parade through the Bowery to the steamship Grand Republic, while Martin Engel, the Democratic leader of the Eighth Assembly District, marched with them. Two bands played and the captain announced the steamship was full when 3,400 people had squeezed on board. And the 400 more pushed their way up the gangplank. Every spare corner of the ship was "packed with some gambling device". At Donnelly's Grove, there was a scramble for the breakfast table and a feast of clam fritters, eels and cutlets was disposed of in about ten minutes. Two Italian prize-fighters then fought themselves into the ground and then it was back to the gambling and the 122 machines and tables which had been laid out throughout the grove. There was red and black, hazard, sweat, three-card monte, Dewey poker, Klondike, chuke-a-luck, wheel game, faro, roulette, stuss bottle game and craps. Each table owner shouted: "The only straight gambling game here." Police officers of the Seventy-Sixth precinct were hanging around but only to keep the crowds from pushing the gamblers. Tom Sharkey was having more fun at the grove than he was in the ring. "The pugilist was feeling a particularly good humour after having been entertained by numerous admirers," said the New York Times. "Followed by a crowd, he started through Gamblers' Row. He stopped at each table, as if he was going to place some money on the games. But instead he brought his fist down with a bang on the table, making the money fly in every direction. The gamblers and patrons took this in good part, as they had great respect for Sharkey."

At one table, Tom disturbed the dice as someone was playing. The owner called off the bet.

"That ain't fair," protested the young gambler. "I won and that big duffer upset the dice."

"That's Sharkey. Look out!" whispered several people in the crowd. The differences were settled. Tom's playfulness may have been good natured but it appeared to favour Sullivan's game owners!

There was still fight rumour though, first of a third battle with Jeffries. Terms were actually agreed at the end of 1900 for a Nevada contest but those plans fell down.

BLOOD, SWEAT AND TEARS

In February 1901, a legal row broke out in Cincinnati over a planned Jeffries-Ruhlin contest (a heavyweight championship bout which was eventually prevented by the governor of Ohio). Tom went along to the city with "Spider" Kelly and planned to challenge the winner.

There were plans to fight McCoy in San Francisco and discussions about a fight with Maher as, at that time, both Sharkey and Maher claimed to be Champion of Ireland. The authorities were, as ever, in the sidelines though. "The bout will probably take place at Louisville or San Francisco, as these two states are the only two left where a big battle can be pulled off," it was stated.[10]

In the end, Tom found himself in Denver on May 3, 1901, to fight a local champion named Fred Russell, who stood well over 6 feet 2 inches tall. Tom trained for a month in the city getting acclimatized to the altitude for the ten rounds planned for the arena of the Colorado Athletic Association. He entered the ring at 190 pounds, about a stone lighter than Russell. It was a rough, tumble bout, with both fighters clinching and Russell trying and succeeding to throw Sharkey to the floor several times. In the fourth, Sharkey broke away from a clinch and, as he did so, landed right and left swings on Russell's jaw, putting him down. As Russell rose, Sharkey sent in a half-swing on the ear which laid Russell out. The fight was fought under a cloud: referee Frank Cullen declared all bets off before the boxers entered the ring, in order, he claimed, "to protect the club and its patrons". There were rumours that there was an agreement of some sort between the fighters.

Four days later, Tom fought another local fighter at the Olympic Athletic Club at Cripple Creek, a difficult venue and not just because it is at 9,800 feet. While the rumours ahead of the Russell fight had implicated both boxers, only Tom himself would have reason to question what happened at Cripple Creek. He lost in the first round when "Mexican" Pete Everett received a body blow which sent him to his knees. While he was down, it was said, Sharkey struck him on the head and the referee gave the fight to Everett.[11] However, another version of the fight contends that Tom's knockout blow to Everett's jaw was entirely fair.

When the referee called a 'foul', Tom protested and found the referee covering him with a six-shooter.

"I said, 'Foul'," stated the referee from behind the pistol.

"Oh, very well," replied Sharkey.[12]

Despite the local 'support' for Everett, Tom met him outside the ring and offered a rematch at once for $1,000 a side. Everett accepted but their friends dragged them apart.

Fighters were turning to the mat and catch-as-catch-can wrestling. In December 1900, a benefit had been arranged for the family of late sports writer Hugh S Hart at the Grand Central Palace, New York, which featured, among others, Jeffries, John L Sullivan, Sharkey, Corbett, Ruhlin and Maher.

There were challenges and boasts too. Sharkey and Tom Jenkins, the best wrestler in the United States, spent time debating which was best, boxing or wrestling. Jenkins, later a wrestling instructor at West Point, remembered: "I was the undisputed heavyweight champion wrestler of America when friends of myself and Sharkey got into a discussion regarding the relative merits of boxing and wrestling.[13]

"I was firmly of the belief that a good wrestler, using all the holds legalized in his sport, could easily master the greatest of boxers using their special blows, and I felt positive that I could pin any boxer's shoulders to the mat before he had a chance to shoot in his famous punches.

"Tom Sharkey was present and he proposed that we retire to the gymnasium with a few of our friends and give my theory a test. Tom was ever eager to engage in any kind of rough-house stunts, and he was elated to meet me. We stripped and entered the ring, each to battle in his own way. The result - well, I hate to tell it. Sharkey surprised me by doing the unexpected, and so decisively that there was no question as to who was the superior."

Tom kept that bout with the wrestler firm in his mind – he was proud of taking on a man like Jenkins. "It ended just as I expected," he said. "Jenkins thought he had the contest clinched and rushed at me with his arms outstretched just as if he were ready to grab me about the waist, raise me as he would a barrel, and toss me for a goal. Before he had taken three steps, I ran out of my corner, was right on top of him, and, with a few wild wallops, sent him into dreamland. Jenkins acknowledged after that that he thought the half-nelson and hammerlock a splendid defence in wrestling, but agreed that the right or left to the chin, coming with the force that I let loose, was far more effective in the matter of downing an opponent."[14]

On June 11, 1901 the contest was for money. Tom went to Cleveland, Ohio, and a crowd of between 8,000 and 10,000 watched him grapple with Jenkins. They fought on the terms that Jenkins should throw Sharkey twice in an hour. No holds were barred. The first round had gone nineteen minutes when Jenkins threw Sharkey with an upright double Nelson hold. After an interval of fifteen minutes, the second round began. The men struggled for twenty-one minutes before Sharkey's shoulders were forced to the floor a second time.

Tom, and Fitzsimmons and Jenkins, were later challenged by the middleweight wrestler Leo Pardello to a catch-as-catch-can or Greco Roman style wrestle. Peter Maher was on the mat too and, unable to get Maher in the ring for the so-called Championship of Ireland, Tom fought with him at the grounds of the Philadelphia American League Club, Philadelphia on June 21. It ended in a draw. Sharkey won the first fall at catch-as-catch-can in seven minutes and ten seconds. In the second Peter won in two minutes and twenty-five seconds. The third fall was at the Graeco Roman style but although they pulled and hauled away at each other for twenty minutes neither secured the decider. (Tom would eventually meet Pardello – the Italian champion – on the mat on March 10, 1905, before 2,000 fans in Brooklyn. Tom took the honours as Pardello failed to throw him twice within an hour.)

Although threatening to turn his entire attention to wrestling, Tom was still the main contender listed in November 1901 when Ruhlin put up a poor attempt to take Jeffries' heavyweight title. [15] Tom was more confident than others that he would get another match with the champ, though. When Tom said, "While I am waiting to hear from Jeffries, I might as well take on someone else," one boxing writer retorted: "Yes, indeed, while he is waiting to hear from Jeffries, he might as well take on everyone that comes along. He will have plenty of time."[16] All the same, articles were signed for a third dramatic Jeffries-Sharkey fight, this time back on the West Coast. Barney Reich handled the negotiations for Tom and the twenty-round contest would take place before the Yosemite Athletic Club of San Francisco sometime between March 17 and April 30, 1902. It would be the third fight of Tom's career to be billed as a heavyweight championship title decider.

Tom's preparations were eagerly followed by the public and reporters. He trained in a gym at the back of a house called Homecrest in Brooklyn, the home of the Sullivan Boys, boxers William "Spike" Sullivan and his brother, Dave, who Sharkey was training.[17] "Spike" built two punching bag platforms for Sharkey while the contender ran the local roads. But even as Tom trained, there were rumours that Fitzsimmons – with whom Tom fought a five-round exhibition in December 1901 - had finally decided to fight competitively again. Tom feared being frozen out.[18]

"What is all this talk about a match between Jeffries and Fitzsimmons?" he demanded of a newspaper man early in 1902. "Why, I'm going to fight Jeffries and have signed articles, so what chance has Fitzsimmons got to meet him?"

The reporter asked what Tom thought of Fitzsimmons' claim that he was returning to the ring.

"I don't believe it and, what's more, Bob has declared time and again that he is done with the ring. This Jeffries crowd know that and they know that he means it. Besides, why are they so anxious to take on Bob? Jeffries beat him by knocking him out and the best he could do with me was to get the decision and a wrong one at that. If Jeffries wants to fight Fitz, why don't he wait until he is through with me?

"I think he shows by his action that he thinks Bob is easier game than I am or he wouldn't be so anxious to take him on."

Tom, whose training included ninety minutes on the punchbag, the skipping rope and three fast rounds with Bob Armstrong, had lost none of his hope that one day he would lift the title. "I'm going to be the heavyweight champion of the world within a few months," he boasted. "I am going to win from Jeffries decisively this time. After that, it will be time enough for him to talk of fighting Fitzsimmons."

Then, with Jeffries in New York and staying at the Vanderbilt Hotel, Tom travelled to Philadelphia after Maher agreed to his demands for a Championship of Ireland fight. The bout, though, was to be of little credit to a nation with such a rich pugilistic history.

They met on January 17, 1902 and to onlookers, it looked less like a battle for an honoured crown than a fight between two friends, which was what in reality it was. It was scheduled for six rounds, with both men cannily getting a hand each on a cheque for 70 per cent of the gross gate receipts before stepping through the ropes. The fight reached only the third round *before* the referee, Billy Rocap, raised his hand and declared it was not on the level and that he "would officiate no longer". Both fighters had looked in good condition but had delivered only what boxing writers of time termed "love taps". One wrote that "before the battle (they) expressed confidence in their ability to knock out any one or any thing. They succeeded in knocking away a large amount of their prestige, which has been slowly dwindling for the past few seasons."

In Sharkey and Maher's defence, the law in Philadelphia made things as difficult as it did now in New York to hold a full-on contest. Before they had gone into the ring both men had been arrested on a complaint that the law was about to be violated. Hauled up before a magistrate, the two Irishmen had been made to promise there would be no knock-out, no violence and "no infraction of the state laws regarding prize-fights". They were then bound over under $5,000 bonds to keep the peace, and to return to court the following morning to prove to the magistrate that there had been no violation of the law.

The men went back to court the next day and were discharged, having successfully persuaded the magistrate that there had been no "overt act which might be construed as a violation of the statute prohibiting prize-fighting". Tom, though, was livid at his treatment in the city. He angrily denied the bout was a fake and blamed the club officials for deceiving the public.

"Figure out my position," he said afterwards, "and see what you think of it. I was between the devil and the deep sea. Peter and I had forfeits up to box before the club. The police step in and make us furnish bonds not to fight.

"Suppose we had not gone on? We would have lost our forfeit. If we had fought we would have forfeited our bonds. The club officials knew this, and took the money off the public, knowing that we would not be allowed to furnish the sport expected.

"I did my best to furnish a good exhibition and I could do no more. Everybody knows that I am a fighter and not a boxer. It was left to the referee to explain the situation to the audience and he only half did it.

"Does anyone suppose that I intended to fake when I know how it would affect my reputation, and the receipts of my coming fight with Jeffries?"

He offered to fight Maher again somewhere else and added: "If the public will think this thing out I think they will understand my position and see that I did the only thing possible. If there is blame to be attached it must go to the club officials and not to Peter and me."

Whatever happened before the magistrate, it was an unwritten law which affected the boxers' reputation with the public and the fans: the one that 'outlawed' fakes. It seemed Tom would pay for the aborted 'no contest' appearance with Maher: and the price would be his chance to get back in the ring with the champ, Jeffries.

Jeffries and Fitzsimmons were seated close to the ring that night in Philadelphia for the Sharkey-Maher fight. And it would be eventually those two, the spectators that night, who fought for the world championship that summer.

At first, Tom still hoped he would have his man and Jeffries was reported as saying kindly that "nobody save his old friend Sharkey shall have the honour and pleasure of the first thrashing at his hands". Then news came in that the Yosemite Athletic Club had declined the bout because they feared the authorities would call it off. The poor contest between Sharkey and Maher then apparently sealed the fate of the Sharkey-Jeffries fight. Jeffries went on to fight Fitzsimmons in San Francisco on July 25, knocking him out in the eighth round.

Tom Sharkey must have been greatly depressed to miss his chance to fight Jeffries for a third time, although it is doubtful he would have done any better than Fitzsimmons. In fact, by the time that fight took place, Tom had travelled three thousand miles for another vicious ring battle which he would have to win to prove that he was not down and out as a title challenger.

In 1902, a series of events were arranged in London to celebrate the coronation of King Edward VII. England was welcoming visitors from around the world as it marked the end of the Boer War and prepared to greet its new King. Celebration was the order of the day and the carnival of sports was to be the biggest in the country's history, featuring a galaxy of fistic stars such as "had never before appeared within the walls of the historic National Sporting Club of London".

The coronation itself was eventually to be postponed as the public read breathless newspaper reports of the "stricken" King's fight against illness, but the tournament opened on June 21 and lasted for four days. It began with Graeco-Roman wrestling for the world title with competitions between grapplers from Cambridge, Oxford, Yale and a number of public schools taking up the afternoon session. Later, the welterweights, including Canadian world champion, Eddie Connolly, took the ring. Joe Walcott and Tommy Ryan took part in the following days, and on Wednesday, June 25, Sharkey and Gus Ruhlin, who had both travelled from the United States, would again take to the ring to fight each other. "Never before in ring history was such a galaxy of ring celebrities gathered for a display of fisticuffs and the notables who attended the boxing matches were highly pleased," noted *The Ring*, 50 years later, as it previewed bouts planned to celebrate another coronation, that of Elizabeth II.

Back in 1902, in Irish Nationalist Dundalk, there was less of a feeling of celebration over the coming coronation. And any celebration at all was likely to be forced.

On June 7, a letter appeared in the *Dundalk Democrat* from "A Dundalk Nationalist" which gave a view on the future King Edward VII's upcoming coronation from Sharkey's former community and noted that "loyalists" in Ireland would be making "merry" like many in London.

"I believe the Great Northern Railway Works will be closed on Coronation Day and the employees, who are mostly Nationalists, thrown idle and their day's pay stopped. Would not this be a terrible state of affairs, the men's feelings represented by being compelled to keep a holiday in honour of England's King, who has branded them as idolators [sic], and then being at a loss of their pay into the bargain. Surely the men will have spirit enough to protest against this. I daresay the directors of the Great Northern Railway are 'loyalists' but that is no reason why they try to force a display of loyalist sentiment from their Nationalist workmen."

He went on: "There may be some feeble attempts made, even about Dundalk, to misrepresent the feelings of its Nationalist and Catholic citizens, and therefore I would advise the people to keep their eyes open. Nationalist Ireland will not celebrate the coronation of Britain's King but will stand sullenly aloof from all such celebrations until the day arrives when we shall regain what lawfully belongs to us and be able to say, 'We are nation still'."

Sharkey, though, the same paper revealed, had reasons for fighting at the coronation contest which would not put him at odds with the people back home.

"His contest…was inspired by a sentimental determination to wrest from Ruhlin, who is a Dutchman, the Championship of Ireland, which he won from Peter Maher in Philadelphia in March last. Sharkey considers that for a Dutchman to be Champion of Ireland is a stigma on the Irish race. For the encounter, Sharkey has for the past month been giving plenty of work to the bevy of trainers to get him into the best possible condition, having been located at the Two Brewers, Chipperfield."

Local journalists hoped he would add "fresh laurels" to his name in the fight against Ruhlin. "Sharkey's great failing is his shortness of arm but for a man of his inches he is a veritable 'terror'."

There was personal and nationalist pride on the line and big money too. The *Sporting Chronicle* noted: "Naturally, for such an important encounter as this, no less than £1,000 had to be offered to secure the match, in addition to which the men had a side wager of £500, which amount is the largest sum boxed for in England since the memorable encounter between Peter Jackson and Frank Slavin. Both men have brilliant records."

Now aged 29, Sharkey was well-known in England, and so, to a lesser extent, was Ruhlin. As *The Ring* noted: "Sharkey enhanced the prestige to the tournament, though he was past his prime". His reputation was not going to protect him inside the ring. The 32-year-old "Akron Giant" stood 6 feet 1½ inches and weighed over 15 stone (210 pounds).

In Tom's corner was Tommy Ryan, who had been Jeffries' second against Sharkey at Coney Island, Sam Fitzpatrick and "Spike" Sullivan. The legendary Jem "Gypsy" Mace, who had worked with Fitzsimmons and Dan Creedon, were in Ruhlin's corner, along with Billy Madden.

Ruhlin looked "much superior" from the start, but Sharkey was never short of courage and took the fight to him in the early stages, charging his opponent "like a tiger". The problem would be Ruhlin's reach: it would allow the Ohioan to box cautiously, wait for Sharkey to tire and then inflict heavy punishment.

As the *Sporting Chronicle* explained: "From the outset it was apparent that if Sharkey had any chance, it was to force matters. This he certainly did, although his disadvantage in reach severely handicapped him. He had to be several times cautioned for holding and hitting rather low while Ruhlin on the other hand fought with considerable cleverness."

After a slight spar in round one, Ruhlin led with his left but was met with an effective counter to the body from Sharkey. The Irishman clinched and held, and was quickly in trouble with the referee. "Ruhlin slipped down and his adversary became too impetuous, and was nearly disqualified through striking his man before he had gained his feet. Sharkey was very busy when the round ended."

When the fight resumed Sharkey was again cautioned for holding and Ruhlin took control of the centre of the ring. Three times he jabbed the sailor on the face and got nothing back. Sharkey then missed a wild uppercut with his left and before he could recover, his opponent drove a left and then a right home to the head just as the bell rang.

In the third, both men boxed for the head with little success although Sharkey landed one left jab to Ruhlin's face.

Both men were guilty of holding in the fourth but a clean jab to Sharkey's face left him looking "flushed" and "distressed" and he "appeared pleased" when the round ended. Tom came out to take more punishment, but tried everything to disguise the fact that the fight was slipping away from him. "This is not so easy for you as in New York," he told Ruhlin.

The bravado fooled no-one at ringside. In the sixth, Sharkey looked "used up", a nasty cut now worrying him over his eye. "With his usual gameness however he kept going after his big rival in determined style." Sharkey was running on instinct. When Ruhlin backed him into a corner in the seventh, Sharkey showed excellent footwork and got out of danger. In the eighth, he took further punishment and in the ninth, he was forced back onto the ropes and was hit hard with both fists in the ribs.

All the same, in the tenth, Sharkey goaded Ruhlin again: "You could not beat me with a hammer!"

"However, for once," noted an onlooker sadly, "the sailor boy's ideas were wrong."

Sharkey tried to rush Ruhlin but took a hefty punch on the draw, staggered and reeled back his corner.

Sharkey was out on his feet now and when he stood up for the eleventh he clutched Ruhlin around the neck and dragged him around the ring. Eventually they broke and every time Ruhlin struck Sharkey went down. Four times in all. Sharkey got up each time but the last time, he struggled to his feet, he really did not know where he was. As the round ended, Sharkey's corner went to his aid and tried to get him ready for another push. But Tommy Ryan, one of his seconds, knew the game was up. He walked over to Ruhlin's corner and gave in on Sharkey's behalf.

Ruhlin walked across the ring to shake his opponent by the hand and left the ring, some onlookers said, without a scratch on him.

Sharkey remained where he was, tears rolling down his cheeks. "It was somewhat pathetic to see such a game boxer in tears," decided a reporter with the *Sporting Chronicle*. A reporter filing for American newspapers said the fight had been "one of the most determined and desperate struggles ever witnessed in the National Sporting Club".

Some observers said Sharkey, reduced almost to insensibility, then raged against his seconds for their intervention. All agree he was cut, beaten and angry.

Back in Ireland, Tom's family and the old fans who had followed his fistic adventures closely through the pages of the *Dundalk Democrat* read what appeared to be an obituary for that career. The sports columnist known as 'Philistine' wrote that not even "Herculean" Sharkey could continue to take such "thumpings" as that handed out by Ruhlin. "While it is generally thought that Ruhlin must have come on immensely in his form," he concluded sadly, "the usual opinion is that the sailor has gone back very much, and now has not much else but his undauntable pluck to recommend him."

Losing the £2,000 purse and getting beaten by Ruhlin again would have been only part of the disappointment; realising he was no longer the fighter he once was would have poured salt on the stinging wounds, wounds laid open by the realisation he would never have the chance to fight for the world title again; but perhaps on that special night there was a wound that went deeper still. For, there in the crowd, was Tom's father James Sharkey who had come to watch his son in a big fight for the first time. James Sharkey, now 78, had travelled to London to celebrate his son's successes on the world stage, but instead he was watching the sun setting on the brightest period of his career.

CHAPTER TEN
"I'll marry you, but give up the gloves."

The fight game at the end of the 19th Century may have been more brutal, less sleek, than that of today, but much was the same. The fighters were superstars, with public interest in their lives extending to events outside the ring.

Sharkey enjoyed a level of celebrity shared by the top heavyweights of the time, an interest in his life which sports stars in the early years of the 21st Century would recognise.

Like many latter-day stars Tom developed a keen interest in running a business – or, at least, attaching his name to one – and to the race track. Those business affairs, stories about his private life and his relationships with women became a regular source of copy for newspapers and gossip columns.

On August 8, 1900, a piece in the *Brooklyn Daily Eagle* suggested that Tom was taking an "extraordinary interest in groceries" although only "when [a] pretty cashier is around". The rumour was that the Sheepshead Bay-based boxer was planning to marry a Jennie Tuttle, who "deals out change in the grocery store owned by Heffner and Pillion, on Voorhees Avenue, near East Twenty-Third Street", near Tom's home. (Sharkey was living at

126 Voorhees Avenue with his sister, Rose, and a servant. Tom's friend and sparring partner, Bob Armstrong, was at 127.) The boxer had "of late…been seen passing many moments in the store". The report added: "Neither will admit nor deny the rumour and anxious residents in the Bay are waiting for the truth to come out. Miss Tuttle is the daughter of a retired sea captain, who settled in the Bay and became prominent in the affairs of the village." The *Milwaukee Journal* also reported the engagement of Sharkey and 19-year-old Miss Tuttle, who it called 'The Belle of Sheepshead Bay'.[1] The family's connections would have seemed to have suited Tom, who more and more, was mixing with those with one foot on the political rostrum and the other in jail. The Tuttles were close to the family of the late John Y McKane who had been a leading figure on Coney Island and in New York's Tammany Hall political scene until a major corruption scandal which saw him end up in Sing Sing.

However, the stories about Tom and Jennie were just gossip. When Sharkey did marry it was to someone he had known since he was an up-and-coming contender – and to someone who would have a major effect on his now fading career.

Katherine McIntosh was only five feet five inches tall and weighed 120 pounds, but she would do something men the size of great oaks had failed to do - get Tom to abandon the prize-ring.[2]

It did, though, take her some time to get her man.

The couple had first met in the summer of 1896 when Katherine and her mother – the wife of a wealthy Scottish-born farmer, David McIntosh, from Broadaxe, Michigan – had been guests at the Avery House, at Mount Clemens, a pretty little health resort in the state.

Katherine was turning heads. She was just 17, demure, slim and petite, with big dark eyes and long jet black hair.

One day as she sat in the veranda with her mother, she noticed a big, square-shouldered young man, tastefully dressed and quiet and unobtrusive in his manner. He cast a sheepish glance at her but tried not to be too forward.

"Who is that man?" Mrs McIntosh asked a friend.

"I'LL MARRY YOU, BUT GIVE UP THE GLOVES."

"That's Tom Sharkey, the prize-fighter from New York," came the reply.

Mrs McIntosh drew a breath of delight: she had never seen a real live prize-fighter before. Neither had her daughter.

Sharkey did not look as though he would hurt anybody: he was particularly keen about his appearance out of the ring and always dressed smartly.

There would be no harm in meeting him, Katherine coaxed her mother. It would be wonderful! Obviously intrigued herself, Mrs McIntosh quickly gave in and Tom Sharkey was introduced.

The Irishman, it was said later, stammered and blushed like a schoolgirl as he bowed to Katherine and her mother.

At first, he was too embarrassed to say more than, "How d'ye do? I'm pleased to meet you".

However, by the next morning he had recovered his nerve and ventured into a more lengthy chat.

Sometime later, probably during 1902, Katherine McIntosh went to New York to train to be a nurse and she and Tom became friends again.

Eventually, after spending some time with Katherine, Tom who was now in his late twenties, decided to ask her to marry him. Friends said he felt sure the answer would be yes. He was right but only up to a point and the condition Katherine put on her acceptance "almost knocked him out."

"Yes, Tom," said Katherine. "I will marry you provided you never take part in another fight."

The words hit Sharkey like a punch to the solar plexus. He still had not faced up to the fact that his career was on the slide, that the days of his being a world championship contender must be over. He still wanted a third fight with Jeffries.

"I'm within one of the championship now," he told her. "I'm sure I can whip Jeffries in another fight."

Katherine knew her mind.

"No, Tom. You must give it up. You really have all the money you need. There is no reason for you to fight."

The prize-ring had been Sharkey's life. But on February 27,

1904, he went to Philadelphia and stepped inside the ropes for what he promised would be the last time. It was a tough contest in front of 7,000 people and, although Tom had the better of the first round, knocking his opponent to the ground, he was outclassed for the remainder of the fight by a fast improving miner named Jack Monroe.[3] Monroe, trained by McCoy, was as rough and tough as Tom, who was now fading. The fast fist work had the crowd screaming throughout and the "wrestling tactics" exhibited by both men came to a head when Monroe slammed him down on the ring floor.

The bout ended after six rounds with no decision – clearing the way for Tom to surrender to Katherine's soft dark eyes and coal black hair. The promise made, the gloves hung up, Katherine and Tom were finally married at 7pm on June 7, 1904, at St Thomas the Apostle church in West 118th Street.[4]

The celebrations then started over on 144 East Fourteenth Street where a few years earlier Tom had begun concentrating on another area of his life: where to invest the money he had earned in the ring.

To start with, back in 1901, Sharkey's business life initially pitted him against his friend, Tom O'Rourke. They had both wanted the lease on a property in 144 East Fourteenth Street which was owned by a pawnbroker named John Stich. O'Rourke had approached Stich and offered him an annual rent of $5,500. But Sharkey too wanted to get into the saloon business. He teamed up with another friend named Bernard Reich and offered the same rent over ten years and said he would pay for the necessary alterations to the building. Stich shook on the deal and the next day when O'Rourke came to sign the lease he was told that his former fighting protégé had taken the place.[5]

Sharkey's Bar was to attract all sorts of attention with the police staying on full alert to enforce city licensing laws. The *New York Times* of November 24, 1901, described a midnight "sortie" by Acting Police Captain Churchill and fifteen officers of the Bowery and Third Avenue which ensured that by 1am the area was "as dry as the desert of Sahara". Churchill had sent out word

"I'LL MARRY YOU, BUT GIVE UP THE GLOVES."

that the saloons must close at midnight or there would be arrests. "Half a dozen bartenders and one or two proprietors were caught in the dragnet and locked up on the charge of violating the liquor tax law," said the report. Although there were no reported arrests at Sharkey's, it was among the places raided, along with McGurk's Suicide Hall, the Drydock Hotel and Merrimac Hall in Third Avenue. Sharkey's was among those places too which served the Raines Law sandwich. The Raines Hotel Law, passed in 1896, declared it illegal to sell drink on Sundays except with meals in hotels. Consequently, saloons with a number of rooms began calling themselves hotels and left on the tables inedible sandwiches which just got them passed the law. The Raines Law sandwiches, slowly going stale and turning green, were much in evidence in the rear room of Sharkey's where drinks were served, the tables being "embellished and garnished with minute samples of these old-time friends".[6] Drinkers would pretend to nibble at the snacks as police officers went by.

However, the officers only walked on by for a short time. On February 23, 1902, an Inspector Cross led a massive raid in which 100 plain clothes officers crammed into six patrol wagons. They were heading for the city's "disreputable resorts" – those, which according to the *New York Times*, were "most infested with vice and crime". Sharkey's place had already built up such a reputation that, following investigations by an undercover team of detectives, it was the first place visited. The police had decided to arrest all the proprietors, managers and women found in the rear rooms of the saloons. However, the boxer was away watching a prize-fight in Louisville, Kentucky. Ten women from the saloon were taken into custody and charged with disorderly conduct.

However, the *New York Times* in April 1902, described how Sharkey's bar was still taking on the 'dry Sunday' law. As midnight approached one Saturday night, the saloon was "wide open and running in full blast". The reporter on the scene said: "At midnight, the lights in the front saloon and upstairs were extinguished and business at the bar was suspended. But in the rear room, the crowds were so dense that there was only standing room. This resort was the only one on Fourteenth Street that remained open.

"Sharkey was in the saloon, giving orders to a small army of waiters, who worked their way through the dense crowds with trays loaded with drinks.

"The side door was open and anybody could enter without meeting the slightest opposition. Reporters saw a number of policemen in civilian clothes in the place but it could not be learned whether or not they were on police business. They mingled in the crowds, drinking and seemingly having a good time."

As well as the police, saloon owners had temperance campaigner, Carrie Nation, to deal with. She was noted for 'raiding' bars and saloons to crash bottles and glasses to the ground, sweeping them off tables with a hatchet. She would even snatch cigars and cigarettes from smokers' mouths and stamp them under foot. Tom, it was said, feared her more than the police but, although his saloon apparently escaped her attentions, he did not. One day on Broadway, he saw her coming the other way. He prepared himself for the worst but she just smiled and told him: "You're just a big boy and will do better than to fight and drink and gamble some day."

The apparently friendly greeting – by the standards of someone who usually announced her arrival with the swing of an axe – still unnerved Tom. "That's the lady I was afraid of," he said later.[7]

Tom saw other threats to the liquor trade too and was always happy to talk about them. One night he stood outside his saloon and, prompted by the sight of two slim youngsters running down the street, began to grumble to the celebrated sports writer, Robert Edgren, about a new fitness fad.[8] "That's the thing that is knocking out the liquor business," Tom said. "The whole country is getting the athletic bug. Everybody's crazy over these Olympic games. Everybody wants to be an athlete. A fellow can't be a fighter or an athlete and drink at the same time.

"Lots of cafes are going out of business. I notice in my place that there isn't near as much whisky drunk as there was a year or so ago. People who drink, make it beer. I read in some of the papers that people buy beer because it's cheap and because they can't

"I'LL MARRY YOU, BUT GIVE UP THE GLOVES."

afford to buy whisky or wines. That isn't it at all. If a fellow wants whisky he's going to buy it, and if he wants some kind of a wine, he isn't going to drink beer.

"The thing that is doing the most damage to the liquor trade is schoolboy athletics. Now a schoolboy is brought up to be an athlete. He has training ideas hammered into him every day. He's taught that he can't be an athlete and drink or smoke, and that he mustn't drink or smoke. And he doesn't do it when he grows up, either. He likes to keep in good athletic condition. The college boys used to come down in a mob after the big football games and lick up everything in sight. They don't do it any more because the colleges are full of this athletic idea and the college boys have no use for a guy who drinks whisky and gets out of shape."

While the trend was bad for business, Tom recognised the consequences for the nation he loved might be quite different.

"Schoolboy athletics are costing me money every day," he said, "but don't mistake me. The idea is dead right and I'm for it. I've been called a 'tightwad', but I don't want to make money at the expense of boys. I'd rather see every kid in New York an athlete and cutting out booze and cigarettes. I hate to see a boy starting in to drink. If a man wants to drink something now and then when he's out for a good time, I think it's all right, but I'm for this schoolboy athletic business. It's going to make this the healthiest nation on earth!"

As Tom recognised, he had developed a reputation for being careful with his money. In October 1903 when police swooped on the Clarendon Hall at 114 East Thirteenth Street to break up a prize-fight, they made 65 arrests, although most of those detained gave the names Smith, Jones and Brown. A number of local politicians and businessmen came forward to post bail for those arrested. Tom had obviously been involved in the organisation of the fight in some way and the referee rushed round to see him. "Haven't got my check book with me," he was told.[9]

Another tale revolved around a mouse which it was joked Tom kept for "sentimental" reasons. The story went that one night while Tom was asleep the mouse had crawled into his pocket book and chewed up a dollar bill. As Tom so hated to part with a buck, he kept the mouse as a pet.[10]

However, there were at least as many testimonies to his generosity and even the stories where he came out badly, often showed a keen wit. As one fan remembered: "The truth was that Sharkey wasn't a fool with his money and didn't like to be made a sucker out of. But he was open-handed enough when it came to helping deserving cases and when making the rounds with the boys, paid up like a man."

Once, while sitting with a boxing writer in the back room of his saloon, Tom was disturbed by a "flashily dressed chap (who) rushed…to Tom with the intention of making a hurry-up touch".

"Tom," said the man excitedly. "Pass me a twenty quick! I've a swell dame waitin' in a cab outside, promised to take her to dinner – and I find I've forgotten my wallet."

Sharkey gazed at him, unconvinced.

"Hmm," he said. "Ye have a swell dame, hey? An' ye want to take her to dinner?"

"Sure, Tom, that's it. But get a move on, won't you?"

"An' ye want twenty dollars," said the boxer, still friendly. "Well, say me bucko, what was yer figurin' on feedin' her? Goldfish?"[11]

Stories often praised Tom as a 'funny man' but some took the tone of the 'dumb Irishman' stereotype. It was rumoured that wily Tim McGrath, an Irishman himself, used to meet Tom with the takings after he had fought and would place a high stack of one-dollar bills and a smaller stack of larger notes on the table. Tom, so boxing legend goes, always took the bigger stack because as he said he "did all the fightin'". Nice tale, but the fortune he massed up suggested that he knew which stack would have had the most value.

During a severe storm in August 1904, a big flagpole on Tammany Hall – home to many of Tom's political friends in the Democratic Party - opposite Tom's saloon, was struck by lightning and three feet of wood with a large big ball on top fell into the street. Tom ran out, carried it inside and said it matched another pole he already had in his place after it, too, had been struck from the building the year before. He told drinkers the event was

"I'LL MARRY YOU, BUT GIVE UP THE GLOVES."

"a sign of good luck for the Democratic ticket".

The decor had been the topic of conversation when Jim Corbett had visited Tom's saloon soon after it had opened.

"Nice place, Tom," Corbett told him. "Except it needs a chandelier."

"And who would play it?" came the reply.[12]

Just as 21st Century celebrities both seek and complain about attention, Tom could too. Once, while training on Staten Island, he was approached by an over-enthusiastic young fan, intrigued by the tattoo of the three-masted ship which Tom had had on his chest since his navy days.

"I see you've got a ship on your chest," said the man.

There was no reply from the fighter known to the boxing world as "Sailor" Tom. He continued getting a rubdown.

The man spoke again, a little louder: "I see you wear a ship across your chest."

But there was still no reply.

Unfazed the young man raised his voice a little more. "I see you've got a ship there on your chest," he said.

Sharkey did not turn to him but he, at last, opened his mouth. "Son," said the sailor flatly, "you knew the ship's there because you've seen it. But I'd know I had a fool talking to me even if I was looking the other way."[13]

As well as the dollar bill eating mouse, dogs often feature in the Sharkey legend. One animal which Tom apparently tried to groom in his own image was a pit bull terrier which typically the Irishman thought could "lick" anything which came at him. One day Tom was out training in the country with the terrier at his heels when a shaggy old farmer's dog leapt out of the hedge and set about Tom's animal. The pit bull slunk off and Tom decided he would get another.[14]

A rather more gentle, shaggy-dog-tale made the *New York Times* in June 1909, when Tom posted a message in the 'Lost' column to recover a two-year-old black cocker spaniel, which had been given to the boxer by a friend. Tom only had the dog a few weeks and it had escaped from a kennel in his stables. "The dog slipped its moorings and got adrift," explained the old sailor. "It's all the fault of my stable boy, who tied the dog with a granny knot instead of a regular half hitch."

Journalists obviously liked to hang around Tom and, like his peers in boxing then and now, he was not afraid to try to get publicity anyway he could. When his career faded, that sometimes took more elaborate forms than getting into the ring to make wild pronouncements and challenges, and on one occasion got him into trouble. In January 1904, Tom was arrested on the East Drive of Central Park after a confusing incident in which he had apparently had an argument with a man and floored him with a punch. With his opponent on the ground, and with a crowd now watching, Tom had bowed and allowed himself to be taken to the police station. However, when the Officer Cavanagh discovered the injured party was a man named Gus Pixley, an actor from the Majestic Theatre, and when Pixley withdrew the complaint and apologised to Tom for being in his road, Cavanagh and his sergeant began to smell a rat. Their fears that the whole charade was just a publicity stunt were then confirmed when they realised Sharkey was, at the time, preparing for his up-coming fight with Jack Monroe. Cavanagh was not pleased as he let the men go: "My notion is that I made a fool arrest and that I heard a frozen laugh of a press agent from behind a bush when I was leading my prisoner to the Arsenal. First thing you know, Sharkey will be playing the part of the human spider in a drama for children. Next time I meet a bunch like that making a row in the park, I'll swing my club and then send for three ambulances - one for the prize-fighter, one for the actor and another for the press agent." Although the police were red-faced, the stunt undoubtedly worked: it made the *New York Times*.

As well as publicity stunts, Tom was also happy to do endorsements. In April 1905, billed as "one of the world's best boxers", he was seen in American newspapers promoting Radium Radia, a treatment for back problems. In an open letter to the company, featured in the ad, Tom said the liniment had been recommended to him after a recent "attack of lumbago in the back, which was

"I'LL MARRY YOU, BUT GIVE UP THE GLOVES."

so painful, and disabled me to such an extent that for several days I was unable to bend over to tie my shoes". However, "after two good rubs with your liniment, the Lumbago entirely left me and I have not since suffered a return of it". In addition, Tom said he had taken on wrestling legend Leo Pardello that March and had wrenched one of his knees so badly that "it swelled to such an extent and was so painful that I was in great misery for several days". Two or three applications of Radium Radia, though, and the pain was relieved. "I lose no opportunity," added the man whose body had been battered and pounded for 15 years or so, "in recommending it to athletes of all kinds." He had heard nothing but good from all who had used it and "I must say it is the quickest cure for relieving soreness and stiffness of the muscles I have ever used."[15]

Endorsements aside, perhaps the most fascinating parallel with today's celebrities involves cosmetic surgery. Despite choosing to put his body through some of the most gruelling sporting contests known to man, and despite the brutal physicality of his appearance, Tom admitted to being extremely sensitive about that "one blemish on my anatomy – my left ear".

The ear, onlookers said, was indeed something to be ashamed of, having being turned into a ghastly mass of deformed flesh that jutted out from the side of his head like the "gas lantern of the flank of a coach."

Of course, Tom had not been born like that. The transformation of his ear came as a 'gift' of Gus Ruhlin in the two men's fight at Coney Island in June 1900. When he left the ring that night, Tom's ear had swollen up to something close to the size of a "large orange" and turned "very blue in colour." Fights often left Tom scarred, bruised and battered - his style was such that he took extremes of punishment but hoped to win by dishing out more to the other guy. This time, though, while the swelling and discolouration again eventually mended, the ear itself did not return to its normal shape.

Tom figured he could learn to live with it but, each time he fought, the poundings damaged and enlarged his ear. After knocking out Fred Russell in 1901, he told a *Denver Post* reporter: "If it keeps on this way, I'll have to button it back."

He became so self-conscious that he began wearing an oversized cowboy hat to cover the ear. "I am not ashamed of being a fighter," Sharkey told a friend, James Delaney. "But I am distressed that people who don't even recognise me can tell at once that I am a fighter, just by looking at my ear."

Eventually, after the Russell fight, Tom felt the time had come to take action. Never shy at coming forward, he placed an advertisement in a New York City newspaper which read: "I will pay the sum of $5,000 to the person who can provide me with a new ear, or do a suitable job on the one I have."

Not surprisingly, several doctors, including "some of wide reputation" and who probably thought they could enhance it further by 'fixing' the famous "Sailor" Tom, answered the appeal. Invitations arrived inviting him to their offices to be examined.

Tom, though, was the star, and instead insisted they come to his rooms at the Carlton Hotel on Broadway. He set aside three full days, making himself available to any doctor willing to accept that challenge. On the first day, no fewer than twelve medical experts "pulled, pinched, tapped and scrapped away" at the ear. In the following two days, a further 27 did the same. When the examinations were complete, only six of them were willing to attempt "corrective measures".

One New York surgeon, Dr Richard Muller, reported: "The ear can be treated by either tapping, dissection to remove any false growth, by bleeding, or by outward applications to reduce tumefaction. I do not consider that any of these methods would be especially dangerous. The trouble is entirely external and has nothing to do with the internal anatomy of the ear."

A noted eye, ear and nose specialist, Dr Joseph Bell, pronounced: "I have treated several persons to correct what is commonly called "Cauliflower" ear. The surest method is by lancing and I have prepared a sketch of the operation to show its simplicity. I shall be delighted to treat Mr Tom Sharkey's ear, and I believe I can guarantee success. The operation is not very painful."

"I'LL MARRY YOU, BUT GIVE UP THE GLOVES."

It was Dr Bell's analysis that Sharkey liked best and he invited Bell to operate. An agreement was made: Tom and his ear would arrive at Dr Bell's surgery at 9am on August 6, 1901. The boxer would pay one half of the $5,000 fee before the operation and the balance "when I see for myself that he did the job".

However, as the operation date grew near, Tom began to have doubts. Whether it was the money, the thought of the operation or attachment to scars of battle, that caused his change of mind has been a matter of speculation, although the latter seems most likely as Tom is known to have gone to his friend and sparring partner, Bob Armstrong, and asked: "Bob, does this ear make me look ugly?"

"No, Tom, I don't think so," replied Armstrong, who had taken some punches himself. "It makes you look exactly like what you are – a fighter."

"Yeah," nodded Tom. "It's an honour when people look at me on the street and say, 'There goes Tom Sharkey, the great fighter."

On the morning of August 6, Dr Bell's surgery was clean and bright and awaiting the celebrity's arrival. He told the reporters who had gathered outside that he was "going to make Tom Sharkey look as handsome as 'Kid' McCoy".

However, Tom had given up on the operation and was already more than 200 miles away, sleeping soundly on a night train to Chicago, his left ear still horribly twisted forward at the top and as hard as rock.[16]

It maybe that Tom regretted the decision to run out on Dr Bell. Many years later he was still grumbling about his "tin ear".

"It made me mad all my life," he said.[17]

Another Sharkey story saw him come to the rescue as a genuine strong-armed hero. The date was July 31, 1904 and the scene 141 East Fifteenth Street. It was on the third floor to be exact and a Dr Nagle from Bellevue Hospital had rushed to the scene to help a 38-year-old vaudeville actress named Elizabeth Drew, who had suffered an "aneurism of the neck". Rev Father William O'Reilly, of St Ann's Church in East Twelfth Street, near Fourth Avenue, was already helping the woman when Dr Nagle arrived and decided she needed to go straight to hospital.

However, Mrs Drew weighed 160 pounds and neither the priest nor the doctor could get her down the three flights of stairs.

"Wait a minute!" said Father O'Reilly. "And I'll see if I can't find you a strong man."

Fortunately, as the priest reached the street, Tom was passing by with Katherine. Tom worked with boys in O'Reilly's parish so the priest knew him well.

"Hello Tom," he called. "You're just the man I want. Will you help carry a sick woman to the ambulance?"

"Sure, Father," said Sharkey. "I'm right on the job."

Sharkey mounted the stairs behind the priest and addressed Dr Nagle.

"Father O'Reilly tells me you want a lift, Doc."

Nagle looked at Sharkey's sturdy build and nodded. "Guess you might as well do the whole job," he said.

Sharkey stepped over, picked up Mrs Drew as if she was a baby and slowly walked down the stairs.

"Don't be afraid," he told the actress. "I'll go just as slow as you like. I could carry you a thousand miles."

Reaching the sidewalk, Sharkey found that a crowd had gathered, blocking his way to the ambulance. Two police officers tried to shift the onlookers but couldn't.

Sharkey had more weight with them. "Gents," he announced, "will yer please git a move on."

The way was quickly cleared. With Mrs Drew on her way to Bellevue, the priest tapped the broad shoulders gently.

"Thanks, Tom" said Father O'Reilly.

"Don't mention it, Father," replied Sharkey, offering his arm to Mrs Sharkey as they continued on their way.[18]

Tom's work at St Ann's involved training the boys of the Holy Name Society in athletics. In March 1905, they performed on the drill floor of the Ninth Regiment Armory for Mayor McClellan and School Commissioner PM McGowan. It was a very proud night for Tom who had worked with hundreds of boys for the contest. The children's adherence to discipline and the inspiration

"I'LL MARRY YOU, BUT GIVE UP THE GLOVES."

they took from Tom surprised the mayor.

The boys were equally impressed too when they discovered the man looking down on them from the box was the mayor of the city.

Tom wandered among the ranks of young athletes, whispering: "Easy boys, keep your nerve. Never go into the ring the least bit excited or it's full count for yous in the first round."

When the performance was over, the mayor clapped and told the youngsters: "It has filled me with wonder to witness the way you have conducted your exhibition. It has been a revelation to me to be a witness of that manly spirit which is in the future to dominate this city. The boy who goes in for good, clean athletics will make a good, clean citizen. I want your instructor to continue to encourage you in the future as he has done in the past."

Tom beamed with pride. "I'm as proud o' them boys as if they was my own," he told friends. "Tell you, there's some amateur champions in this bunch. It looked fierce sometimes tonight but nobody got hurt."

Tom supported a special event at Madison Square Garden in May 1906 in aid of victims of the San Francisco earthquake and was due to take to the ring in an exhibition with Ruhlin. He was prevented from doing so by a boil on the neck. Later in his life, he used his continuing fame to support a number of causes, including the United Jewish Campaign for the Relief of Jews in Europe, sharing a stage in 1926 with Al Jolson and Sophie Tucker.[19]

The performances also continued in the theatre. Boxers often treaded the boards during the period – as they would try their hands at 'acting' in the cinema in the years to come. In February 1904, Sharkey traded blows on stage with Terry McGovern, Bob Fitzsimmons and Hughey Dougherty in a presentation called The Pit.[20] Two years later, he appears to have had a small role in a musical comedy called Happy Hooligan's Trip Around the World at the Murray Hill and Thalia theatres.[21]

Later in 1906, he and Katherine were guests at a special charity fair in aid of the hospital in Englewood, New Jersey.[22] They were treated like royalty, walking down lines of staff in the grounds, and 1,500 – around half of them women - crowded to see Tom referee the boxing bouts which formed one of the main entertainments. While the local lads tried to lay gloves on each other, many of the spectators' eyes were on Sharkey, who was wearing the large diamond which he and his wife had bought during a recent trip to Paris. He, himself, watched the fighters through a cloud of cigar smoke. During one of the bouts, with the blood flowing from both fighters, there was a lot of concern about the "many pale faces" of female members of the audience. Tom separated the boxers and told them: "Ease up, boys, you're fighting before ladies."

Later in the week-long event, Tom, who had proved such a popular attraction, returned to spar and it was noted that he walked among the 'fine' folk of Englewood, carrying himself, with "great modesty". To one of the women to whom he was introduced, he stated that he would never have thought of "butting into society" if it had not been "for the sake of sweet charity which, madam, makes all the world akin". A matron approached Tom and he hurriedly took off his hat and hid his cigar behind his coattails. Tom asked her how she liked the fights and she said that she did not approve of them.

"But the last was a beaut and if I hadn't stopped it there would have been a knockout," he said. "You ought to have seen it. A little too lively, perhaps, for women folks and do you know, I never saw so many at the ringside before. Eaglewood is a fine place for fighting and I'm glad it's going to make your hospital rich.

"You must come and see me spar Thursday night," he added, eager to enthuse the matron. "I won't hurt the other fellow but he'll know that he's been in the ring. Good night lady!" he said, got into his forty horse power car and drove off.[23]

In July 1910, "looking like the proverbial advance agent of prosperity", Sharkey took Katherine to see his California, to the Mare Island Navy Yard and the scenes of his first fights. "Vallejo's favourite pugilist" was met by a large delegation as he arrived from San Francisco on the ferry boat *Napa Valley*. His first words as he stepped ashore from the big steamer were: "Ah, but it is good to be back in the only place on earth." At the Hotel St Vincent, the couple was surrounded by Sharkey's "old time friends and admirers".

"I'LL MARRY YOU, BUT GIVE UP THE GLOVES."

"You can have San Francisco, Chicago, New York or any of the big places, but dear old Vallejo is mine every time," he said. "I expect to return here someday to make my future home, but in the meantime, I act as a kind of Chamber of Commerce and always keep boosting Vallejo to Eastern people who want to know about California."[24]

As well as the saloon, Tom launched an athletic club, or more precisely a boxing club. This, too, attracted the attentions of the police in January 1906 after a fighter named "Kid" Groog died in a fight at another club on 130th street and Third Avenue. Groog's death prompted Police Commissioner Bingham to launch a new investigation into prize-fighting and one of his men, a Captain Handy of the West Sixty-eighth Street Station, told him about a series of fights which had been held at the Sharkey Athletic Club in Sixty-Fifth Street, near Broadway. Bingham decided the law on these fights needed a test. He ordered for people at the club to be arrested and the issue to be settled in court.

Two detectives went along to Sharkey's club and paid a membership fee of $1. They, then, arrested the doorkeeper, Cornelius A Crow, a referee named James R Buckley and two men named Julius Mack and Frank Rowe, who were to be seconds in a fight which was due to start between two featherweights from Brooklyn, Edward Cantwell and Eddie Wallace. The fighters were taken away too and later bailed. Tom was at the club but escaped arrest.

Sharkey's club hosted a number of well-attended fights including one in front of 1,200 local men, US sailors and members of the British Royal Navy on November 17, 1905. This so-called battle of the "fleet champions" was refereed by Tom but it was all over in less than ten minutes with the visitor, E Cockayne, laying Jack Riene, of the *Iowa* out on the floor. Sharkey, a former champion of the US Navy, was disgusted by the American's performance, saying Riene was not, by any means, a representative American fighter. "Why the feller knew precious little about the game but the Englishman, he knew nothing about fighting. He won by his grit and strength."[25]

In 1923, during a look back at the history of boxing, the *New York Times* noted that saloons all over the city were hosting or promoting prize-fights during the first decade of the twentieth century, including those owned by Corbett and McCoy. It harked back to "classic" saloon fights of the 1860s, it said.

Sharkey's place would have a distinguished visitor, the artist George Bellows, a leading figure in what became known as the Ashcan School, which concentrated on gritty images of the urban slums. Bellows studied the boxers at Sharkey's and the crowds who went to see them and, in 1909, produced his famous painting 'Stag At Sharkey's', which is now at the Cleveland Museum of Art. According to the museum, the painting "embodies the grittiness, violence and masculinity" of New York at the time. "Athletic clubs such as Sharkey's were the equivalent of Prohibition's speakeasies - illegal, but they did a booming business. In Bellows' boxing match, the spectators are vulgar; their expressions indicate that they are at least as violent as the match they are watching. But the boxers themselves are reminiscent of stags in nature, still graceful while locked in combat."[26] Another Bellows' work, 'The Knock Out', which was based on a scene the artist witnessed at Sharkey's in 1907 came up for auction at Sotherby's in 2004. The pastel and ink artwork, showing a referee holding up an exhausted fighter as he struggles to get at his downed opponent, sold for just over five million dollars.

Bellows created an enduring image of the clubs. The unenviable reputation of the bar itself would last too. In 1933, during a debate on licensing laws in New York State and whether drinkers should be allowed to use bars where they could sit down, Senator Dunnigan said: "Most of us well remember such notorious places as The Haymarket, The German Village, Tom Sharkey's....The drinking in those places was done exclusively sitting down. And many remember the bad names those places had, the raids conducted on them and the vice that thrived within their doors."[27]

Drinkers and prostitutes were not the only ones who frequented these bars. There were plenty of other kinds of criminal too, and sometimes Tom would fall victim. One fellow took Tom for

$50 for advertising space in a magazine which did not exist while, in 1907, Tom's wealth again got him the wrong kind of attention at his home in East Twenty-Seventh Street and Forest Avenue: one morning that summer his housekeeper came down to find the house had been broken into and the whole lower floor had been stripped of valuables, including two paintings by old masters worth $500 and silverware and cut glass worth $300. Tom told everyone he was determined the burglar would be caught, even if he had to do it himself.

The police raids had come to a head at Sharkey's in 1913 and, this time, Tom found himself facing the full weight of the law. That October, Special Assistant District Attorney Train began an investigation which resulted in a new and dramatic raid on the premises a week before Christmas. Sixteen policemen guarded the exits of the saloon opposite Tammany Hall as a police lieutenant named Ross pushed open the doors, walked right up to the ex-boxer who was standing at the cash register and placed him under arrest. Andrew Osborne, the saloon manager, and a waiter were also arrested. Ross was carrying a warrant issued by a magistrate which accused Sharkey of keeping a disorderly resort. It had been drawn up on evidence collected by three patrolmen who had been assigned the job of watching the saloon after complaints to the police from, among others, the Gramercy Park Association. The three prisoners were taken to the East Sixth Street Station but were later released on bail. Meanwhile, the police took the names and addresses of all those in the saloon and an officer was left to keep the back room of the saloon closed.

On February 9, 1914, Tom appeared before Justices Russell O'Keefe and Collins in the Court of Special Sessions for being the "proprietor of a disorderly resort". The testimony that was to convict him came from Charles S Briggs, a member of the Committee of Fourteen, which was set up to root out prostitution. Briggs testified that he had gone to Sharkey's and had seen all three defendants (Osborne would also be convicted but the waiter was acquitted). He said the place was "disorderly", and was backed up by a Mr Murphy, of the Church of the Immaculate Conception, and

WF Edwards, of the Gramercy Park Neighbourhood Association.

Sharkey took the stand and vehemently denied the charge.

"Why, everybody knows my place," he said. "People from all over the world come here, including the most respectable people in New York City."

"Is there ever any profanity used in this place?" he was asked.

"Why, if any persons used profane language in my place I'd have them thrown right out, whether they were men or women," replied Tom indignantly. "I run the most respectable place in New York City. I've been hounded and hounded. Why, I don't know, because I'm a good, honest man. I'm a married man, too. The people who are pushing me to the wall have charged that I keep my place open after hours, but that is a lie. The people who accuse me were drunk on the night in question."

Six character witnesses testified to the good reputation of Sharkey and Osborne, who himself denied that he had permitted unescorted women to come into the place except in the daytime "when they come from the shopping district". The guilty verdict came after just 30 seconds of deliberation by the justices and a few days later, Tom heard his sentence. Father Mechan, of St. Ann's Church, asked the justices to show clemency as Sharkey had contributed $600 to build a gymnasium for the boys of the parish and had "done much to keep youngsters from going astray by giving them free boxing lessons several times a week". However, Tom was going to jail. He was fined $500 and was sent to the city's main prison, the Tombs, for 30 days. He spent the next few days shovelling snow in the prison yard and working for the dormitory squad whose duties were to make the beds and sweep the corridors. His legal team made an application to appeal to the Supreme Court. Justice Cohalan told lawyers that there could be only two specific grounds for an application - the admission of improper evidence and the insufficiency of the evidence – and that it was "absurd" to suppose that Sharkey was not aware of the character of the place he was running.[28]

Tom was eventually released on March 17, after serving his time and paying his fine. "I never felt better in my life," he said outside,

"I'LL MARRY YOU, BUT GIVE UP THE GLOVES."

"but I'd hate to stay there any longer."

Rumours had started about more work in the theatres, where most of the other heavyweights were making handsome incomes. "No, I'm not going on the stage," said Tom, "although I will admit I have been approached by theatrical managers."

Tom might have been buoyant on his release from jail but a month behind bars was sadly not the worst that 1914 had in store for him.

On the afternoon of May 2, Tom returned to his home in Sheepshead Bay and found Katherine unconscious in the bedroom. The boxer called a doctor but there was nothing that could be done. Katherine McIntosh Sharkey was dead. Her death was sudden and was attributed to apoplexy (a stroke). She was 35 and the couple had been married a month short of ten years.

The marriage had been far from smooth and Katherine had, in fact, filed for separation in July 1912. But the couple had been quickly reconciled after what Tom had called "short-lived domestic difficulties". He had said at the time: "There isn't any woman in the world like her and I didn't intend to let her get away from me - no, not for all the Carnegie and Morgan millions in the world."

On her death, Tom appeared to throw himself back into business, reopening a saloon at a new venue. In June, he held a quiet opening night party for his Cronin Café Company at 723 Third Avenue between Forty-First and Forty-Second Streets. Tom had bought out the previous owners and had received the licence shortly before going into jail. However, he had lost his licence when he was sentenced to jail and he now claimed the new bar was actually owned by his younger brother, John, now 33. The brothers were paying about $50,000 a year rent on the property.

But the venture was dogged with problems – including a legal battle with builders carrying out the refurbishment – and was to signal only a deepening spiral in the Irishman's fortunes... and fortune.

Before jail and Katherine's death, Sharkey was worth an estimated $500,000.[29] But by June 1916, he was owing so much, to so many across New York, that he was adjudged to be bankrupt.[30]

Making his Federal Court appearance in San Francisco, where he had obviously gone to make a new life away from the creditors, Sharkey heard his attorney state that the ex-boxer was now owing a massive $299,556. Sharkey's only asset, the attorney pleaded, was a note for $20.50 from a Sergeant of Marines at the Mare Island Navy Yard, who had borrowed money off Tom many years ago. The attorney said Sharkey had lost money on real estates and his New York businesses had failed after his jail sentence.

There were suggestions much later that some of Tom's problems might have been down to a falling out with the New York politicians he had previously courted – and who had courted him. One review of this period noted that Sharkey's saloon was "a prosperous concern until Tom unfortunately got in bad with the ruling Tammany powers and in the end was driven to the wall and obliged to close up".[31]

Another point not mentioned at the bankruptcy hearing was Tom's gambling habit. Next door to his saloon was the Mauretania Club, an establishment which was known to gamblers across New York City as The Bastile because of its impregnability to police. However, in August 1911, the police led by Commissioner Dougherty breached the defences and found 230 people, including Tom, inside. The officers arrived in a furniture van so as to maintain a surprise. They jumped out to tackle the look-outs and then spent half-an-hour knocking through a steel door. Inside they found a scene like something out of *The Sting* and went round collecting scrawled up betting slips and racing charts, and collecting evidence from around the building's two roulette wheels. Many of the men inside were prosperous businessmen. Only five people were arrested, being on outstanding warrants for other matters, and Tom was not among them. Outside, a detective who had gone undercover as a gambler to expose the club was attacked by a mob.

But there had also always been the racetrack. Well before his career in the ring had ended, he had become interested in light harness horses and had began to buy up a string of the animals. The Speedway was a big event at Sheepshead Bay and Tom liked to be seen at the track in a light green suit, strolling among the

"I'LL MARRY YOU, BUT GIVE UP THE GLOVES."

crowds. He appeared smartly-dressed and refined at the races, as he would on the lawns of Avery House when Katherine first set eyes on him, but lost all airs and graces in the betting ring. Some sent commissioners or friends to place bets for them but not Sharkey: he dived straight through the crowds and always got to where he wanted to go. Whether the horses he backed always did what he wanted them to do seems doubtful considering his eventual levels of debt.

Later it was estimated that the saloon had been making between $60,000 and $75,000 a year and that it should have seen Sharkey, "set for life". "However the Wall Street crowd that had used his place as a half-way house uptown found that when the new sub-way was finished it was just as easy to go on to Time Square – and the Sharkey establishment gradually faded out. He made total profits of $575,000 during these years, lost it all on the horses and is still playing the ponies every day in San Francisco as if nothing had ever happened. The scale is lower but the ambition remains intact."[32]

He was a competitor on the track too, driving his horse, Merry Pat, regularly and often mixing it with some old friends from the ring. On March 30, 1902, for instance, Sharkey, Fitzsimmons and Terry McGovern all took part in heats at the Brooklyn Speedway. On April 7, 1902, the *Brooklyn Daily Eagle* went so far as to describe Tom as a "confirmed roadwayite" who "handled the ribbons skilfully". However, a week later, fortunes changed when the horse appeared "erratic", rearing up and forcing Tom to find "good use for his powerful shoulders and forearms". The horse rode on half-a-mile on one occasion with Tom desperate to stop it and having to spend the next ten minutes retracing their course to pick up his hat, laprobe and other pieces of equipment which had flown off. He abandoned Merry Pat soon after and drove other horses, often for other owners. He also challenged others, like boxer McGovern, to side bets on races, and had other riders taking the reins for him at other trotting races.

Sharkey's move to California, as explained above, came as the creditors closed in over in New York. But there were two other reasons.

Firstly, Tom had been thrown a lifeline by an old friend, big Jim Jeffries, who had offered him $50 a week to manage his saloon. Secondly, Sharkey had a new bride, Florence Camille Manzoni, a pretty Irish-Italian woman who was 23 years his junior and who appeared to have designs on a career in the cinema.

Of the two relationships at the centre of his new start on the West Coast, only one was destined to last.

Tom had known Florence's family for sometime and they started going out the year after Katherine's death. They moved to California together and got married at St Patrick's Church, Mission Street, San Francisco.

During 1916, the new Mrs Sharkey's "unusually good photoplay features" appeared to be on the verge of getting her into the movies. It appears the 19-year-old, using the stage name Rita Gardner, was getting some work at one of the Hollywood Studios with actor Harry McCabe and was perhaps on the verge of a big break.

However, by the summer of 1917, not only were the Hollywood dreams in tatters, the marriage was over. Sharkey was again in court as Florence sought alimony.[33] It was an unpleasant affair during which Sharkey blamed a friend of Florence's, Marion Ridgeway, for the break-up of his marriage.

"I am not trying to keep anything from the little girl," he said. "There's another woman in the case, Mrs Ridgeway. She has ruined my little girl, taken her out at nights until two or three o'clock in the morning."

Florence flushed indignantly at the courtroom attack but came back with her own. She accused Sharkey of "cruelty consisting of blows and alleged attempts on her life". She said he was jealous of Mrs Ridgeway and said his attack on her friend was "bunk".

"I am white, free and over 21 - I don't need anyone to take me around," she shouted at him outside.

"You can have Mrs Ridgeway now," Sharkey replied.

There is no way, now, of exploring the allegations of cruelty against Sharkey. He was a man who had made a living with his fists and it is certainly not impossible that he may have been violent towards Florence. It is equally possible that these were allega-

"I'LL MARRY YOU, BUT GIVE UP THE GLOVES."

tions constructed simply to support Florence's claim for alimony.

That Sharkey was jealous of the time Florence spent with Mrs Ridgeway is perhaps more likely. His complaints about Marion Ridgeway echo those made during problems with his Katherine which he attributed to "certain persons...taking advantage of his wife's high-strung nature and [trying] to prejudice her against him".[34] Tom may also have become jealous of the attention his young wife was getting in the film business. "It's a great business, this movie game," Tom had told one reporter in California when Florence was trying out for films. "I never thought I'd care for it but, well, the wife, she's a star now and I kinder like to hang around and watch her act." He had added, perhaps only half in jest: "Then I guess no guy'd try to get fresh with me on the job. I've still got a punch or two left."[35]

The alimony court heard that Tom had fresh personal debts of $3,000, loans made to tide him over and to meet medical expenses. Florence "looked after the details of a handsome tombstone for the first Mrs Sharkey", the court heard.

Since the separation, Florence had pawned a locket set with fourteen diamonds for $65 in order to live. It had been a gift from her husband.

"Are you superstitious of the number 13?" the court asked Sharkey.

"No, Your Honor," he replied.

"Well, I make the order $12 a week."

Florence, who was now working as a book-keeper, had wanted $20 a week in order to start up a business career. The first week's alimony was paid in court.

One thing Sharkey appeared to maintain throughout his life was his pride at having served in the US Navy. For instance, at some point during Teddy Roosevelt's time as twenty-sixth president of the United States, Tom was apparently invited to the White House. On his way through an outer office to meet the keen boxing fan, Tom passed a white moustachioed man whose face struck Tom as familiar although he could not get the name. The boxer and the president talked for an hour or so about Tom's fights with Fitz and John L and, as Tom left, the president introduced him to the elderly gentleman. It was Admiral George Dewey, the hero of the recent Spanish-American War and perhaps the most famous American sailor in history.

"So," said Tom, "you are a sailor, too?"

"Yes, I am a sailor, but I don't think as good a one as you were, Tom," replied the highest ranking sailor in the country.

"You can't convince me of that," declared Tom with some pride at Dewey's attention. "An admiral is a better fighter than a common sailor any old day."[36]

This sort of patriotism also meant that he often found himself rubbing shoulders with old foes from the law. In April 1906, for instance, Police Commissioner Bingham and Deputy Commissioner Waldo were installed into Garrison 35, Regular Army and Navy Union, an organization of current and former soldiers and sailors. Sharkey was not only also a member of the garrison but he occupied the seat next to Bingham on stage and applauded as the commissioner described the values of "loyalty, patriotism and unselfishness, exemplified in the American soldier". The police officer said a good soldier was a good Christian as well as a good citizen. Money sometimes does not bring happiness, he said, and newspaper notoriety did not either, but friendship and comradeship did.

Tom's pride in his military connections never left him. In 1912, *Police Gazette* owner Richard K Fox published *Navy Drill*, a 73-page book by Sharkey with a list of exercises to keep the serviceman in shape. The following year, when war between the United States and Japan looked possible, he said he was ready to rejoin. "I've seen some officers of the navy and I can jump right back into my old berth as master-at-arms," he said proudly. "If there is a scrap, I'll go. That's the life for me. I'd like nothing better than the old hard work and the fine condition it would get me into."[37]

An elderly lady was once asked by Tom if she liked a fundraising exhibition bout they were watching together. She said it was all very interesting if the men had not looked so angry and if there had been no blood.

"Why, lady," he told her, "they were only playing. It was a game

"I'LL MARRY YOU, BUT GIVE UP THE GLOVES."

of love taps. The blood was an accident. Now, madam, I did not catch your name but I see you have a fine son with you. Mighty fine looking boy - but I wouldn't own him if he were a coward nor would you and I tell you every boy ought to be taught how to fight. I don't mean that he should go looking for it but he ought to know how if anybody should insult his mother."[38]

Tom would have no child himself, but Katherine and he did adopt one of his nephews after a visit home to Dundalk. The family back home – after regaining contact with Tom in 1897 – had enjoyed some of the fruits of his success. He had bought them a more comfortable home across the road in Hill Street.[39] However, on March 10, 1906, Tom's father, James, died. He was 83.[40] There was a large turnout at the funeral of this "universally liked" man who had worked at the Great Northern Railway Company for more than fifty years. His prize-fighting son returned from New York for the service and stayed until late in June. Tom's parents had been looking after a grandson, Patrick Joseph Carroll, who had been born in 1894 to their daughter, Elizabeth, and her husband, John Carroll, ever since Elizabeth's death in 1898. Now, a decision was made for Patrick to go and live with his rich uncle, Tom, in New York. Tom not only adopted the boy but changed his name. He became Joseph James Sharkey, or Joe.

In Joe, Tom could combine the pride of having a 'son' with his own pride in military service. He also, of course, taught him the "manly art". Aged about 23, Joe joined the United States Army as the country joined the struggle against Germany in the Great War. After initial training, he crossed the Atlantic to serve.

Tom was obviously inspired. In 1918, the YMCA was recruiting for people to go to France to run army canteens and support the wounded and the refugees. In mid-July with the First World War still raging, Herbert L Pratt, Vice President of Standard Oil, claimed that New York City would raise 2,000 volunteers. Tom was one of the applicants who arrived at 347 Madison Avenue, saying he wished to go to France as a physical director. He had been introduced to the idea by a long distance runner, Thomas F Gallagher. According to at least one source, the fact the prize-fighter and former owner of a notorious bar was now aligning himself with the YMCA had "left the sporting world aghast". Sports writer Paul Purman said: "The surprise was not that Sharkey was on his way to France - Tom was always a fighter - but that he was with the YMCA. Tom's ways and the ways of the YMCA have always been on two widely divergent paths."[41]

Back during the heyday of Sharkey's career, movie picture records of his fights had made him rich while the lights that lit the cameras made him sweat. The Jeffries fight had brought in thousands and film of Tom's victory over McCoy in New York had even been shown in St Stephen's Hall, Westminster, with the crowds who turned up forcing exhibitors to show the film twice a day.[42] Then, Sharkey and the other fighters were pioneers, some of the first sporting stars of the big screen. Many traded on this to find careers in the cinema.

Tom's was fairly shortlived. He appeared in three films which were released in 1925: *The Range Terror*, directed by William James Craft, *Bashful Buccaneer*, a comedy director by Harry Joe Brown, and the rather more notable, *Capital Punishment*. The latter starred Clara Bow, was directed by James P Hogan and was written and produced by BP Schulberg, a future head of Paramount Pictures. Sharkey played an unnamed convict in this socially-aware melodrama about an innocent man facing the electric chair.

As silent cinema prepared to breathe its last, Tom had a character name, Luke Hatton, but only a small role in the Ken Maynard vehicle, *The Grey Vulture*, and was 'Pedro Sanchez' in another western, *Fighting Jack* (both 1926).

The following year, there was more action out west in *Born to Battle*, starring B-movie lead Bill Cody but memorable only for Sharkey's character's name, Bulldog Bangs, chest-beating melodrama in *The Cruise of the Hellion*, and even more woe in *The Thirteenth Juror*, in which Tom played a prisoner. The latter featured future star Walter Pidgeon and was made at Universal.

Tom's career continued in much the same vein in 1928 with *Isle of Lost Men* and *Good Morning, Judge*, in which his understandable typecasting as a tough continued with the role of 'second crook'.

"I'LL MARRY YOU, BUT GIVE UP THE GLOVES."

The film featuring Tom which got most attention came out when cinema found sound. *Madison Square Garden* (1932) was directed by Harry Joe Brown and starred Jack Oakie. Centring around the famous New York venue, the plot had a number of famous ex-sports stars – including Tom and Jack Johnson - coming in at the end to beat off the heavies.[43] The *New York Times* described the Paramount picture as a "mirth-provoking pugilistic tale" but noted that its efforts to "contrast the sporting days of the old Madison Square Garden with those of the new structure [are] none too convincing fashion".[44]

In June 1926, businessman and head of MGM Marcus Loew threw a special dinner in New York for his friends in the entertainment and sporting world. He wanted three special guests at the head of the table and invited a trio he had admired as a young man when starting out in the nickelodeon business: the dinner reunited Jim Jeffries, Jim Corbett and Tom Sharkey.

CHAPTER ELEVEN
Down But Not Out

Old fighters never quite fade away; they are always there in somebody else's corner.

Tom Sharkey was Jim Jeffries' man. It was a friendship forged in 45 rounds of bruising, bloody fighting. And when Jeffries needed him, he would be there. In 1910, Jeffries needed all the help he could get.

Jeffries had retired a few years earlier, claiming to be unable to obtain suitable opponents, and had proclaimed that Marvin Hart and Jack Root should fight for the vacated throne, with himself as referee.

When Hart knocked out Root in the twelfth round, he was proclaimed new champion but, as Nat Fleischer later noted in his *Pictorial History of Boxing*, "dissension arose". Why had Jeffries been allowed to decide? Why had only Hart and Root had the chance to compete when there were "other excellent heavies in the field"? One excellent heavy was a 23-year-old Canadian who fought under the name Tommy Burns. He challenged all comers in various parts of the world and beat them. Fans began to recognise him as the champion. In 1906, Burns finally got Hart into the ring and won on points after 20 rounds. Having won, he knew he had a new great boxer, Jack Johnson, breathing down his neck, so he took off on a world tour to make some money from the crown before Johnson could catch up with him.

But Johnson, who would now become of focus in the mind of Sharkey and Jeffries and the whole white-skinned and prejudiced boxing world, did catch up with Burns. They fought in Australia on December 26, 1908, with Burns guaranteed a $30,000 pay packet. He got the money but lost the title.

Now began one of the most fascinating and unpleasant periods in boxing history.

Johnson – the new world champion - was a dominating physical presence. He had taunted Burns, and his victory had not only ended the white domination of the heavyweight championship it had also horrified many white Americans. Johnson frightened them further, refusing to conform to the racist rules of white society. He simply 'did not know his place'. His marriage to a white woman resounded like a blistering uppercut through conservative white America.

And so the call went out for a 'Great White Hope', the man who could put Johnson 'back where he belonged'. This was not about backing a new contender; it was about finding someone to 'defend a race'.

Pressure mounted on Jeffries and Sharkey played his part. "If I were Jeff, do you know what I'd do?" said Sharkey. "I'd line Jack Johnson and Tommy Burns up in the same ring on the same night and guarantee to knock them both out. And just to prove my championship calibre. I'd also agree to take on 'Philadelphia' Jack O'Brien as a consolation bout in case I took too little time in settling the other two.

"Johnson can't beat that big fellow. No-one in this whole wide world can. If Jeff will undertake the contract that I have suggested, I will gamble every dollar that I possess in the world that he does the trick.

"Don't you fool yourself about his dissipation. He's not an idiot. Jeff is always in striking distance of his crown and in mighty fair sort of shape to defend it, too. There never was a fellow in the world like the big fellow, and there isn't going to be one in a hurry, either. All this talk about his being an easy victim for that big colored fellow is rot."

So, asked an eager reporter, would Jeffries fight Johnson? "You can just bet he will and you can just bet he'll beat the darky," said Sharkey. "Too big, I tell you. Too big altogether for those fellows. He kills a man with those big fists of his.

"I sampled them and I do believe I know. I never expected to see the light o' day after he got through with me in the last romp of ours. He hit harder than Maher, Choynski, Fitz, or any of those fellows. He didn't hit as cleanly or, at least, he didn't appear to, but the receiver-general of one of his body smashes certainly did have private ideas about the force of them. Jeff threw every ounce of his weight into one of shuffling pokes on the ribs.

"He's all right. Don't listen to anything against the big fellow. He'll be on deck when it's up to him to fight any of those fellows, and he'll knock them forty-seven ways for Sunday. That's what Tom Sharkey thinks about the situation."[1]

Sharkey no doubt spoke with two motivations: firstly, with a greater respect for Jeffries than for any other boxer; secondly, with the prejudice which ran through the sport and the society of the time that black fighters – black people – were inferior to white people. A century later it makes for deeply unpleasant reading but the prejudice was widespread – routine - during Johnson's tenure as champion.

Sharkey's heroes Sullivan and Jeffries – during his pomp as champion- both refused to take on black fighters. "I will never fight a Negro," Jeffries had said. And in his biography of Johnson, *Unforgivable Blackness,* Geoffrey C Ward claims that Sharkey had stated in 1900, after being challenged by the black fighter Ed Martin: "I have never barred nobody outside of a nigger. I will not fight no nigger. I did not get my reputation fighting niggers and I will not fight a nigger. Outside of niggers, I will fight any man living."

Sharkey's prejudices no doubt mirrored those of the time and are indefensible. However, as pointed out before, one of Sharkey's friends, next-door neighbour and sparring partner, was Tennessee-born Bob Armstrong, a very good black fighter. They had fought at least ten exhibition matches going back to May 1897, although Armstrong like other black fighters had to contest a "coloured" heavyweight championship. As reported in Chapter Six, Sharkey also laid down a challenge after beating Goddard in December 1897 that he would take on anyone "regardless of their colour". And, in February 1900, he had been eager to fight in a fundraising testimonial for his friend, George Dixon, another black boxer. Both events would appear to contradict the deeply unpleasant comments from 1900, as quoted by Ward.

Sharkey went on to make a number of challenges to Johnson himself. In March 1909, with Jeffries still not willing to come out of retirement, the Irishman blustered: "I have not had a glove on for five years, but I am not an old-timer and I don't think much of the heavyweights of today. Give me three months and I could get in condition to give any of them a go for their money."[2] A year later, as a guest at a dinner of the Road Drivers' Association in Shanley's Restaurant, Times Square, Sharkey repeated the challenge to fight "the Negro". Sharkey – then working as a second to Italian boxer Frank Picato - said he was only thirty-six and could be in condition inside a month. His announcement was greeted by "loud cheers" from the Road Drivers and was reported in the *New York Times* under the headline 'Sharkey to the Rescue'.

In September 1909, Sharkey was ringside in San Francisco to see Johnson take on local favourite and sparring partner Al Kaufmann, 'The San Francisco Dutchman'. Kaufmann (sometimes spelt Kaufman) liked to enhance his punching power by "judicious use of hand-wrappings".[3] At the time, there were not many regulations as to what fighters could wear to protect their fists inside their gloves. Kaufmann liked to wind heavy black tape around his hands. Sharkey watched with amazement as strand after strand of tape was bound on by Kaufmann's seconds. Finally, unable to contain himself any longer, Sharkey blurted out: "This guy's no fighter, he's an electrician!" Johnson beat Kaufmann easily.

The call went out for a 'Great White Hope' to defend a race. And the callers quickly turned to Jim Jeffries who was in retirement. After two years of pressure, he agreed to come back to show that the white man was superior to the 'Negro'. The million-dollar fight, which pitted race against race and captured the public imagination, took place in Reno, Nevada, in July 1910. Armed police guarded the venue and no guns were allowed inside. Such hatred had been whipped up against Johnson that he'd received death threats – but he would answer the bigots in the ring.

Sharkey organized one of the special trains which was laid on to carry fight fans to Nevada from New York. It was combined with one for black fight fans.[4] Before the fight Tom, now 36, was one of the big time boxers paraded before the crowd and he seized his moment to challenge the winner.

In the summer sunshine, though, Sharkey was to witness a brutal display of power from Johnson.

Jeffries started well but by the end of the sixth round he was tired, frustrated and looking like a man who had come back from retirement to face a much better foe – a foe who was fitter, younger and had fought regularly at the highest level since Jeffries had last officially stepped into the ring.

In round 14, Jeffries was knocked down twice but referee Tex Ricard allowed the fight to continue until Jeffries was left slumped at the ropes. Jeffries - the Great White Hope - was beaten. Interracial violence flared around the country.

Johnson went on but the knives were out. He opened a nightclub in Chicago and mixed in some questionable circles. The Bureau of Investigation (later the FBI) set out to get him and eventually charged him under a law barring taking a female across a state line for "immoral purposes". He was convicted in 1915 and fled the country.

Sharkey never personally followed up his challenge to Johnson. Instead, he claimed for a short while to be nurturing a new "white hope", Jim Barry, but the Chicago heavyweight was quickly out of the running.[5]

Early in 1925, Sharkey approached Californian boxing commissioner Louis Almgren to apply for a licence to fight again. He was 51. Almgren granted the licence and Sharkey contacted another veteran, Frank Fields. Together, they fought a series of the three-round exhibition bouts, beginning in Watsonville and continuing through central California.[6] *The Ring* editor Nat Fleischer was less than enthusiastic with the news of the return of a Sharkey now "old with age, his muscles covered with layers of fat, his eyes no longer sparkling as of old".

He added: "Not by the slightest stretch of imagination can one conceive how Tom expects to compete with the young, powerful well-trained youths of today without making a mockery out of boxing and possibly sounding for California the death knell of a sport which has been revived legally only four months after a ten-year lapse.

"Should Tom Sharkey be permitted to fight and an injury to his person result, boxing in California would receive a black eye and bills for the repeal of the law would undoubtedly follow."

Fleischer could not see, he said, why Sharkey – "reputed to be prosperous" and a "frequent visitor to the Tijuana race track" – would consider a comeback, other than because "like many other fighters of the old days, [he] refuses to acknowledge that the youth of today is his superior".

Fleischer concluded: "Age will take its toll, and not even a Tom Sharkey can prevent it."[7]

However, there are comebacks, and there are comebacks. And a year later there was much more excitement about a new pairing. In June 1926, the *New York Times* reported: "Jim Jeffries and Tom Sharkey, former heavyweight boxing champions, are to tour the Loew theatres in a vaudeville act, closing, naturally with a sparring exhibition."

To fight fans, it was like reuniting Laurel with Hardy or Butch with Sundance after they had been apart for more than a quarter of century.

Both men had made and lost fortunes in the ring. Jeffries had invested unwisely in oil wells and unprofitable gold mines and when he was visited by a promoter who wanted to put the two prize-fighting legends together again, he jumped at the chance.

The plan was quickly put into action with a debut fight in Buffalo to be followed by a talk with the audience afterwards. In fact, the plan was so rushed by the promoter that Jeffries and Sharkey did not have time to time to map out an act and Tom did not reach Buffalo in time for a rehearsal.

So they met in the ring, both determined to put on a show and to prove to the audience they still had what it takes. "All of a sudden it was Coney Island all over again," wrote Kelly Richard Nicholson in *A Man Among Men*, a book about Jeffries. Sharkey, paunchy and bald like Jeffries, went at his opponent like it was "the twenty-sixth round of that fight", remembered Jeffries later. The Irishman feinted and swung a left haymaker at Jeffries who responded with right to the ribs.

Sharkey remembered they were "using great pillows of gloves" but that: "We took up right where we had left off 26 years before. I crashed at him with the old left, and Jeffries came out of his crouch and battered my ribs, and so we went, puffing and groaning."[8]

At the end of the first round, the shocked referee told them they were going to beat each other to death within a week at this rate. Wisely, they took the foot off the gas and fought more gently through the remaining two rounds. "In the dressing room, the two men compared painful notes and agreed to tone down the act in mutual interest," said Nicholson.

Sharkey said: "The reception we got everywhere was a tonic to us. Like a schoolboy Jeff was, when the crowds cheered him and showed him that the greatest heavyweight champion of all time was not forgotten. We took off the fat, made some money and had a grand time."[9]

Sharkey, said Jeffries, was a "fine fellow, a loyal and devoted friend; still a sailor at heart – ready to battle anyone from a rival crew but readier to fight for one of his own mates".

The tour continued throughout the summer in New York before ending in Los Angeles. It had been such a huge success that it was repeated two years later.

This time the two fighters would be fighting on sawdust, having signed up for 36 weeks with the famous Al G Barnes Circus. They started in Los Angeles on March 15 and were set to "visit nearly all the small towns in the nation from coast to coast". The *Los Angeles Times* reported: "This will be the first time many old-timers in the hick villages have ever seen either man in the flesh, although they have been reading and talking about them for years."[10] Jeffries later described the experience as "one of the funniest and most interesting of my life". The circus' publicity photographs show elephants, zebras and horses, and the "king of the clowns", Austin King. One photograph shows Jeffries "taking on" Fitz, the kangaroo, in a ring – both are wearing gloves. Another shows Jeffries and Sharkey – who wears a striped suit and cap, sitting outside a cage with a chimp called "Jiggs, the jungle man".

Jeffries and Sharkey fought each other across four decades. But astonishingly, Sharkey once revealed that, on their first meeting, they had both balked at the chance to trade gloves.

The two men, said Sharkey, had first laid eyes on each other in 1896 when the Irishman was in training at the old Seal Rock House in San Francisco. Tim McGrath was making money allowing fans to see the up-and-coming Sharkey knock down "third-raters" in sparring matches. However, the third-raters did not like being the fall guys for so little money.[11]

"So finally I ran out of training partners and I got tired punching the bag and told Tim to go out and grab off some great big gink that I could plaster but who wouldn't get scared every time I sent him into sleep land," said Sharkey.

One day, two local movers, "Oakland" Billy Gallagher and Billy Carkeek, began boasting about a new fighter they had discovered.

"He's as big as the side of a livery stable," Carkeek told McGrath. "He has a pair of hands on him like sugar cured shoulder hams. His arms are as long as flails and his shoulders as broad as the back of a hack. Coach him along and he'll be a wonder."

McGrath looked at Sharkey.

"That's just the fellow I want," he said. "Send him out to the Seal House Rock and let him workout with Sharkey and I'll pay him as a sparring partner."

So, a deal was agreed, a spar arranged for what would have been a first meeting of Sharkey and Jeffries.

However, on the way to Oakland, Gallagher "stops and takes more than is good for him", something which upsets Jeffries.

"Right then and there, Jeff took a dislike to Gallagher," remembered Sharkey. "McGrath and I saw the three drive up in the buggy. Jeff loomed up like a giant in the rig, alongside Carkeek and Gallagher."

McGrath said: "He sure is big, Tom."

"Too big!" said Sharkey.

Gallagher got out of the buggy and started into the house. "But," remembered Sharkey later, "Jeff reached over and took the reins and turned the horse around and with Carkeek arguing with him, drove on back to 'Frisco. It developed afterwards that Jeff was so sore at Gallagher that he wouldn't go through with the proposition."

Years later, Sharkey overheard Jeffries' trainer Billy Delaney telling McGrath: "I'm mighty glad Jeff didn't become Sharkey's sparring partner that time. Tom would probably have rocked him to sleep and broken his spirit and, in that case, I wouldn't have the champion of the world today."

Sharkey, nursing wounds from two of the biggest fights of his career, shouted: "Yes, and I wouldn't have a couple of fanned in ribs, either."[12]

Sharkey, bolstered by the reception that he and Jeffries had got, continued to live on his reputation.

In January 1930, he fought an exhibition match with Pat Maguire in Miami Beach – and was photographed in the ring with a fan – the baseball star "Babe" Ruth.

In Chicago in 1934, he was a headline act with another great boxer, one he had never fought in anger – Jack Johnson.

Fighter Chuck Burroughs, who was 19 at the time and fighting exhibitions, later remembered one backstage scene at Dave Barry's Carnival of Champs event.

"One hot afternoon, Tom Sharkey and I were alone in the dressing room," he said. "We were sparring open-handed while he was teaching me to hook off the jab. We were both in street clothes. This dressing room had a toilet which the spectators had to use.

"I said to him, 'Hey, Tom, I read in a sports magazine that when you fought Jeffries for the title in 1899, that the last few rounds the ends of your busted ribs were sticking out through your skin. Is that the truth or just some crap they put in the papers?'

"He snorted, yanked up his shirt and held it under his chin and said, 'See these little white scars on my ribcage?' I saw about four little white scars about as big as kitchen matches. 'Feel 'em!' he said."[13]

Even in the late 1930s, in his mid-sixties, he was still trading on his strength, doing a strong-man act at the San Francisco Fair. One observer noted: "All anybody has to do, who doubts the ability of the old-time pugs, is to say Old Thomas a sassy word and forget to run. An ordinary man could be killed by the sort of punch he is capable of throwing even at his advanced age."[14]

He was a special guest at the Golden Gate Exposition to celebrate the opening of the famous bridge in July 1939. Sharkey took part as an actor in the pageant and then "revived scenes familiar [from] the Gay Nineties" when he sparred for three rounds as part of the climax to the event. He was only months away from his 65th birthday.[15] It was originally intended that Sharkey and Jeffries would fight, and a permit had been applied for, but Jim had to pull out.[16]

Tom regularly went to fights, particularly the big ones, and was seen at the heavyweight championship contests between Jack Dempsey and Jess Willard in Toledo in 1919 and between Joe Louis v James Braddock at Chicago in 1937.[17]

He had been honoured when a Lithuanian-born fighter adopted his surname and became Jack Sharkey. The pair sparred together for the cameras before Jack took on Dempsey in New York in July 1927.[18] The jazz trumpeter and band leader Sharkey Bonano, from New Orleans, took his name from Tom as, most probably did Victor McLaglen – later a famous film actor, particularly in John Ford movies – who boxed and wrestled under the name Sharkey McLaglen.

Conan the Barbarian creator Robert E Howard wrote a tribute to Sharkey (now lost) while PG Wodehouse mentioned Sharkey in his 1925 book, *Sam the Sudden* (known as *Sam in the Suburbs* in the United States).

But away from the occasional photocall and pre-fight soundbite, Sharkey had to earn a living and he drifted through a range of jobs. At some point, Tom – like many others – had tried his luck in the gold mines of Alaska. He probably went there in the early 1920s, after things went bad in New York. He certainly had some success, too, bringing back for one of his good friends a "chunk of gold an inch long and a half inch wide". The friend, JD Tucker, a onetime Mayor of Sheepshead Bay, wore the piece of gold in his tie.[19]

He worked at the Tijuana race track after getting a job through former boxing promoter and racetrack owner, JW "Sunny Jim" Coffroth, who had previously put on fights which featured many top fighters, including Sharkey and Jack Johnson.[20] Sharkey was said to be Coffroth's favourite fighter for many reasons, including his sense of humour. During the 1899 fight with McCoy, in which Tom was struck repeatedly with a left for four rounds, Sharkey leaned over the ropes in an interval and said to Coffroth: "Don't tell me this guy's a scientific boxer. A scientific boxer wouldn't keep hitting in the same place all the time!"[21]

At Tanforan, he sold options to guys like himself who followed the horses and whiled away the days getting round gambling laws down at the track. During World War II, he got a job as a civilian guard on army property and later, aged 73, he patrolled as a San Francisco waterfront guard, with a badge on his chest and a pistol at his side.[22] He was a special policeman at Bay Meadows racetrack, California, during 1949.[23]

He had been living in various hotels along Fourth Street, San Francisco – perhaps mostly at the Keystone Hotel at number 54 - becoming known as the 'Mayor of Fourth Street'.

However, with the passing of time came the new foes. This time, his opponents were "old age, feebleness and loneliness".[24]

Ever since he had been 25, Sharkey – a man who had spent long nights on cold, wind-beaten boats and long minutes being battered in the ring - had suffered with rheumatism. Back then, he sought the soothing waters of Sulphur Springs, Rochester. Now, he took to his bed in San Francisco. He claimed the condition was worsened by a fall as he got out of a taxicab on New Year's Eve, 1932.

During 1937, while refereeing a fight in California, Sharkey showed signs of illness after the summer heat overcame him and he stepped aside.[25]

On April 30, 1938, he was admitted to Laguna Honda Home for the Aged as an invalid.

The *New York Times* reported: "Tom Sharkey one of the famed figures of earlier day boxing and once possessor of a fortune of $250,000 today became an inmate of the Laguna Honda Home – San Francisco's haven for the aged, infirm and destitute. He still carries his head high but he's broke, this old-time gladiator, who came out of the United States Navy to fight them all."

Sharkey, it said, the man who boasted, he "wasn't afraid of any man alive", was going to receive treatment for an infected foot. At the hospital, he told reporters: "I'm down but not out."

He came out of the hospital, "just as he had always got up from the canvas," in the words of a 1947 article in *The Eagle* magazine, the publication of the Fraternal Order of Eagles. The Eagles is a social and fundraising organization which supports charities across the United States and Canada. Sharkey had joined in 1946, becoming a member of the San Francisco Aerie, where he once welcomed the Grand Worthy President from Milwaukee, Wisconsin, to give a major keynote speech. Having sat down, the guest turned to Sharkey and asked him if he had enjoyed the talk. The Irishman gave him the same look that used to unnerve opponents in the ring and replied; "It was all right, but I'm not sure it was worth travelling 2,000 miles to give."[26]

In January 1950, Tom heard of the death of his friend Tim McGrath. He was getting weaker himself, too.

On February 8, 1952, Tom suffered what was first thought to be a heart attack in his hotel room in San Francisco. He was rushed to hospital, seemingly gravely ill. Subsequent tests showed

DOWN BUT NOT OUT

he had been laid low by a congestive condition rather than from a coronary attack, doctors said. However, it was later confirmed he was suffering from heart disease.[27] That June, he was still in the hospital, and was visited by Jimmy Bronson, one-time adviser to Gene Tunney and Billy Cavanaugh, a former boxing coach at West Point. A period of grumbling about the then current fighters and reminiscing about the old days then followed. "But [my light] weight never meant anything to me. The bigger they were, the better I liked it. I knew I always could cut them down to my size."[28]

Sharkey left hospital for a short period but by August, was back with the doctors and was said to be "fighting a serious and possibly his final battle".[29] He re-entered San Francisco County Hospital penniless but his friends came to his aid. Two bankers, Parker Maddux and Louis Lurie, had started a committee to raise funds to pay for Sharkey's treatment. Fighters, promoters, old-time newsmen and followers were to contribute. "When he had the money, he dished it out to those less fortunate," noted one observer. "Never has he asked for charity. The old ring gamester, whose sun is surely setting, could use some help today."

Sharkey would be in and out of the hospital ten times during those last years as his heart condition got worse. On January 31, he was admitted for the last time and was on a ward with thirty seven other patients because "hospital officials said he liked company".[30]

The hospital was to be the last home, and his fellow patients were to be the final companions, of the adventurer and battler, "Sailor" Tom Sharkey.

CHAPTER TWELVE
No Crown, Only Glory

Jim Jeffries died on March 3, 1953 at Burbank, California. He was 77.[1] When Tom heard the news of his old friend, he said: "Well, I finally beat him."[2]

Within six weeks, Tom Sharkey's remarkable life was over too.

He died in his sleep in the early hours of April 17, 1953. He was 79. That big, strong heart had finally given out.

The man who had tested his physical and mental courage to the absolute limits in so many brutal ring contests died "easily" in a bed at San Francisco County Hospital.

The *Mexia Daily News* called him "one of the last of the great old time heavyweight prize-fighters" and the "uncrowned heavyweight champ".

The *New York Times* said Sharkey had become a legend in California. "He was well known to thousands of San Franciscans, many of whom made it a practice to stop him on the street to question him about the boxing greats of a half-century ago and to enjoy his appraisal of the present crop of heavyweight fighters as no more than good enough to serve as sparring partners for those of his day," it wrote.

The Times of London reported that "Sailor Tom Sharkey [had been] penniless but not entirely without friends, [and] belonged to one of the golden periods of the ring – golden, that is in fighting ability and personalities, if seldom in financial reward." He had been the "toughest and most formidable slogger of his time".

The *Irish Independent*, said he was the "last of the ring's great men of the 1890s", adding: "The game little slugger, who won $250,000 fighting John L Sullivan, Jim Corbett, Bob Fitzsimmons and Jim Jeffries and others, died penniless."

It was the Californians, of course, not the Irish, who knew the Dundalk-boy best now. The *Humboldt Standard* reported sadly: "Colourful, twinkly-eyed Sailor Tom Sharkey is dead. In his heyday, the scourge of four heavyweight champions, has gone to report to the place where all good sportsmen go…"

The writer, Fred F Thevenin, said Sharkey - "the last of the great ring gladiators of the long ago" – was "proud of his claim that he feared no man in the ring and never took a backward step while in action". He added: "Always a sucker for a touch, Tom Sharkey was broke soon after he retired. No money, but thousands of friends throughout the world."

The *Los Angeles Times* said the death of the "barrel-chested battler" had "rang down the curtain on a long-gone era of pugilism". It noted the irony that it followed so closely on Jeffries' demise, "Sharkey's greatest rival".

He was buried on April 21, 1953, with military honours in Golden Gate National Cemetery, San Bruno. The grave is simple. Sharkey's date of birth is incorrect, taken as it is from the records kept at the navy when he signed on. The inscription reads: "Thomas Sharkey, California, MAAS US Navy, January 1, 1871 - April 17, 1953." No mention that he was a boxer; but how proud he was of his service as a master-at-arms. Later, an effort was made to move Sharkey's remains to the family plot in the old Haggardstown graveyard, Dundalk, but it was never done.

Tom claimed to have "fought and whipped, perhaps, three thousand men in the ring and in rough-and-tumble fights" during his lifetime.[3]

Professional ring records show he scored 40 wins in 54 fights, knocking out his opponent 37 times.

It was an exceptional record. He was shorter and lighted than most of opponents – 5 feet 8½ inches at most and averaging around 180lbs – and survived on pure courage, a virtue always stressed by his admirers.

In his tribute in *The Ring*, Jersey Jones said: "He was all beef and brawn, with tremendous shoulders and ham-like fists, and his burly physique was supported by boundless energy and implicit confidence in an ability to whip any man in the world."

In 1945, the Helms Athletic Foundation of Los Angeles had presented to him a medallion inscribed: "His ring courage will be a lasting memorial in the history of boxing."

To Jeffries, he was always quite simply, "the toughest"[4], a "physical wonder"[5] and the "bravest man who ever lived".[6]

After one Sharkey fight, one expert had commented: "[He] would be pronounced a fighter even by a man who never saw a professional pugilist. He has the deep-set eye and the massive under jaw of one and the brute in him that knows no beating was manifested at every stage of the fight last night."[7]

He was also a man of immense personality, one of "most popular battlers the ring ever has seen".[8]

His courage, at the dawn of modern boxing, harked back to the older days. He was a "fighter ready always for a battle, a relic of the days of long ago when John Morrisey *[sic]*, Bill Poole and other bruisers used to fight with bare knuckles".[9]

The era in which Sharkey fought, at once added and detracted from his legend and legacy.

It was an incredible era for the sport, packed with some of the greatest names in the formative period of the sport.

This was the "golden era of the new prize-ring, a period in which great boxers of all weights simply tumbled over each other in the race for titles and the moderate purses that went with them". Here, the fighters "had to fight it out between themselves and the general result was not only a series of worthy champions but a standard of ability upon which the boxers and spectators alike could base their estimates... Then it was not only difficult to keep a good boxer down but next to impossible to keep a bad one standing up."[10]

Sharkey was among the best of that golden era named by *The Times* of London. It also listed the champions who brought the sport into the new century.

And Sharkey fought 'em all. Four champions in a row. The first four champions under Marquis of Queensberry rules. John L Sullivan, James J Corbett, Bob Fitzsimmons and James J Jeffries.

But while the history books cannot find a place on the congested summit of the heavyweight game in the 1890s, Tom is there or there about.

He was, after all, included in a parade of champions past and present in 1937 when the *New York Times* noted Sharkey was "the old sailor, who though never a champion, nevertheless will always rate among the ring immortals".

Colonel Harvey L "Heinie" Miller, an executive secretary of the National Boxing Association, noted in 1950, that Sharkey was a top-notch fighter who came along at a time of great heavyweights. "He probably would have won the title at any other time," said Miller.[11]

"He never held the championship but if he had met different competition, if he had been born a little earlier or a little later, he would be immortal," wrote Donald Barr Chidsey.[12]

Another writer, S De Cristofaro, said: "Sharkey was a giant in an era of giants and could acquit himself against the best in the world."[13]

Sharkey, according to the *Los Angeles Times*, was "pound for pound one of the greatest fighters of all-time".[14]

In 1925, Sidney McNeill Sutherland wrote: "[Sharkey] embraced in that short, stocky body, a fearless, honest heart, and in that bullish head a ring wit of no mean order. What a pity he is not with us now, to show up the mediocrities of the heavyweight crop and to earn some of the large purses his fighting prowess entitled him to. And how long a journey 'twould be worth travelling to see the sailor touch gloves with Jack Dempsey."[15]

In the *Cyber Boxing Zone Journal*, November 1998, boxing historian Tracy Callis listed a collection of descriptions made of Sharkey. He was "game and aggressive to the core", "one of the most durable heavyweights of the golden era"; he was "regarded by some as an uncrowned champion". W Diamond, in *Kings of the Ring*, had written: "Tom Sharkey was a veritable nightmare to heavyweights. He never became champion, but with a little luck he might have been."

John Durant and O Bettman in their *Pictorial History of American Sports* stated: "Sharkey was a tough, squat battler who had the misfortune to appear when there were many great heavyweights on the scene. He fought them all but could never quite win the crown."

Callis himself concluded: "It is the opinion of this writer that Sharkey was a Rocky Marciano 'look-a-like' and a 'near-equal' of the great 'Rock' in ruggedness, power and size. He had the bad luck to fight when Jim Jeffries, Bob Fitzsimmons, and Jim Corbett were around. Had he fought in any other period of history, he probably would have been a champion."

Callis believes Sharkey belongs to a "special class of power punchers" along with Sullivan, Marciano and Mike Tyson.

In 2003, 50 years after he died, Sharkey was finally included in the International Boxing Hall of Fame, at a ceremony in New York.

David Hannigan, writing in *The Sunday Tribune* at the time, said: "Regarded as one of the finest fighters never to hold the world heavyweight title, and often compared in style and build to Rocky Marciano, a rare extant photograph of Tom Sharkey in his prime bears eloquent testimony to the passions of his life. A crude tattoo of a masted galleon stretches across his ample chest, his left ear is bent into the shape of a cauliflower by so many concussive blows, and his nose is the typically crooked construct of the weather-beaten pugilist. ...It was his misfortune to be around during one of the more competitive eras in the division."[16]

The 1899 fight with Jeffries holds, as boxing writer Mike Casey has said, a special place in the pioneering stage of modern boxing, which produced "special men who risk their very lives on breaching unchartered territory and setting new milestones in bravery and endurance".

"It was a fight for the ages, which proved in time to be so much more," he stated. "It was a long, brutal confrontation that showcased outstanding talent and unrelenting courage. It forged a deep mutual respect between two of the hardiest men in the boxing universe and ultimately led to a trusting and enduring friendship." The fight "combined all the essential and sometimes mystical elements of the noble and savage art".

Tracy Callis believes "this was the greatest heavyweight bout ever".

Sharkey had almost taken the title in that fight. The great boxing writer, Charles P Mathison of *The Ring*, who covered the fight as sports editor of the *Detroit Free Press*, said that if it had been a twenty rounder, as the one in California, "Sharkey would have won the crown". However, it had gone on five rounds too long in which "Sharkey received the worst beating…ever handed out in a heavyweight title bout".[17]

That marked the beginning of the end of his title hopes. He was never the same fighter again.

There were allegations of dirty fighting, but that affected all fighters at the time.

In the November 1898 Corbett fight, for instance, both men had agreed not to hit in the clinches and to step back when ordered by the referee. Sharkey was the "only one to comply", noted the *Brooklyn Daily Eagle*. Following the fight, as onlookers went out of their way to describe Sharkey's clean fighting and technique which did everything to avoid a foul, Corbett tried to besmirch his name, claiming, "Everybody could see that Sharkey was hitting too low."

Sharkey, a no-nonsense figure, was less likely to grumble or complain.

The day after getting beaten by Sharkey, McCoy wrote to a Cincinnati newspaper claiming he had been "repeatedly fouled" by the Irishman. But, as the *Brooklyn Daily Eagle* noted, "McCoy cannot go back on what he said as soon as the fight was over on Tuesday night. Then, he made no complaints and admitted he had been beaten fairly."[18]

During the 1899 Jeffries contest, the same newspaper recorded: "Sharkey never complained to the referee…when there was rough work going on, while on a number of occasions Jeffries called

Siler's attention to the tactics of his opponent. It did not indicate that the sailor is a gamer man. It simply meant that when Sharkey is in the ring he has a mind for one thing, fight. The way it comes matters little to him."

Sharkey started with a bad name and kept it until the fans were won over by his courage. Early criticism of his lack of technique certainly caused some opponents – Corbett and McCoy among them – to underestimate him.

There was also always a need for fans to hate the fighters. Sharkey was hissed at times, so were many others, Corbett included, when he arrived only as a spectator for the Sharkey-McCoy fight.

Tom's pride in being a member of the United States Navy and of his adopted homeland perhaps contributed to his being forgotten back home. In Dundalk, only a pub next to the house Sharkey bought his parents in Hill Street, marks Sharkey's life. The owner of Byrne's, John Byrne, is a descendant of Sharkey family friend, James Gosling. The seats at the fireplace in the front bar of the pub are called Sharkey's Place and a mural of the boxer has been painted on the pub ceiling. In contrast in Hawaii, scene of some of Tom's first fistic encounters, there is a complex called the Sharkey Theatre in his honour.

Tom Sharkey, being the colourful character he was, could talk like he could fight, and so he left many fine phrases of his own.

"Give your best in whatever line you follow, my lads, and the rest will take care of itself," he once said. "The fight game was always good to me, and I never was the champion. The best I can say for myself is that I was always in there trying. All I can say is that when the champions got through with Mrs Sharkey's little boy, Tom, they knew they had been in a fight."[19]

And in a poem written at the time of the Golden Gate Exposition in 1939, he stated: "I've lived the life of a man of the world, I've had all its ups and downs.

"I've shook the false hand of the fair-weather friend, I've seen fortune's smiles and frowns; I've led a life of both pleasure and pain and I'd gladly live that same life over again."

THE CREED OF A MAN OF THE WORLD

I've lived the life of a 'man of the world',
I've had all its ups and downs;

I've shook the false hand of the fair-weather friend,
I've seen fortune's smiles and frowns.

I've led a life of both pleasure and pain,
And I'd gladly live that same old life over again.

Altho' there are things that I have done I'd like to forget,
And there are deeds that I've done I have lived to regret,

There are deeds of darkness that shadow our lives,
No matter how much, to avoid them a fellow strives.

Then there are other deeds of which I am proud,
But of these I don't care to boast and brag of aloud.

When I could, I have lent the helping hand –
When poverty's voice has made its demand.

To help, I have given in the hour of need,
To help, and to help gladly, has been my creed.

I have always helped my friends in a needy hour,
I have given little, but it was all in my power.

'Tis the deed of kindness that makes the heart light
And the wintry days seem summery bright.

I've found that a deed well done, is a battle won,
And victory is ours over the strife that has begun.

I believe in loyal hearts and spirits brave
and souls that are pure and true,
And that if you give the world the best you have
That the best will be sure to come back to you.

Then give love, and love to your heart will blow,
It will give you strength in your utmost need.

Have faith and a score of hearts will show
Their faith in your word and deed.

Whether you be a king or a slave,
'Tis just what you are and what you do,

Then give to the world the best you have
And the best will come back to you.

I am just a plain man of common clay
Like the man you meet on the street every day.

I have tried to live on the level and on the square,
And treat everyone honestly, kindly and fair.

And when my journey on this earth is ended,
If there be any of the many I've befriended

Who stands by my grave when I have crossed the 'Big Span',
Let them mark my tombstone, 'Here lies a MAN'.

Yours truly,
Sailor Tom Sharkey

NOTES

Tom Sharkey's first person memories of his early life up to and including his 1896 fight with John L Sullivan, and the reports of conversations during this time, are mainly taken from a series of articles called "Fighters I've Met" which Tom wrote for a US newspaper called the *Evening Herald*. We have been unable to ascertain the place or dates of publication.

CHAPTER ONE: SAILOR TOM
1. Gambling on horse racing was legalised in California in 1933, after being outlawed since 1909.
2. The site of the house where Tom was born is now occupied by a new building housing a pizza take away and a motor accessories business.
3. James already had one family. Records show he had fathered a child, Maria. when only a teenager. The mother was Ann Gallagher.
4. Tom Sharkey's date of birth has been recorded as being as early as January 1871 and will be discussed later.

NOTES

5. The act was to return soon after following the murders of Lord Frederick Cavendish and the under secretary Mr. Thomas Burke in Dublin.
6. James and Margaret's efforts for their family were noted in a court custody hearing when they applied to take in a niece, Jane. Margaret Sharkey, it was said, was "possessed of some means being the wife of a signalman", Dundalk Democrat, January 2, 1892. The family took in Jane and she was still living with them at the time of the 1901 Census.
7. This description of Hill Street in the 1870s comes from Tempest's Jubilee Annual, 1909: Dundalk and District.
8. Thubber Holmog, Dundalk Democrat, May 7, 1881.
9. 'Celtic Fighter of the Sea', by George T Pardy, *The Ring*.
10. 'Sailor Tom', by Donald Barr Chidsey, *The Eagle* magazine April 1947.

CHAPTER TWO: MASTER AT ARMS

1. The fight officials that day included Bat Masterson, once sheriff of Dodge City and later the boxing expert of the *Morning Telegraph* of New York.
2. *Prize-Fighter, The Life and Times of Bob Fitzsimmons* by Dale Webb.
3. 'Tom Sharkey Was A Victim Of His Times', by Michael A Glick.
4. Chidsey.
5. Frederick S. Harrod, *Manning the New Navy*.
6. In a colourful interview in the *Coshocton Tribune*, October 1, 1950, Harvey "Heinie" L Miller, claimed: "(Tom) was plenty smart on the ring but not so good out of it. He couldn't read or write."
7. There would, of course, never be any records of these first fights on board ship or in the dockyards. It is generally claimed that Tom was undefeated or at least had by far the better of these fights. His subsequent record in the professional game would obviously support that.

NOTES

However, an obituary for 53-year-old Father William Henry Ironsides Reany, 'The fighting chaplain of the US Navy', which was published in the New York Times on November 19, 1915, claimed: "He was said to be the father of boxing in the Navy and also introduced other athletics among the sailors. Fr Reany was always ready to put on the gloves with the sailors and was a very proficient boxer. It is related of him that he was the only man in the navy who ever defeated Tom Sharkey. The story is that Sharkey was obstreperous and interrupted divine services and the priest 'called him down'. As soon as the services were over he reproached Sharkey for his disturbance and the upshot of the matter was that they put on the gloves. Fr Reany with his clean hitting and scientific knowledge of the sport, soon placed the pugilist hors de combat and from that time on never had any further trouble with Sharkey." The obituary provoked a strong response from a Helen Manzone, of Brooklyn, who was angry not at the claim that Tom might have been beaten but had been rude. She wrote to the newspaper's editor: "I have read your tribute to Fr Reany. I take pleasure in attempting to correct that statement relative to Tom Sharkey. You have put it before the public that Fr Reany had to upbraid Tom Sharkey for being turbulent. That is false. Such thing is against Tom Sharkey's principle."

8   The fight was recorded in the *Daily Bulletin* (Honolulu) as having happened later in the year, around June 21, 1894. The newspaper details Sharkey's dominance of the fight and says that he had almost knocked out Langley in the third.

9   There was probably a third fight with Thompson, a four-round contest won by Sharkey that August: the *Hawaiian Gazette*, August 7, 1894.

10 *The San Mateo Times and Daily News Leader*, May 18, 1932.

11 Contemporary coverage of Sharkey fights in United States newspapers before 1896 is hard to find (even with the internet). Tom's claim, made forty years

later, that his father was reading about him before then in Irish newspapers is unlikely to be true.
12 According to Dale Webb, James was actually a ship's purser who had been sent to Australia to escort middleweight champion Jem Hall to the California Athletic Club. While there, he offered to take Fitzsimmons too. Fitzsimmons said he would have to ask his wife, Alice. She jumped at the chance to go to the States, as she wanted to pursue her own theatrical career.
13 Sharkey may not be the only unreliable recorder of events and dates. At the same time the *Daily Bulletin* reported he was fighting Barrowich for the second occasion, the *Hawaiian Gazette*, also of Honolulu, said he was fighting Langley.
14 The description of this fight comes from Sharkey's memories in his series of articles for the *Evening Herald*. It seems likely that this fight was in fact a rematch, Sharkey having conveniently forgotten that Washington had knocked him out earlier that year: The *Daily Bulletin* (Honolulu) carried a brief report on February 8, 1894, of a fight at a "certain place last night" at which "Geo Washington, the colored pugilist, knocked out Sharkey".
15 Mare Island remained a major centre for shipbuilding until well into the twentieth century. The last of the more than 500 vessels built there was the nuclear submarine USS Drum which launched in 1970.
16 Chidsey.
17 *Brooklyn Daily Eagle*, October 28, 1896.
Sharkey later gave the cane to his father.

CHAPTER THREE: "SHARKEY: YOU'RE PURE GOLD"
1 "Spider" Kelly would enjoy a 40-year partnership with McGrath, continuing long after the end of his own fight career which peaked in a battle with champion Joe Gans in New York in October 1899. Having turned pro himself when under 20, Kelly was a remarkable character,

NOTES

regularly fighting 40-round bouts. He lived most of his life in San Francisco and died on November 1, 1927 after suffering a blood clot on the brain. He was 55. At the time of his death, the Los Angeles Times described McGrath and Kelly has having been "probably the greatest team of seconds the game has known". They were always full of tricks. Once, as Kelly seconded for Fitz Holland, he watched as the boxer staggered back towards his corner. As an attendant shoved a stool under Holland, Kelly kicked it out of the ring, quipping: "If he sits down he'll never get up." The fighter went on to earn a draw.

2 *Sports History*, November 1988.
3 The Mechanic's Pavilion was similar to modern indoor sports arena in that it was central to the community and used for sporting and non-sporting events. It hosted some of the world's greatest fights until 1906 when it was destroyed in the fires which followed the San Francisco earthquake.
4 Eugen Sandow, 1867-1925, was the strong man 'Father of Modern Bodybuilding' who became extremely famous during the Victorian era and wrote several books, including *Strength and How To Obtain It*.
5 It is not clear if Sharkey ever fulfilled his half-promise to referee these fights.
6 In the opening bouts that night, Sam Bolan beat Joe Hopkins over four rounds; Bob Armstrong defeated Tom Forrest, of Sheepshead Bay, when the bout was stopped in the second round; Billy Richards, of Newark, and Young Foley, of the United States Navy, Tommy White, of Chicago, and Jack Burge, of Mount Vernon, Bob Armstrong, of Chicago, and Fred Morris, of New York, and Paddy McGuiggan, of Newark, and Johnny Banks each fought four-round draws.
7 AD Phillips seems to have first related this when writing the article 'When Sharkey First Met the Great John L' for the July 1922 issue of *The Ring*.

NOTES

Chapter Four: The Fight He Won Flat On His Back
1. *San Francisco Examiner*, December 3, 1896.
2. Ibid.
3. *San Francisco Evening Bulletin*, December 5, 1896; *Wyatt Earp: The Life Behind the Legend* by Casey Tefertiller.
4. December 16; Tefertiller.
5. *San Francisco Bulletin*, December 1896; Tefertiller.
6. *Brooklyn Daily Eagle*, December 19, 1896.
7. *Brooklyn Daily Eagle*, December 28, 1896.
8. Tefertiller.
9. *The Ring*, April-May 1961.
10. *The Sunday Times*, June 23rd, 2003.

Chapter Five: A Celebrity Homecoming
1. *Irish News*, July 1897.
2. *Liberty*, June 3 1939.
3. This was about £3,000 sterling at the time, according to the *Dundalk Democrat*.
4. Kingstown is now called Dún Laoghaire.
5. *Dundalk Democrat and People's Journal*, July 3, 1897.
6. Queenstown is now called Cobh.
7. The purse being fought for in some of the local and national contests shows just how big the game had become in America. An Ulster championship fight in 1897, for instance, not an insignificant bout, attracted a purse of around £50, about one-sixtieth of what Sharkey would fight for at the time.

Chapter Six: Hard As Nails
1. Three Veriscope cameras had been used to film the Corbett-Fitzsimmons title fight earlier that year. The subsequent film played to packed-out audiences in the US and Britain. Box office receipts were estimated at more than $750,000, or about $16m in today's money.
2. Pete Ehrmann, in correspondence with the authors, explained that Baker's grisly nickname stemmed from his

NOTES

job in a meat packing plant. He also stated that Baker met an unpleasant end himself when, in around about 1910, he was decapitated while working on the railroad at Kansas City. "Or at least somebody claiming to be Henry Baker did," added Pete. "Up to 1960 there are reports of Baker or somebody using his name appearing at old-timers nights. Another great boxing mystery."

3 The Greater New York Athletic Club was not happy that the fight ended so quickly. It later took the two fighters to court, claiming they had not lived up to their contract and that Ruhlin had faked a knockout. The judge ruled in favour of Gus Ruhlin for $776 and Tom Sharkey for $2,101 for prize money due them. Reporters noted that the club apparently "had as much difficulty in convincing the court as it would have in proving to anyone who saw the fight that Ruhlin was not in a genuine trance after Sharkey landed the right hook on the jaw". There was almost a fight in the courtroom, according to the Brooklyn Daily Eagle, when a Mr Dowdell, the head of the club, invited Ruhlin's, Emmanuel Friend, to meet him outside. "Friend and Ruhlin went outside and Dowdell had disappeared, not however without having left a farewell message. It read, so it is said: 'You can whistle for your money.'" Eight months later the club tried to reorganise under the name New Coney Island Athletic Club allegedly to avoid meeting a number of debts – the main a "balance of about $2,500" due to Sharkey and Ruhlin.

Chapter Seven: Fair And Square

1 McCoy's life was colourful outside as well as inside the ring. He fought off and on until 1916 when he retired to run a saloon and a gym, act in movies and work as a detective. He was married a reported eight times and in 1924 was jailed after shooting the woman he was living with. He served seven years in prison before he was released on parole. He committed suicide in Detroit on April 18, 1940. He was 67.

2 The fight apparently arose from a series of challenges to Sharkey which followed McCormick's stamping out of the Sharkey training camp the year before. McCormick went on and on until the sailor went to Philadelphia and knocked him out. McCormick gained a bit of notoriety later in 1899, however, with a first-round knock-out of 'Kid' McCoy, delivered with a "ridiculous" lucky blow.

3 The competitive fights planned for this period seem to have fallen through for a number of reasons. For instance, a six-round bout with Corbett, which was to take place in Chicago on March 7 was abandoned when the city's Mayor Harrison emphatically vetoed the proposition, saying as long as he was Mayor the "two burly sluggers who cannot help but give a brutal exhibition" would not meet in the Windy City.

4 *Brooklyn Daily Eagle,* November 2 1899.

Chapter Eight: Ninety-Nine Minutes of Hell

1 This figure of 200 arc lights came from contemporary newspaper reports. Later references, possibly based on a claim made by Sharkey in *Liberty* in 1939, place the figure at 400.

2 It is believed the official footage of the fight has been lost, but film still exists thanks to the work of bootleggers who smuggled a camera into the club in a stall selling cigars. In 2007, some of this footage was available on the You Tube website.

3 There was another loser of a quite different kind that night. Fight fans in the US Navy were especially excited about Sharkey's shot at the title. In July 1953, *The Ring* recalled a story from reporter Charley Van Loan, who was in Manila at the time of the fight. Getting news from Coney Island to the Philippines at the time was a complicated process: a cable would be sent from New York to London, from London to Hong Kong, and from there to Manila,

NOTES

and news would often arrive a day or two late.

Manila was full of sailors, who "went haywire betting on Sailor Tom…No sailor picked Jeff to whip the Pride of the Navy".

Charley Fagan was a star sports writer in Manila, although he was not an entirely straight one. "Like many scribes of his day, he was a heavy drinker and couldn't stick to one job long enough to make the post a steady one, but shifted from one paper to another and every now and then he would pick up some easy money by trimming some gullible sucker."

On the day of the fight in Manila was bedlam. Everyone expected the papers to carry at least a line of the winner, but not a word was received. The editors were frantic.

About an hour before the *Manila Press* was to go to press, Fagan got an idea and ran to the editor's office.

"I understand that you have no report of the big fight," he said.

"That's so," replied the editor, a young man who had recently arrived from St Louis. "Do you know anything?"

"Well, I've seen a private message. It came over a cipher," panted Fagan. "I not only know who won but I've got the fight by rounds and all that happened. Some of my friends have engineered the deal to keep the news out of Manila so that they can make a clean-up in the betting. But you can have it if you'll pay what it's worth."

The editor was amazed. "I can't understand how such a thing could be done but if you've got what I want I'll give you fifty dollars for the story," he told Fagan.

"Fifty eh? Don't make me laugh."

"That's all I can pay," came the reply.

Fagan made the deal and was told to write the story as fast as he could.

"Sharkey won by a knockout in the eighth round," said Fagan excitedly.

309

"That's a peach of a story for us. Get busy in a hurry."

Fagan banged away at a typewriter, faking up a good and thrilling round-by-round yarn.

The young editor, who had been told about the shady side of Fagan, came out of his office and asked for a copy of the cable.

"Not a chance", replied Fagan. "No one sees it. My friends expect to clean up a lot of dough on this beat and I'm taking no chances. I've done these fellows a good turn and they wanted me to get in on the scoop. That's how I got the cable."

"Who are these men?" asked the editor.

"There are two and both are big time gamblers. That's all I can tell you."

Fagan went back to writing the bloody details of the fight. He had Jeffries leading in the first six rounds before Sailor Tom came tearing back to cut big Jim to ribbons.

The paper came out with its exclusive and thousands of dollars changed hands. "Fist fights and beer bottle battles followed the celebration of the sailors who had trimmed the soldiers…The other Manila papers were scooped and scooped properly. It was an angry group of scribes that gathered in the sportsmen's bar cussing the failure of the cable service."

Late in the evening, a rival reporter bumped into Fagan and found the crafty hack had bought a ticket on a boat to Hong Kong.

"You finally leaving Manila?" asked the rival. "Why so soon?"

"For my health," replied Fagan. "I need a change of air."

It was not until Fagan had left that the first genuine cable report of the fight arrived in Manila.

There was nothing anyone could do as the bets had been paid.

An angry mob bore down on the newspaper which had printed Fagan's story.

NOTES

The windows of the office were smashed and the editor was unable to leave without a bodyguard.

Less than a fortnight later the young editor packed his bags and left for America.

CHAPTER NINE: BLOOD, SWEAT AND TEARS

1. The big money involved in the motion pictures meant they were never far from controversy. In February 1900, WJ Fisher was in Chattanooga exhibiting pictures when he reported to the police that the films and electric machinery had been stolen from the exhibition room by two of his own employees. It was reckoned they had headed for Cincinnati and the police there were on alert.
2. After this final bout with Sharkey, Goddard only entered the ring three more times before a bizarre incident ended his career and his life. During the Republican primaries in New Jersey in July 1902, Goddard was travelling from poll to poll. At the polling station in Pensauken, he got into an argument with a black constable named Robert Washington. When Goddard attacked Washington with a baseball bat, Washington shot him in self-defence. The bullet hit Goddard in the head and he died from his wounds on January 21, 1903. Source: boxrec.com)
3. *Dundalk Democrat*, June 16, 1900. Lord Claremount was an 18th Century Irish landowner who had owned estates in County Louth and been a founder member of the Jockey Club.
4. *Brooklyn Daily Eagle*, June 4, 1900.
5. *Dundalk Democrat*, June 30, 1900.
6. *Brooklyn Daily Eagle*, August 24, 1900.
7. *The Milwaukee Journal*, December 8, 1907.
8. Jeffries and Fitzsimmons would eventually meet July 25, 1902, in San Francisco when for nearly eight rounds Fitzsimmons hammered the giant mercilessly with both hands, breaking his nose, cutting both cheeks to the bone, and opening gashes over each eye.

There was no surrender from the champion though and eventually a crashing left hook to the jaw would leave Fitz spread out on the canvas in the eighth.

9 *New York Times*, September 11, 1900.
10 *Brooklyn Daily Eagle*, March 8, 1901.
11 Some reports state that the fight ended early in the second round.
12 *The Milwaukee Journal*, February 2, 1910.
13 'Boxer vs. Wrestler-Records Show Pugilists Superior to Grapplers in Mixed Bouts', by AD Phillips, *The Ring*, March 1923.
14 Interestingly, newspapers were soon making their own comparisons between the two sports, although they were hardly favourable. Tom – and Jenkins – were involved in this debate too. On December 23, 1902, the *Brooklyn Daily Eagle* ran a piece headline, 'Will wrestling go the way of boxing?', after Tom was punched during a George Bothner-Tom Jenkins wrestling match at Grand Central Palace. Tom was the referee. The trouble started when Bothner was declared the winner because Jenkins did not throw him four times in an hour. Billy Elmer, one of the winning man's seconds, and Tom Sharkey had "a little mix-up" which had the crowd in an uproar. Despite Bothner's victory, his seconds felt Sharkey had favoured Jenkins. The police eventually pulled the men apart and Captain Lantry was heard to vow that "to guard against a similar occurrence he would issue no more permits for wrestling bouts in his territory". The timely intervention by the police, noted the *New York Times*, "prevented what might have become a general free fight and the spectators were dispersed without any further acts of violence occurring".

The *Brooklyn Daily Eagle* was indignant, blaming fighters like Sharkey who were in danger of being left "stranded all along the shore" after the reforms and end of the Horton Law. "Love of the roped arena never dies," it stated. "In the minds of all, a squirming, struggling wrestling match is merely an apology for the biff, biff of the prize-ring. It is considered better than nothing, however, and each bout of prominence held within striking distance of Greater New York always sees a gathering of the old guard outside the ropes, following the progress of the mill with a mingled expression of amusement, toleration and superiority."

It added: "Wrestling will soon drift into as much disfavour as boxing unless those managing the various bouts take warning."

15 "Ruhlin was pitifully outclassed and the wonder is that he was ever induced to enter the ring with Jeffries." *Brooklyn Daily Eagle*, November 17, 1901.
16 'Vigilant' writing in the *Brooklyn Daily Eagle*, December 5, 1901.
17 *Brooklyn Daily Eagle*, January 5, 1902.
18 Little was reported about this fight with Fitz. It took place in Manhattan and was investigated by the authorities following the recent changes in New York law. The police ruled the fight was an exhibition and therefore within the state law.

CHAPTER TEN: "I'LL MARRY YOU, BUT GIVE UP THE GLOVES."
1 August 8, 1900.
2 Katherine is sometimes referred to as Catherine or Kate.
3 This fighter's name is sometimes spelt Munroe. He had become famous overnight when he fought Jeffries in an exhibition in Butte, Montana, in 1902. Monroe is alleged to have floored the champion. Jeffries hotly denied it, but Monroe's backers milked the incident into a title shot on August 26, 1904, and an angry Jeffries put him out in two.
4 *New York Times*, June 8, 1904; *Milwaukee Journal*, 1904.
5 According to a gossip column back home in the *Dundalk Democrat*, Tom had been "given an interest in (the) saloon…for the use of his name." When

his partner Reich heard of Tom's June 1902 defeat to Ruhlin in London, it was claimed, he had the big illuminated 'Sharkey' sign taken down!

The story was probably a case of knocking a celebrity while their star was fading: the bar continued to be known as Sharkey's.

Sharkey's fame would mean that Bernard Reich's misdemeanours would also make the news. In April 1903 the *New York Times* reported how a Mr Samuel Schneider was suing the "partner and backer of Thomas Sharkey" for $25,000 damages for the "alleged alienation of the affections of his wife, Dora. Mr Schneider, who had been married 17 years, said he and his wife had lived happily together until 1898 when Dora met Reich and had become "infatuated by him".

6   *New York Times*, November 25, 1901.
7   *The Ring*, December 1923.
8   *The Milwaukee Sentinel*, June 2, 1912.
9   *New York Times*, October 12, 1903.
10 *The Ring*, June 1923.
11 *The Ring*, 1936.
12 Story told by Harvey "Heinie" L Miller, of the National Boxing Association, in the *Coshocton Tribune*, October 1, 1950.
13 *The Milwaukee Journal*, May 6, 1903.
14 *The Ring*, June 1923.
15 Tom's injuries against the mighty Pardello were not exaggerated. Although Tom claimed victory because Pardello only managed to get him to the mat once and onlookers said the Italian was "puffing like a porpoise", the *New York Times* of March 11, 1905, noted that "Sharkey had to use all his strength and ingenuity in the balance of the match and was badly winded when the bout ended."
16 This story was told extremely colourfully in *Boxing Illustrated* in 1964 and was one of the many articles kindly provided for the authors by Pete Ehrmann.

NOTES

17 *Collier's Magazine*, May 13, 1939.
18 *New York Times*, August 1, 1904.
19 *New York Times*, June 28, 1926.
20 The boxers appear to have taken part in a one-night-only special of this event which was produced by Billy Brady. According to the Internet Broadway Database one of the young cast members of the full eight-week run of the play was Douglas Fairbanks.
21 Pember W Rocap also refers to a 1900 theatre appearance by Sharkey alongside Jeffries in *Around New York in Eighty Minutes*.
22 *New York Times*, September 18, 1906.
23 This is probably the same car which Sharkey would later have stolen from outside his house – an event which lead to strange little meeting between Tom and the great opera singer Enrico Caruso. Following the car's theft in March 1910 the boxer went to the Adams Street Court in Brooklyn to get a warrant for the arrest of "the guy that swiped me motor at Sheepshead Bay". Caruso was there to testify in the case of two Italians who were accused of being part of a Black Hand attempt to extort $15,000 from him. The *New York Times*, noted that the packed court "gazed wide-eyed, awed by the presence of such greatness", Caruso, "he of the gold voice and the other Mr Thomas Sharkey, is of the Gibraltar-like chest and the cauliflower ear". There had been rumour, the reporter said, that Tom was there as the tenor's bodyguard but they met as strangers and Tom, with warrant in hand, then left court with "never so much as a look or a word of appreciation of the presence of his fellow artist".
24 *Vallejo Evening Chronicle*, July 10, 1910.
25 *New York Times*, November 18, 1905.
26 The Cleveland Museum of Art.
27 *New York Times*, March 28, 1933.
28 *New York Times*, February 25, 1914.

NOTES

29 According to measuringworth.com this would have given him a fortune of around $10m by early 21st Century standards.
30 *New York Times*, June 24, 1916.
31 Pardy.
32 *Collier's Magazine*, May 13, 1939.
33 *Los Angeles Times*, August 7, 1917.
34 *New York Times*, July 27, 1912.
35 A San Francisco report quoted in the *Milwaukee Sentinel*, December 3, 1916.
36 This story – attributed to journalist Spike Webb - appeared in *The Ring* in 1922, but the authors could find no report of it nearer the time the meeting must have taken place. Teddy Roosevelt was president of the United States of America between 1901 and 1909.
37 *The Milwaukee Journal*, April 30, 1913.
38 *New York Times*, September 18, 1906.
39 The new home was across the street from the thatched cottage in which Tom had been born. It was next to a public house ran by James Gosling, a councillor and property developer. The pub was at Number 10. Gosling sold the house at Number 11, now an off licence, to Thomas Sharkey who wanted the house for his parents. "These would have been a better quality house," according to Hugh Smyth, of Dundalk Museum.

Goslings pub is now called Byrne's and is run by John Byrne, James Gosling's great-grandson. Mr Byrne told the authors in 2006: "The front of our bar has a fireplace which would have been in Number 10, against the wall of Number 11. We call the seats there Sharkey's Place."
40 A contemporary newspaper report states 84, but this possibly refers to his "84th year" as was often the style of the time. Dundalk Democrat, March 17, 1906.
41 *The Beloit (Wisconsin) Daily News*, July 30, 1918.
42 *The Times* of London reported on April 20, 1899: "One of two defective parts of the films have been cut

316

out, and the pictures as shown are an improvement on others previously exhibited. This is said to be the first time that fight at night time has been shown by means of the cinematograph. A vivid representation of the contest is given, the whole of the ten rounds, being seen in every detail."
43 In his fascinating book, *Unforgivable Blackness, The Rise and Fall of Jack Johnson*, Geoffrey C Ward notes that in the climatic brawl Johnson is the only one of the former ring stars who does not throw a punch. "Hollywood evidently still thought it best not to let Jack Johnson be seen hitting a white man on screen," he states.
44 *New York Times*, October 23, 1932.

Chapter Eleven: Down But Not Out

1 *The Milwaukee Journal*, November 12, 1907.
2 *New York Times*, March 31 1909.
3 *The Great White Hopes*, by Graeme Kent.
4 *New York Times*, June 12, 1910.
5 *New York Times*, July 31, 1911 and August 9, 1911.
6 *Los Angeles Times*, April 25, 1925.
7 *The Ring*, June 1925.
8 *The Saturday Evening Post*, September 12, 1936.
9 Ibid.
10 *Los Angeles Times*, January 6, 1927.
11 Tom ended the careers of at least one of the fighters who sparred with him. Edward C Currie, later a senior New York boxing official, abandoned the ring after Sharkey broke three of his ribs.
12 *The Ring*, August, 1922, 'When Jim Jeffries Balked at Becoming Tom Sharkey's Sparring Partner', by Vernon Van Ness.
13 From a letter written to Pete Ehrmann from Burroughs, May 4, 1985.
14 'Only Punks get Punch Drunk', *Collier's Magazine*, May 13, 1939.

15 *Los Angeles Times*, July 10, 1939.
16 *Los Angeles Times*, June 2, 1939, and June 22, 1939.
17 Tom O'Rourke, with whom Tom had had a falling out, died of a heart attack in the dressing room of Max Schmeling at the Yankee Stadium just before the German fighter met Joe Louis in the ring. He was 82. *New York Times*, June 20, 1936.
18 *New York Times*, July 10, 1927.
19 *New York Times*, January 21, 1945.
20 Tom had long been a regular punter at Tijuana. On December 23, 1924, the *Vallejo Evening Chronicle* reported he could be "found each day at the Tijuana races and he has quite a bit of success picking winners" After a series of bets that afternoon, it stated, he had bought a big Christmas box, "loaded with attractive presents and rounded out with some of California's famed fruits", and sent it to his family back in Ireland.
21 *New York Times*, February 7, 1943.
22 Chidsey.
23 *San Mateo Times*, September 16, 1949.
24 *Long Beach Press Telegram*, August 13, 1952.
25 *Modesto Bee and News Herald*, July 3, 1937.
26 Jeffries was a member of the Los Angeles branch of the Eagles.
27 *Los Angeles Times*, February 10, 1952.
28 *Los Angeles Times*, June 11, 1952.
29 *Long Beach Press Telegram*, August 13, 1952.
30 *New York Times*, April 18, 1953.

CHAPTER TWELVE: NO CROWN, ONLY GLORY

1 Jim Corbett had died in February 1933. Sharkey paid tribute to him in the *New York Times* on February 19, 1933: "He was a grand man, always a gentlemen and a real credit to boxing. He was the most clever man I ever fought."
2 *The Ring*, February 1994.
3 *Liberty*, February 4, 1939.

NOTES

4   *New York Times*, April 15, 1946.
5   *New York Times*, April 24, 1910.
6   *Sports History*, November 1988.
7   *New York Times*, January 11, 1899.
8   *The Ring*, July 1922.
9   *New York Times*, January 1899.
10 *The Times*, June 17, 1935.
11 *Coshocton Tribune*, October 1, 1950.
12 *The Eagle* magazine, April 1947.
13 *Sports History*, November 1988.
14 *Los Angeles Times*, June 11, 1952.
15 *The Eagle* magazine, August 1925.
16 *The Sunday Tribune*, January 19, 2003.
17 *The Ring*, July 1944.
18 *Brooklyn Daily Eagle*, January 12, 1899.
19 *The Saturday Evening Post*, September 12, 1936.

BIBLIOGRAPHY

Books:
  Anderson, Roger, *The Fighting Irish*
  Cooper, Henry, *The Great Heavyweights*
  Corbett, James J, *The Roar of the Crowd*
  Fleischer, Nat, *Pictorial History of Boxing*
  ------, *The Heavyweight Championship*
  Kent, Graeme, *Boxing's Strangest Fights*
  ------, *The Great White Hopes*
  McQuillan, Jack, *Voices of Dundalk*
  Mee, Bob, *The Heavyweights*
  Miletich, Leo N, *Dan Stuart's Fistic Carnival*
  Myler, Patrick, *Gentleman Jim Corbett, The Truth Behind A Boxing Legend*
  Nicholson, Kelly Richard, *A Man Among Men – The Life and Ring Battles of Jim Jeffries*
  Rocap, William H & Rocap, Pember W, *Remembering Bob Fitzsimmons*
  Sante, Luc, *Low Life*
  Ward, Geoffrey C, *Unforgivable Blackness: The Rise and Fall of Jack Johnson*

BIBLIOGRAPHY

Webb, Dale, *Prize-Fighter, The Life and Times of Bob Fitzsimmons*
Wilson, Maureen, Ross, Noel and Power, Patrick F, *Dundalk, Images and Impressions*

ARTICLES:
  Real Story of the Sharkey-Fitz Fight: Why Gun Fighter Earp Was Selected as Referee and Why his Kind are No Longer Wanted, by Robert Edgren, various US newspapers 1912
  When Sharkey First Met the Great John L, by AD Phillips, The Ring, July 1922
  When Jim Jeffries baulked at becoming Tom Sharkey's sparring partner, by Vernon Van Ness – The Ring, August 1922
  Sharkey Meets Admiral Dewey, The Ring 1922 (month unknown)
  Boxer vs Wrestler: Records show pugilists superior to grapplers in mixed bouts, by AD Phillips – The Ring, March 1923
  Unnamed article about boxer's pets, The Ring, June 1923
  When Tom Sharkey Was Fearful, The Ring, December 1923
  As We See It, by Nat Fleischer, The Ring, June 1925
  For The Fight Fan, by Sidney McNeill Sutherland, The Eagle Magazine, August 1925
  The Jeffries-Sharkey Fight, by Nat Fleischer, The Ring, June 1926
  Fight for the Championship of Ireland Results in Everybody Going to Jail, by Tim McGrath – The Ring, December 1926
  Unnamed article, The Ring, September 1927
  Unnamed article, The Ring, August 1930
  Tom Sharkey, poem by John Harvey Belanger, The Ring 1930 (month unknown)
  Sharkey, once Ace of the Ring, now Option Seller, The San Mateo Times and Daily News Leader, May 18, 1932
  Fighting the Champions, by Tom Sharkey and Morrow Mayo, the Saturday Evening Post, September 12, 1936
  Only Punks Get Punch-Drunk, by Kyle Crichton, Collier's Magazine, May 13, 1939

BIBLIOGRAPHY

We Need Red-Blooded Men, by Tom Sharkey,
    Liberty Magazine, May 13, 1939
Sailor Tom, by Donald Barr Chidsey, The
    Eagle Magazine, April 1947
Coronation Gala Planned, by Nat Fleischer,
    The Ring, January 1953
Around Our Town, Humboldt Standard, April 18, 1953
Sharkey Initiated Ring Career Here After Navy,
    Vallejo Times-Herald, September 16, 1954
Tom Sharkey's Famous Ear, Boxing Illustrated,
    1964 (month unknown)
Sailor Tom Sharkey: The Jerry Quarry of his Day, by
    Patrick Myler, The Ring, February 1994
Fighting Eagles, The Eagle Magazine, August 2004
The Right Stuff: Jeffries and Sharkey at Coney Island, by
    Mike Casey, boxingscene.com, August 24, 2006
Boxer vs Wrestler, by George Bothner,
    The Ring (date unknown)
Tom Sharkey Was A Victim Of His Times, by Michael
    A Glick (publication and date unknown)
Celtic Fighter of the Sea, by George T Pardy,
    The Ring (date unknown)

NEWSPAPERS:
Brooklyn Daily Eagle, 1896-1902
Milwaukee Journal, 1900-
Milwaukee Sentinel, 1912
New York Times, 1895-1953
New York World, January 11, 1899
The Beloit (Wisconsin) Daily News, 1918
Modesto Be and News-Herald, 1937
Reno Evening Gazette, 1943
San Mateo Times, 1932, 1949
Coshocton Tribune, 1950
Long Beach Press-Telegram, 1952
Mexia Daily News, 1953

BIBLIOGRAPHY

Daily Bulletin (Honolulu) 1894
Hawaiian Gazette, 1894
Dundalk Democrat, 1873, 1893-1900, 1953
Irish News
Irish Times
The Times (London), 1914
South Wales Echo, 1902
The Times (London), 1899-1953
Western Mail, 1902

VARIOUS DOCUMENTS:
Letter from Chuck Burroughs, author of Come Out Fighting, to Pete Ehrmann, dated May 4, 1985 (unpublished);
Vallejo Directory, 1897;
Tempest's Jubilee Annual, 1909: Dundalk and District
United States Navy records: The National Personnel Records Center (Military Personnel Records), St Louis, Missouri.

WEBSITES:
Cyberboxingzone.com
sfmuseum.org (The Virtual Museum of the City of San Francisco)
grandslampage.net (Run by boxing writer and historian Mike Casey)
boxrec.com
hotboxingnews.com
eastsideboxing.com
boxingscene.com
ibhof.com (The International Boxing Hall of Fame)
foe.com (The Fraternal Order of Eagles)
fitzsimmons.co.nz (Everything Bob Fitzsimmons)
brooklynpubliclibrary.org/eagle (A fascinating collection of issues of the Brooklyn Daily Eagle)
ibdb.com (Internet Broadway Database)
imdb.com (Internet Movie Database)

AUTHORS' NOTE

Tom Sharkey was alone in the centre of the ring; we had plenty of help in our battle to tell his story.

In particular, we would like to give special thanks to boxing writer Pete Ehrmann for so much help - he went above and beyond; boxing historian Tracy Callis, of the Cyber Boxing Zone and the International Boxing Research Organisation, for giving us a phenomenal amount of time and encouragement; Robert J Clooney and his daughter Karen Ehatt, relatives of Tom's in Maryland, for generously sharing their information and for being so enthusiastic; Pember W Rocap, for helping out right at the beginning; and Chris LaForce, of the International Boxing Research Organisation, who was generous with his research and is working on a biography of Joe Choynski.

Thanks also to James Kern, Executive Director, Vallejo Naval and Historical Museum; Pat Hatfield, of the Colma Historical Association; John Byrne, of Byrne's Bar, Hill Street, Dundalk (a fine place for a pint); staff at Dundalk Museum; Alan Hand, of Dundalk Library; staff at the National Library of Ireland, Dublin; staff at the National Archives of Ireland, Dublin; Kalisma Alayon and Louise Merriam, of the YMCA (US); Nick Sharkey (Dublin); Noel Ross, of County Louth Archaeological and Historical Society; Sergei Yurchenko; Jack Green, of the US Navy Historical Centre; Brian Lawrence, of Alabama, for contacting us about his relative Florence Manzoni; Renée Williams; Len Mullins; Mary Silk (Isle of Wight); Mike Casey; F Gwynplaine MacIntyre.

We are also indebted to the newspaper reporters throughout the years who followed Tom's life, recorded his quotes, spent long hours phoning in and typing up copy; who lived and breathed the fight game – this is their book too.

Thanks to Mary Sharkey (for proofreading) and Leo (for encouragement and enthusiasm), Declan and Louise (for always being great hosts in Dublin) and to Clive, Mary and Mark for their continuing support.

The idea for this book came about after a night out in Ireland when Colm Sharkey asked, 'Why isn't there a book about, Tom?'

Well, Colm, now there is. Finally.

INDEX OF PEOPLE AND PLACES

Allen, George, 76, 80, 94, 95, 98
Armory Hall, Vallejo, 33, 37
Armstrong, Bob, 114, 115, 145, 157, 173, 184, 185, 221, 222, 226, 229, 238, 248, 259, 280, 305
Asbury Park, New Jersey, 159, 174
Australia, 8, 18, 29, 75, 100, 130, 148, 278, 304
Australia (steam ship), 29, 30

Baker, Henry "Slaughterhouse", 152, 306, 307
Baltimore, Maryland, 69, 145, 185, 222
Bangor, 133
Barrington, Jim, 28
Beecher, Harry, 164
Belfast, 10, 14, 75, 131, 132, 136
Bellows, George, 264
Braddock, James, 286
Brady, Bill, 53, 55, 68, 69, 113, 142, 184, 186, 193, 199, 214, 315
Broadway, 70, 157, 158, 204, 224, 252, 258, 263, 315

Broadway Athletic Club, 114, 222
Brooklyn, 8, 65, 211, 237, 238, 263, 269, 303, 315
Brooklyn Navy Yard, 25
Brown, Alex (referee), 153
Brown, Charles "Sailor", 33, 34, 47, 124, 216
Burley, Nick, 29-31, 36, 216
Burns, Tommy, 277, 278
Burroughs, Chuck, 285, 317
Bush Street Theatre, San Francisco, 46, 47
Cape Horn, 20, 35
Carr, Frank, 57, 58, 62
Carroll, Patrick Joseph (Joseph James Sharkey), 273
Carson City, 107, 110, 111, 114, 131, 133, 149, 159, 214
Casey, M, 135, 136, 138
Cattanach, Jack, 117
Cavanagh, John J, 152
Chicago, 62, 65, 112, 153, 156, 209, 214, 226, 259, 263, 281, 285, 286, 305, 308
Childs, Frank "The Crafty Texan", 38

327

INDEX

Choynski, Joe, 47-50, 62, 63, 69, 79, 99, 111, 114, 115, 117, 122, 124, 126, 142, 143, 145-148, 154, 173, 182, 184, 222, 226, 279, 325
Claremont Villa, 225, 226
Clark, John S, 221
Cleveland, Ohio, 237, 264, 315
Clifton, Lord Talbot, 50-51
Cohen's Hotel, 231
Colorado Athletic Association, 235
Colville, Jimmy, 116, 117, 120, 121
Coney Island, 111-113, 153, 185, 187, 188, 191, 203, 204, 209, 214, 215, 217, 220, 224, 226, 227, 231, 243, 248, 257, 283, 307, 308
Connolly, Buck, 117, 121, 133, 142
Connolly, Eddie, 241
Conroy, "Stockings", 133, 223
Considine, George, 161, 163, 165-168, 219
Corbett, James, 23-25, 38, 44, 47, 51-66, 68-74, 75, 76, 85, 86, 99, 105-107, 109-111, 113, 114, 117, 124-126, 128, 131, 142, 147, 149, 151, 153, 155-168, 172, 174, 175, 182-187, 200, 203, 204, 207, 213, 220, 222, 225, 227, 232, 233, 236, 255, 264, 275, 292, 294-297, 306, 308, 318
Corneille, Marguerite, 168
Craig, Joe, 134, 136, 137
Creedon, Dan, 112, 173, 243
Cripple Creek, 235
Cullen, Frank (referee), 235

Daniel, Dan, 104-106, 212-214, 216
Davies, Parson, 62, 67
Delaney, Billy, 61, 156, 193, 285
Dempsey, Jack "Manassa Mauler", 286, 294
Dempsey, Jack "Nonpareil", 75
Denver, 87, 114, 235
Derry, 14, 15, 19
Detroit, 220, 221, 307
Devery, Chief of Police, 159, 161, 164

Dixon, George, 145, 162, 184, 192, 193, 222, 280
Dublin , 10, 14, 15, 29, 118, 130, 131, 302
Dundalk, 8-14, 16-20, 25, 26, 64, 76, 91, 108, 118, 125, 128-130, 134-137, 141, 144, 158, 241, 242, 273, 292, 297
Dundalk Museum, 316
Dunkhorst, Ed, 225
Dunn, Jim, 33, 34

Earp, Wyatt, 77-81, 83-96, 98-108, 114, 115, 153, 182, 224
Eckhardt, Johnny, 185, 221
Edward VII, King, 241, 242
Everett, "Mexican" Pete, 148, 235, 236

Finnegan, Jack, 220
Fitzpatrick, Sam, 243
Fitzsimmons, Bob, 29, 44, 53, 64, 68-70, 74-77, 79-100, 102, 103-107, 109-111, 114-117, 124, 126, 128, 131, 133, 138, 142, 146, 147, 149, 152, 153, 155, 156, 159, 168, 169, 174, 182-186, 192, 193, 211, 213, 215, 223-225, 229-233, 237-241, 243, 261, 269, 292, 294, 295, 302, 304, 306, 311
Fitzsimmons, Rose, 231
Fleischer, Nat, 24, 104, 151, 206, 216, 277, 282
Foley, Ted, 165
Fort Dearborn Athletic Club, Chicago, 226
Fox, Richard K, 24, 76, 272

Gans, Joe, 39, 145, 222, 304
Gardner, Jack, 28
Gibbs, Jim, 39, 53, 80, 93, 103, 105
Goddard, Joe, 38, 114, 142-145, 148, 155, 169, 182, 184, 221, 280, 311
Gosling, James, 126, 297, 316
Grand Central Palace, New York, 236, 312
Graney, Ed, 49, 50, 105

328

INDEX

Gray, George, 165, 166
Greater New York Athletic Club, 111, 112, 153, 307, 313
Great Northern Railway, Ireland, 14, 242, 273
Green, George, 57
Greggains, Alec, 45-47, 105, 151
Groom, Jim, 39, 53, 88, 93, 95, 103
Guilder, Jim, 232
Gunst, Moses, 49, 79, 88, 96

Hall, Jem, 304
Hall, Jim, 100, 113
Hallen, Fred, 70
Harrison, Billy, 46, 47
Hartford, Connecticut, 222
Hart, Hugh S, 236
Hart, Marvin, 277
Harvey, Charley, 162
Harvey, Jim, 28
Heenan, John C, 186
Herford, Al, 39
Herman, Paul, 34, 38, 39, 62
Holtman, Jake, 112
Honolulu, 28-31, 33, 36, 48, 303, 304
Horton Law, 112, 123, 133, 159, 225, 229, 232, 233, 312
Hotel Bartholdi, New York, 75, 184
Hotel Warwick, Broadway, 70

Ice Palace, Manhattan, 159
Industrial Hall, Philadelphia, 221

Jackson, Peter, 24, 34, 148, 243
James, Tom, 29, 36
Jeffords, Jim, 192, 221, 222
Jeffries, Jim, 148-152, 156, 157, 182-188, 191-217, 219-221, 223, 225-227, 229, 231-241, 243, 249, 270, 274, 275, 277-286, 291-296, 310, 311, 313, 315, 317, 318
Jenkins, Tom, 236, 237, 312
Jester, Louis, 152

Jimmy Wakeley's Saloon, New York, 66, 67, 72
Johnson, Jack, 151, 275, 278-281, 285, 287, 317
Jordan, Billy, 57, 80
Julian, Martin, 77, 80, 83-86, 90, 92, 93, 95, 96, 99, 105, 106, 156, 184

Kelly, "Honest" John, 105, 158, 161-166
Kelly, Margaret (Tom Sharkey's mother), 11, 14, 302
Kelly, "Spider", 33, 48-54, 56-58, 150, 156, 235, 304, 305
Kenny, "Yank", 223
Kilrain, Jake, 24
King, Alva, 39, 49
Knickerbocker Athletic Club, San Francisco, 142

Langley, Jack, 28, 216, 303, 304
Lansing, Tom, 114, 117, 122
Lavigne, George "Kid", 112
Lazay, Vic, 41, 42
Lenox Club (Manhattan), 157, 159, 165, 167, 169, 185
Lewis, Warren, 111-113
Lexington Avenue, Manhattan, 114, 157
London, 18, 19, 129, 133, 182, 241, 242, 245, 292, 294, 308, 314
London Prize Rules, 19
Louis, Joe, 286, 318
Louisville, Kentucky, 235, 251
Lowry, Pete, 117, 121, 124
Lucky Baldwin's Hotel, San Francisco, 89, 103
Lynch, Danny, 52-54, 56, 66, 68, 70, 71, 77, 80, 90, 93-95, 97-99, 101, 105-107, 111, 113, 122, 129, 133-135, 142, 145
Lynch, Tom, 135

Mace, Jem "Gypsy", 243
Madden, Billy, 153, 243

INDEX

Madison Avenue, 273
Madison Square Garden, 66, 71, 117, 168, 220, 229, 232, 261, 275
Maher, Peter, 29, 68-70, 76, 111-113, 115-124, 126, 128, 130-133, 138, 139, 141-143, 146, 148, 149, 153, 155, 160, 172, 173, 181, 182, 232, 235-237, 239, 240, 242, 279
Manhattan, 157-159, 313
Manzoni, Florence, 270, 271
Marciano, Rocky, 295
Marks, Jack, 33
Marquis of Queensberry Rules, 79, 100, 134, 154, 294
Martin Hotel, Broadway, 157
Masterson, Bat, 77, 87, 105, 106, 302
McAuley, Jack, 33
McCarty, Dan "White Hat", 50
McConnell, Sammy, 135, 136
McCormick, Frank, 188
McCormick, Jim, 183, 222, 308
McCourt, Pat, 137
McCoy, "Kid", 148, 153, 155-157, 160, 165, 168, 169, 171-185, 187, 210, 222, 229, 232, 233, 235, 250, 259, 264, 274, 287, 296, 297, 307, 308
McFadden, George, 193
McGovern, Terry, 222, 261, 269
McGrath, Tim, 41-44, 45-48, 51-54, 56, 58, 113-115, 117-124, 150, 156, 184, 188, 193, 254, 284, 285, 288, 304, 305
McIntosh, Katherine, 248-250, 260-262, 267, 269-271, 273, 313
McKane, John Y, 248
McKittorick, Tom, 135
McLaglen, Victor, 286
McVey, Con, 161-167
Mechanic's Pavilion, San Francisco, 51, 56, 76, 79, 102, 142, 149, 305
Miller, Colonel Harvey L "Heinie", 294, 302, 314

Miller, Jerry, 223
Miller, John "The Terrible Swede", 42-44, 45, 124
Mitchell, Charley, 24, 168, 183
Monroe, Jack, 250, 256, 313
Mulverhill, Martin, 36-38

Nation, Carrie, 252
National Athletic Club, San Francisco, 55, 69, 77, 85, 90, 94, 103, 105, 106
National Sporting Club, London, 241, 245
Nealon, Fred, 48
Needham, Danny, 52-54, 65, 70, 74, 76, 80, 83, 92-94, 101
Nevada, 107, 124, 234, 281
New Orleans, 23-25, 286
Newry, 14, 125, 137
New York City, 15, 17, 25, 35, 66-71, 73-74, 75, 76, 79, 90, 92, 97, 99, 112, 114-118, 120, 124, 131-133, 141, 142, 144, 146, 152, -158, 160, 164, 166, 168, 174, 183, 185, 187, 212-214, 220, 221, 223, 225, 226, 232, 233, 236, 239, 244, 248, 249, 253, 258, 263, 264, 266-269, 273-275, 281, 283, 286, 287, 295, 302, 304, 305, 308, 313, 317

O'Brien, Dick, 65
O'Brien, "Philadelphia" Jack, 278
O'Donnell, Steve, 68, 157
Olympic (ship), 33, 34
O'Neill, "Reddy", 27
O'Rourke, Tom, 67, 145, 155, 160, 165, 172, 174, 180, 184, 185, 193, 195, 200, 206, 207, 209, 211, 213, 217, 219, 223-225, 227, 228, 232, 250, 318

Palace Athletic Club, New York, 113, 120
Pardello, Leo, 237, 257, 314
Pardy, George T, 19-21
Parks, Tom, 137
Parks, TV, 134, 135, 136, 137, 139

330

INDEX

People's Palace, San Francisco, 47
Philadelphia, 74, 116, 158, 169, 183, 220, 221, 237, 239, 240, 242, 250, 308
Philadelphia American League Club, 237
Pickett, J, 28
Poole, Bill, 293

Quinn, "Scaldy" Bill, 65
Quinn, John, 111, 121, 124, 153

Raines Hotel Law (New York), 251
Reich, Barney, 238, 250, 314
Rocap, Billy (referee), 239
Roche, Billy, 193
Roeber, Ernest, 214
Root, Jack, 277
Ruhlin, Gus, 43, 148, 152-156, 173, 182, 184, 187, 210, 222, 226-230, 232, 233, 235-237, 241-245, 257, 261, 307, 313, 314
Russell, Fred, 235, 258
Ryan, Paddy, 23
Ryan, Tommy, 183, 187, 188, 193, 200, 241, 243, 244

Sagamore Hotel, Coney Island, 189
Salt Lake City, 51, 112
San Francisco, 18, 24, 33, 34, 36-39, 42, 46-48, 50, 51, 53-55, 60, 61, 65, 69, 70, 74, 76, 79, 86, 90, 91, 97, 100, 102, 103, 106, 108, 110, 128, 133, 142, 144-149, 152, 153, 157, 158, 164, 167, 188, 229, 230, 235, 238, 241, 261-263, 268-270, 280, 284, 286-289, 291, 305, 311, 316
Scanlon, Jim, 152
Scully, Pat, 117, 121
Seaside Sporting Club, 224, 228, 229
Sharkey, Elizabeth (Tom's sister), 11, 273
Sharkey, James (Tom's father), 11, 13-15, 139, 245, 273, 301, 302
Sharkey, James (Tom's brother), 11
Sharkey, John (Tom's brother), 11, 125, 138, 139, 267

Sharkey, Mary (Tom's sister), 11
Sharkey, Owen (Tom's brother), 11
Sharkey, Patrick (Tom's brother), 11
Sharkey, Richard (Tom's brother), 11
Sharkey, Rose (Tom's sister), 11, 248
Sharkey's Bar, 250, 251
Sheepshead Bay, 113, 221, 225, 226, 247, 248, 267, 287, 307, 315
Siler, George, 153, 167, 188, 189, 194, 198, 199, 201, 206-217, 223, 225, 226, 297
Sing, Sing, 248
Slavin, Frank, 68, 243
Smith, "Australian" Billy, 38-42, 44-46, 76, 80, 93-95, 98, 124
Smith, "Denver" Ed, 114
St Louis, 112, 142, 309
Stuart, Dan, 111
Sullivan, Dave, 162, 238
Sullivan, Jeremiah "Yank", 116
Sullivan, John L, 23-25, 44, 63, 66, 67, 70-73, 75, 99, 117, 124, 153, 163, 186, 203, 204, 206, 215, 222, 236, 279, 292, 294, 295, 301
Sullivan, Senator Tim, 121, 162, 164-167, 203, 233, 234
Sullivan, William "Spike", 238, 243
Sweeney, Eddie, 188

Tammany Hall, 121, 164, 248, 254, 265, 268
Tanforan racetrack, 7, 50, 105, 287
Tate, Bill, 33, 216
Tattersall's, Chicago, 226
Tenderloin, 158
Thompson, "Rough", 28, 216, 303
Thorne, Jeff, 184
Tuttle, Fred, 221, 248
Tuttle, Jennie, 221, 247, 248
Tyson, Mike, 295

US Navy, 8, 9, 18, 25-27, 34, 35, 38, 40, 41, 57, 59, 128, 130, 154, 255, 262, 263, 268, 271, 288, 292, 297

INDEX

USS Drum, 304
USS Independence, 40, 41
USS Philadelphia, 26, 29, 31, 33-38, 40, 41, 43, 51, 62, 128
USS Saginaw, 35

Vallejo, 33-35, 38, 39, 41, 43, 53, 56, 109, 143, 147, 262, 263
Van Buren's Hotel, 112
Van Court, DeWitt, 53
Vanderbilt Hotel, 239
Vaughn, Punch, 142
Vermont (ship), 26

Walcott, Joe, 145, 241
Walsh, Jack, 28
Warrenpoint, 125, 137
Washington, George (boxer), 31, 32, 304
West Baden Springs, 159
Westchester, 112, 113, 224
West Point, 236, 289
White, Charley, 159, 162, 230
White, Johnny (referee), 228
White, Tommy, 112, 305
Whitman, Police Captain Charles W, 80
Willard, Jess, 33, 286
Williams, Jim (Salt Lake City), 51, 52, 99, 112, 124
Woodward's Pavilion, San Francisco, 146

Yosemite Athletic Club, San Francisco, 238, 240